T0317642

"Complicated subject? Not if you let Bill Beagles explain it to you! Essential reading."

John Foyle, Deputy Chief Executive, LIFFE

NYSE Liffe

NYSE Liffe is the brand name for the global derivatives business of NYSE Euronext – the world's largest and most diverse exchange group. NYSE Euronext operates futures and options markets in both the US and Europe.

European markets

In Europe, NYSE Liffe runs futures and options markets in Amsterdam, Brussels, Lisbon, London and Paris where every day approximately two trillion euros worth of derivatives business is traded by customers from around the world. NYSE Liffe offers a broad choice of derivatives products including short-term interest rates, single stocks, indices, swaps, government bonds, commodities and currencies – all available to trade via state-of-the-art electronic trading platform.

W.A. Beagles graduated in economics in 1984, before starting his City career with Lloyds Bank as an FX trader and going on to help establish the bank's presence on the LIFFE trading floor. In 1986, Bill joined AOT, a specialist option trading firm, for whom he traded a range of option products on LIFFE and LTOM in London, the MATIF in Paris, the EOE in Amsterdam and the electronic DTB (fore-runner of Eurex) in Germany. Following in the footsteps of many successful traders before him, Bill "went local" in 1994, making markets in the FTSE 100 Index option on LIFFE. When the open outcry trading floor closed in 2000, Bill had the honour of ringing the closing bell for the final time.

Joining up with Simon Hart and Andy Swaine, two long term friends and fellow traders, Bill then set up K2 London, a trading company that combines day-to-day derivatives trading with fund management, education and consultancy. Since 2000, Bill has provided specialised education and consulting services to a wide range of institutions including LIFFE and the LSE in London and to a range of government agencies and major companies across the globe.

Bill's combination of current market knowledge and educational experience allows him to present the complex subject of options in a clear and intuitive fashion.

Equity and Index Options Explained

For other titles in the Wiley Trading Series
please see www.wiley.com/finance

DISCLAIMER

The views expressed by Bill Beagles are those of the author and should not be construed as necessarily reflecting those of NYSE Euronext or any of its subsidiary companies ("NYSE Euronext"). NYSE Euronext disclaims all responsibility and liability (to the extent permitted by law) for information contained in this publication which is for information purposes only and does not constitute investment advice.

Potential users of products that are traded on the exchanges operated by NYSE Euronext should familiarise themselves with the full contract specification of the product concerned and any associated information. It is the responsibility of the individual user to consider his legal and regulatory position in the relevant jurisdiction, the risks associated with trading such products and to ensure that the use of this information and the subsequent making of any investment does not contravene any such restrictions or applicable laws and regulations of any jurisdiction.

You should always bear in mind that:

- The value of investments and any income from them may go down as well as up. You may not get back all of your original investment.
- Past performance is not necessarily a guide to future performance.
- Rates of exchange may cause the value of underlying investments to go up or down.
- Tax arrangements may change.
- All stock market based investment is exposed to a degree of risk.

EQUITY AND INDEX OPTIONS EXPLAINED

W. A. Beagles

A John Wiley and Sons, Ltd., Publication

A catalogue record for this book is available from the British Library.

ISBN 978-0-470-69717-7 (HB)

Typeset in 10/12pt Times by Aptara Inc., New Delhi, India.

Contents

Foreword   vii

Preface: Trading Language and Products   ix

1   Option Basics   1

2   Option Specifications   9

3   Exercise and Assignment   13

4   Option Uses   19

5   Option Price and Value   31

6   "Moneyness"   39

7   Pricing Options   43

8   Skew   61

9   Option Pricing Revisited: the "Greeks"   71

10 Basic Option Strategy   95

11 Option Spreads   105

12 The Collar (Fence)   107

13 Long Call Spreads (Bull Call Spreads)   119

14   Long Put Spreads (Bear Put Spreads)   127

15   Short Call Spreads (Bear Call Spreads)   139

16   Short Put Spreads (Bull Put Spreads)   147

17   Selling Naked Puts versus Selling Put Spreads   151

18   Long Verticals versus Short Verticals   157

19   Long Straddles   161

20   Long Strangles   167

21   Short Straddles   173

22   The Iron Butterfly   179

23   Short Strangles   185

24   The Iron Condor   187

25   Calendar Spreads   193

26   Long Call Calendars   195

27   Short Call Calendar Spreads   201

28   Long Put Calendar Spreads   205

29   Short Put Calendar Spreads   209

30   Diagonal Spreads   213

31   Yield Enhancement   219

32   Gamma Trading   223

33   Resources   233

34   Summary   235

Glossary   237

Index   247

Foreword

As the title suggests, this book aims to explain the subject of equity and index options. The challenges involved in explaining this subject lie not in the complexity of the subject matter but in the sheer volume of it. A bit like a foreign language, very few of the individual pieces of the jigsaw are difficult to understand but that doesn't mean that putting it all together is easy. Many people know bits and pieces of information about options; they know, perhaps, that options "erode" or that selling options can be dangerous. They have picked up these nuggets of knowledge without understanding the bigger picture, without understanding the context – and that can be costly.

The aim of the book is to move the reader steadily towards a full understanding of this wide-reaching subject. From absolute basics to advanced trading techniques, the book aims to explain both the theory and practice of equity options in clear, accessible terms. This is not a mathematical textbook; equations and formulae are avoided wherever possible. Rather this is an options text aimed at every man and every woman, whether professional investor or part-time "punter".

As a professional options trader since 1984, I have learnt about options from a practical perspective. Accordingly, the book includes plenty of real-world examples, along with practical trading tools (including a pricing model) and resources. As a professional options consultant and teacher since 2000, I have learnt to anticipate key questions, to anticipate those subjects that cause students the greatest difficulty. During the many courses that I have delivered, I have learnt that interaction is of prime importance. I have tried to point delegates towards solutions, to make them comfortable with the right methods, with good practice. To that end, the book includes plentiful exercises of varying degrees of difficulty, all designed to direct the reader towards a truly intuitive understanding of the subject.

The book breaks down into two broad sections: theory and practice. While there is some overlap between the two areas, the first part of the book deals mainly with the necessary theory while the second part of the book focuses largely upon option trading in practice. It would be nice to be able to ignore the drier theory and go straight to the livelier subject of trading but that would be (forgive the pun) to "sell the reader short".

For those readers with some existing knowledge and who therefore wish to skip some of the early, more basic chapters, it may be an idea to run quickly through the exercises. If these exercises present no problems, then the reader may safely move on. If, on the other hand, the reader struggles with the exercises, then working through the preceding text seems sensible. Remember, this is a big subject. If the foundations are not solid, then what follows is built on shaky ground.

Chapter 1 is prefaced with a short section on key trading terminology and some of the exchanges and products that are mentioned in the main body of text. Those with trading experience may elect either to skim or skip this section.

Technical language and market jargon are explained in plain English as and when appropriate. Where necessary, chapter glossaries are provided relating to the subsequent text. Further, a full, option-specific glossary may be found before the index at the end of the book.

Preface: Trading Language and Products

The table below represents a simplified version of a trading screen, the sort of screen that a professional trader might use to view and to access the markets. The exact nature of the prices shown is irrelevant; the price could apply to a share or an index or a commodity, it really doesn't matter. What does matter is that we understand what the various numbers mean.

BID SIZE	BID	LAST	OFFER (ASK)	OFFER SIZE
220	4211	4212	4213	390

Currently, the highest price at which anyone is prepared to buy is 4211. This is known as the *bid*. The best bid at the moment is 4211. If we look at the *bid size*, we can see that the bid is for a total of 220 units (shares, futures, options, it doesn't matter). This might be one person looking to buy 220 units, two people looking to buy 110 each, 220 different buyers, each wanting to buy 1 "lot" each, or any other combination that adds up to a total of 220. We really don't care how the "bid size" breaks down, it doesn't matter.

Currently, the lowest price at which anyone is prepared to sell is 4213. This is known as the *offer* or *ask*. The best offer at the moment is 4213. If we look at the *offer size*, we can see that the offer is in a total of 390 units (shares, futures, options, it doesn't matter). Again, this might be one person looking to sell 390 units, three people looking to sell 130, 390 different sellers, each wanting to sell one "lot" each, or any other combination that sums to 390. Again, we really don't care how the "offer size" breaks down, it just doesn't matter.

Currently, the *bid/offer spread* is "4211 bid, offered at 4213".

The last price that actually traded was 4212. This happens to be midway between the current bid and offer, but that need not be the case. If we ask our broker for the current "touch", the best price available at the moment, we will be told something like "the market is 4211 bid at 4213, last traded 4212".

If we want to buy, we have various choices. The only way to guarantee that we buy is to "hit the offer", to pay up to the current best selling price of 4213. Alternatively, we can "join the bid"; place an order to buy at 4211. Or we can improve on the current best bid and pay 4212. Either way, if we join the bid or bid in the middle of the spread, we are not guaranteed to trade; not certain to be "filled".

The same applies to selling. If we want to sell, we have similar choices. The only way to guarantee that we sell is to "hit the bid", to sell down to the current best buying price of 4211. Alternatively, we can "join the offer"; place an order to sell at 4213. Or we can improve on the current best ask and offer at 4212. Either way, if we join the offer or offer in the middle of the spread, we are not guaranteed to trade; not sure to be "filled".

In the real world, trading screens are more complex than the simple snapshot shown above. The prices are likely to be moving around, sometimes at high speed. The extreme of this, when prices are moving at a furious speed, is known as a "fast market". It may be difficult for brokers to secure a meaningful option quote under such conditions.

Traders talk of having a "position" or "book". This is the trader's cumulative holding in a given asset, whether "long" or "short".

If, starting from a zero or "flat" position, we buy XYZ, then we are *long* of XYZ.

Starting from flat, if we buy 10 XYZ, then our position is "long 10". If we then buy 5 more XYZ, we are "long 15". If we then sell 7 XYZ, we are "long 8". And if we sell those 8 XYZ, we are back to "flat" or zero.

If, starting from a zero or "flat" position, we first *sell* XYZ, then we are *short* of XYZ.

Starting from flat, if we sell 150 XYZ, then our position is "short 150". If we then sell 50 more XYZ, we are "short 200". If we then buy back 75 XYZ, we are "short 125". And if we buy those 125 XYZ back, we are once again back to "flat" or zero.

The following timeline shows how a position may move from being long to short and vice versa.

Starting position: Flat (zero)

Trade 1: Buy 25 XYZ
          Resulting position: Long 25 XYZ
Trade 2: Buy 75 XYZ
          Cumulative position: Long 100 XYZ
Trade 3: Sell 150 XYZ
          Cumulative position: Short 50 XYZ
Trade 4: Buy 50 XYZ
          Cumulative position: Flat (zero)

As we will see, the ability to "go short" is a key feature of derivatives such as futures and options. We cannot "go short" of something *physical* such as a house. We can only sell a house if we own it. But we can use *derivatives* based on a house (e.g. property futures or an option on a house) to "go short", to sell before buying back.

Derivatives may be traded upon a recognised investment exchange, such as LIFFE (the London International Financial Futures Exchange) or EDX, the derivatives arm of the LSE (London Stock Exchange). A list of the major European and US exchanges may be found in Chapter 33.

Any derivative that trades *away* from a recognised exchange is known as an *OTC*, an "over-the-counter" product. This book focuses upon options traded upon exchanges since most readers are likely to trade *ETOs* (exchange traded options) rather than OTCs. However, the vast majority of points made through the book apply generically to options, regardless of *where* the trading takes place.

There are two main advantages to trading upon an exchange rather than OTC. The first is the removal (or at least reduction) of counterparty risk due to the presence of the "clearing house", a central counterparty for financial transactions. For example, the *guarantor* for all trades executed on LIFFE and the LSE is LCH Clearnet. The existence of the clearing house reduces concerns that the counterparty to a trade may default.

The second main advantage of trading on an exchange is *transparency*, the fact that we can see the best prices available upon an exchange at any particular moment, something that *cannot* be said of all OTC markets.

Derivatives now trade on a bewildering array of underlying assets and commodities. As the title suggests, this book concentrates upon options based upon equities and stock indices. Examples of *stock* options used in the text are taken from the LIFFE market, well-known names such as BP and Lloyds TSB. The *index* option chosen for illustrative purposes is the FTSE 100 Index option, also traded upon LIFFE. The exact equities and indices used are of no great importance; the vast majority of points made through the book apply generically to equity and index options, regardless of the exact nature of the underlying asset.

1
Option Basics

An option contract is a financial instrument; specifically, a type of derivative. But what is a derivative?

The clue is in the name. A derivative derives from an underlying asset, such as an equity, an interest rate or a commodity. The price of a derivative is derived from the price of the underlying asset.

So a coffee *futures contract* (a coffee "future") is a derivative of *physical* coffee.

A dollar/euro *option* is a derivative of the *spot* or *cash* dollar/euro rate. BP *futures* or *options* are derivatives of *cash* BP shares, as traded on the LSE.

Derivatives, whether options or futures, are contracts. When we trade a future, we are trading a futures *contract*. When we trade an option, we are trading an options *contract*. In the context of derivatives markets, the word "future" is an abbreviation of the term "futures contract". The word "option" is an abbreviation of the term "option contract".

These contracts are transferable, they are tradable between market participants. We can buy an option from one person and sell it to a different person. Trades are executed via the exchange and the related clearing house, such as LIFFE and LCH Clearnet, respectively. Trading is *anonymous*. We don't know who we have traded with and nor do we care; it is irrelevant.

When we buy 5 futures and then sell 3 of them, we do not have two positions. We are not long of 5 futures *and* short of 3 futures. Rather, we have a *net* position of long 2 futures. There may also be a profit or loss, depending upon the prices at which we traded, but our position is simply the net result of the two trades. Furthermore, we can trade in and out of derivatives positions as and when we want, at any time while the market is open up until expiry. Futures and options positions do not have to be held until expiry. We may buy some options this morning and sell them an hour later ("intra-day" trading). Or we may buy some futures or options today and sell them tomorrow or next week or next month, any time until the contracts expire.

There are three basic types of derivative: futures, options and swaps. Here, we are concerned with options, but it is worth giving a brief explanation of the difference between physical, forward and option trades. Consider the following everyday example.

Imagine that we want to buy a house for £100K. We pay £100K in cash to the house vendor; the vendor hands us the deeds to the house. This is an example of a "physical" or "cash" or "spot" transaction. "Physical" because we are buying something tangible, a physical house in this case. "Cash" because we are paying for the house in cash. And "spot" because we are paying the price right now, we are paying "on the spot".

Now consider that we want to buy the same house for £100K, but don't wish to complete the transaction for 3 months. If we wait 3 months to buy the house, the price may have changed, so we make a contract with the house vendor to buy the house for £100K in 3 months' time. This is an example of a "forward" or "future" transaction. The cash is not exchanged for the house right now. Rather we have agreed to exchange cash for the house on a forward date, on a date in the future.

Now consider that we want the option to buy the same house for £100K in 3 months' time. Unsurprisingly, this is an example of an option transaction, an example that is expanded upon in the following section.

Options convey the right, *but not the obligation*, either to buy or sell an asset. Hence the name option, because option ownership conveys *choice*.

There are two types of option:

1. *Calls*, which convey the right to *buy* something. For example, a BP call conveys the right but not the obligation to *buy* BP shares.
2. *Puts*, which convey the right to *sell* something. For example, a Vodafone put conveys the right but not the obligation to *sell* Vodafone shares

Before considering equity options in detail, consider an everyday example of a call and a put:

EVERYDAY EXAMPLE: A CALL OPTION ON A HOUSE

We want to buy a house and, on the first day of our property search, we find a suitable house on offer at a price of £100K.

We are now in something of a quandary. This is the first and only house that we have looked at so far. What about all the other houses on offer? We want to look at other houses on the market, but don't want to miss out on this one. How can we retain the right to buy this house but also have time to look at the alternatives? How can we "have our cake and eat it"?

The solution is to ask the house seller if we can have a month in which to look at other properties on the market. We want to be able to come back in a month's time and have the choice of buying the house for £100K (in the event that we have found nothing better in the meantime) or not buying the house (in the event that we *have* found a better choice). We want time. We want choice. We want an option to buy the house; a *call option*.

Not unreasonably, the seller of the house wants something in return for giving us this time and flexibility. After all, by giving us a month in which to decide whether or not to buy the house, he has to take his house off of the market and may miss out on a quick sale.

To compensate the house seller for this missed opportunity, we agree to pay him £500. This is the price of the call option, the price of time and choice. This price of £500 is non-refundable, non-returnable. It is the price of the option, also known as the *option premium*. At which point an important point must be made. We have paid £500 for an option. We have paid away cold, hard cash but – we now have control; we are *proactive*. We decide whether or not to exercise our right to buy the house.

On the other side of the transaction, the option seller is entirely *reactive*. The option seller has received the same £500 in cold, hard cash but he is now entirely reactive. Specifically, the option seller must wait for our decision as to whether we do or do not want to buy the house for £100K.

Furthermore, in giving us the month in which to make our decision, he is taking on risk. Specifically, he is taking the risk that the property market will move significantly in the next month. Consider the effect of such a move.

As the owner of the call option on the house, what will we choose to do if there is a property *crash* in the next month? Will we still want to buy the house for £100K if we can now find better and/or cheaper alternatives? The answer is "no". We will *not* exercise our right to buy the house for £100K *because we are not obliged to*. We will allow our call option to *expire worthless*. And while the £500 spent on the option has been lost, this is more than compensated for by the saving that we are making on the cheaper and/or "better" house that we can now buy.

Consider this from the option seller's perspective. He has sold us the right (but not the obligation) to buy his house for £100K in 1 month's time. He cannot therefore sell the house to anyone else during this period. If there *is* a property crash during the period, then he knows that we will no longer wish to buy his house for £100K (because there are cheaper alternatives) and he will only be able to sell on the open market at a lower price.

We can see that a fall in property prices will benefit the house buyer and hurt the house seller, but what if property prices *rise*?

As the owner of the call option on the house, what will we choose to do if property prices rise significantly through the next month? Will we want to buy the house for £100K if the alternatives are significantly more expensive? Of course we will! We will *exercise* our right to buy the house for £100K. The call option has cost us £500 but it has protected us against the cost of property rising.

Again, consider this from the option seller's perspective. He has sold us the right to buy his house for £100K in 1 month's time. And if property prices rise significantly through the month, we will definitely exercise our right to buy at such a (now) attractive price. Although the house seller is selling his house at the original asking price, it could be argued that, since he has missed out on the rise in property prices, he has incurred opportunity cost. This point will be revisited at a later stage.

Exercise 1.1

In the above example of a call option, we paid £500 for the right to choose to buy a house for £100K in 1 month's time.

Formally, we paid a premium of £500 for a 1 month £100K call on a house. The price of the option was £500. How did we arrive at this price? What three key factors helped determine this price?

Hint 1: How much would we expect to be charged for a *1 day* option to buy the house?

How much would we expect to be charged for a *1 year* option to buy the house?

Hint 2: How much would we expect to be charged for an option on a *£50K* house?

How much would we expect to be charged for an option on a *£950K* house?

Hint 3: In terms of the underlying property market, what is of most concern to the house seller?

Exercise 1.1: Answers and Explanation

The question asked for the three key factors that might influence the price of a 1 month £100K call on a house. The answers are not given in order of importance but rather in relation to hints 1 to 3 above.

1. **Time:** We would expect to pay far more for a 1 *year* option than a 1 *day* option because we are getting more time, more flexibility. In general then, all other things being equal, the longer-dated the option, the greater the option price.
2. **Underlying value:** We would expect to pay more for an option on an expensive house than an option on a cheap house, simply because there is more *value* at stake. In general then, all other things being equal, the greater the amount of underlying value, the greater the option price.
3. **Probability:** Specifically, probability of the underlying property market moving around. Remember, by selling you a 1 month call option on his house, the house seller is exposing himself to the risk of the underlying property market changing. If there is a property crash, we will not choose to buy the house and the house seller will be left with an unsold house that has reduced in value. And if there is a sharp rise in property prices, the house seller will not be able to take advantage of the increased value of his house as we will exercise our right to buy at £100K. In summary, a significant change in the property market will cause the house seller

either to lose money or to miss out on a profitable opportunity. In general then, all other things being equal, the greater the probability of the underlying market moving, the greater the option price.

CALL OPTIONS: FORMAL DEFINITION

Consider the formal, textbook definition of a call option:

The right but not the obligation *to buy the underlying at a given price on or before a given date.*

At first glance, this may seem a little complex, a little long-winded. However, breaking this definition down into its constituent parts simplifies matters considerably.

The key part of this definition is highlighted: "The right *but not the obligation* to buy the underlying at a given price on or before a given date". It is this element of *choice* that is key to the *optional nature* of an option. Indeed, that is why an option is called an option. Essentially, buying an option confers choice; selling an option concedes choice. This is the basic dynamic of options.

So, a call option is the right but not the obligation to *buy the underlying* at a given price on or before a given date.

Any option to buy is a call. The underlying can be just about anything, as long as it may be priced. For example, a copper call confers the right but not the obligation to buy copper. A FTSE call confers the right but not the obligation to buy the FTSE. And, as in our intuitive example above, a house call confers the right but not the obligation to buy a house. This may seem a little imprecise, a little general, but we will look at this in greater detail in the section entitled "Option Specifications".

To reiterate, a call option confers the right but not the obligation to buy the underlying *at a given price* on or before a given date. Consider the highlighted phrase "at a given price" The price at which the call owner has the right to buy is known as the *strike price*, often abbreviated simply to the *strike*.

Now consider the last part of the definition. A call option confers the right but not the obligation to buy the underlying at a given price *on or before a given date*. All options have an *expiry date*, a date on which they cease to exist.

So, to summarise, we have taken the formal, textbook definition of a call option and broken it down into its constituent parts. A call option is:

The right but not the obligation to buy (because it is a call) a given amount of a given asset (the underlying) at a given price (the strike price) on or before a given date (expiry).

Now, having dealt in basic terms with calls, let's consider the other type of option – puts.

EVERYDAY EXAMPLE: INSURANCE (A PUT OPTION ON HOME CONTENTS)

Put options convey the right but not the obligation to *sell* something. For that reason, they are sometimes a little harder to understand than call options. After all, we are very used to the idea of buying things in our everyday lives. We may buy property, stocks and shares, any number of assets and commodities. We are familiar with the idea of being "long" of assets, of owning them. The opposite, the idea of being "short" of selling things before we have bought them, is less commonplace. For that reason, the best everyday example of a put option is insurance. This comparison is by no means perfect but does have the great advantage of being something with which we are all familiar.

Let's assume that we wish to insure £10 000 worth of home contents. We pay an insurance company £300 for the right to make a claim for up to £10 000. In the event of a fire or a flood, we have the right to (notionally) "sell" our now damaged and worthless home contents back to the insurance company for £10 000. We have choice. We have the right to sell, should we need it. We have a *put option*.

Again, some important observations need to be made. In paying a price of £300 for the option, we have gained control. We decide whether or not to make a claim; we are *proactive*.

The insurance company, the option seller, is entirely *reactive*. The option seller has received a premium, a price of £300 in cash, but is now reactive. The insurer can only wait and react to a claim if and when it is made.

Exercise 1.2

In the above example of a put option, we paid £300 for the right to choose to "sell" our home contents for £10 000 at any time in the next year.

Formally, we paid a premium of £300 for a 1 year £10 000 put on our home contents. The price of the option was £300. How did the insurance company price this insurance? What three key factors helped determine this price?

Hint 1: How much should we expect to be charged for insurance for *1 month*?
         How much should we expect to be charged for insurance for *5 years*?
Hint 2: How much should we expect to pay to insure *£500 worth* of home contents?
         How much should we expect to pay to insure *£1 million worth* of home contents?
Hint 3: How does the *location* of your home affect the cost of insurance?

Exercise 1.3: Answers and Explanation

The question asked for the three key factors that might influence the price of a 1 year £10 000 put on home insurance. The answers are not given in order of importance but rather in relation to hints 1 to 3 above.

1. **Time:** We would expect to pay far more for 5 years' insurance than 1 month's insurance because we are protected for a far longer period. As a general rule, all other things being equal, the longer-dated the option, the greater the option price.
2. **Underlying value:** We would expect to pay far more for insurance on £1 million worth of home contents than insurance on £500 worth of home contents, simply because there is more *value* at stake. As a general rule, all other things being equal, the greater the amount of underlying value, the greater the option price.
3. **Probability:** Specifically, the probability of a claim being made. This is directly related to the *location* of the property. Simply, the greater the probability of a claim, the greater the price of the insurance. As we will see at a later stage, broadly speaking, *probability* in the insurance world translates as *volatility* in the option world. Probability and volatility are closely related. As a general rule, all other things being equal, the greater the probability of a claim, the greater the option price.

PUT OPTIONS: FORMAL DEFINITION

Consider the formal, textbook definition of a put option. This is identical to the definition of a call option except that a put conveys the right to *sell* rather than buy something. A put option is:

> *The right* but not the obligation *to sell the underlying at a given price on or before a given date.*

Again, at first glance, this may seem a little complex but breaking this definition down into its constituent parts simplifies matters considerably.

As with the definition of a call, the key part of the definition is highlighted: "The right *but not the obligation* to sell the underlying at a given price on or before a given date".

Remember, it is this element of *choice* that is key. Buying an option confers choice; selling an option concedes choice. This is the basic dynamic of options.

So, a put option is the right but not the obligation to *sell the underlying* at a given price on or before a given date.

Any option to sell is a put. Remember, the underlying can be just about anything. For example, a copper put confers the right but not the obligation to sell copper. A FTSE put confers the right but not the obligation to sell the FTSE. And, as in our intuitive example above, a home contents put confers the right but not the obligation to "sell" our damaged home contents in the event of some sort of accident. We will look at more detailed examples in the section entitled "Option Specifications".

To reiterate, a put option is the right but not the obligation to sell the underlying *at a given price* on or before a given date. Consider the highlighted phrase "at a given price". The price at which the put owner has the right to sell is known as the *strike price*, often abbreviated simply to the *strike*.

Now consider the last part of the definition. A put option is the right but not the obligation to sell the underlying at a given price *on or before a given date*. All options have an *expiry date*, a date on which they cease to exist.

So, to summarise, we have taken the formal, textbook definition of a put option and broken it down into its constituent parts. A put option is:

The right but not the obligation to sell (because it is a put) a given amount of a given asset (the underlying) at a given price (the strike price) on or before a given date (expiry).

2
Option Specifications

Before going into detail, an important preliminary distinction needs to be made. Options that are traded on a recognised exchange, such as LIFFE or the CME, are known as exchange traded options, abbreviated to ETOs. Any trading that takes place away from a recognised exchange is "over-the-counter", abbreviated to OTC. It is likely that most readers of this book will confine themselves to ETOs for reasons of convenience, simplicity and capital efficiency. Nonetheless, the vast majority of what follows applies generically, to all types of options, unless otherwise stated.

All options are specified exactly in respect of the following:

- Whether it is a call or a put
- The underlying
- Strike price
- Expiry date
- Exercise rights

Let's consider each of these factors individually.

The first point has already been covered; any option that conveys the right to *buy* something is a *call*. Any option that conveys the right to *sell* something is a *put*.

The *underlying* (sometimes known (esp. USA) as the "underlier") can be just about anything, as long as it has a price. In the OTC markets, there are options on an astonishing range of underlying assets, from obvious candidates such as currencies, interest rates, bonds, equities, indices and the like, right through to more unusual underliers such as emissions, satellite load-space and the weather.

The point has already been made that the majority of readers of this book are likely to stick to ETOs, and with respect to ETOs (see above), the underlying is nearly always the corresponding future.

For example, on LIFFE, the underlying of a May Coffee option is a May Coffee future. The underlying of a June Euribor option is a June Euribor future (Euribor derivatives are based upon interest rates on 3 month euro deposits). On the CBOT, the underlying of a March Corn option is a March Corn future. On Eurex, the underlying of a September Bund option is a September Bund future.

The notable exception to this is the equity market. The underlying of a stock option tends to be the *physical shares* themselves, rather than a share future. For example, on LIFFE, the underlying of a June BP option is 1000 BP shares. The underlying of a September Lloyds TSB Option is 1000 Lloyds TSB shares.

Note: There are regional variations in the underlying of equity options. In the UK, the standard number of shares underlying a stock option tends to be 1000. In both the USA and continental Europe, the standard number of shares underlying a stock option tends to be 100, because share values in those regions tend to be significantly higher than in the UK.

As a general rule, *make sure that you are familiar with the exact contract specification* of anything that you want to trade. Brokers and exchange websites can provide such information (detail provided at a later stage).

The *strike price* (often abbreviated simply to the "strike") of an option, that is, the price at which the underlying may be bought (call) or sold (put), will be specified exactly.

All options have an *expiry date* or *expiration*, a date on which they cease to exist, just like an insurance policy, which also expires on a given date. An option's expiry date will be specified exactly, including the *time* at which the option expires on the expiry date. For example, on LIFFE, both FTSE 100 options and single stock options expire on the third Friday in the month. However, FTSE 100 options expire at 10:30 while single stock options expire at 18:30. The extra eight hours of "life" of the single stock option may be crucial!

Note: Most options expire on the same day as the underlying future. For example, on LIFFE, FTSE 100 options expire at the same time and on the same day as FTSE 100 futures. Euribor options expire just 45 minutes after Euribor futures. Most of the exceptions to this rule lie in the commodities field, where *physical delivery* of the underlying commodity may be an issue. Again, as a general rule, *make sure that you are familiar with the contract specification.*

The final feature of an option that will be specified is the type of *exercise rights* that pertain to the option. Essentially, there are two "styles" of option; *European* style and *American* style. This distinction has nothing to do with *where* the options are traded or the currency in which trading is denominated. Rather, the distinction relates to exactly *when* the options can be exercised. The distinction is very simple:

- European-style options can only be exercised *upon expiry.*
- American-style options can be exercised *at any time.*

In this sense, American-style options are more flexible than their European-style counterparts. This extra flexibility should, in theory, mean extra value, extra price. However, in the real world, with one notable exception, there is no significant difference in the prices or values of the two styles of option. The reason for this is that the early exercise (i.e. exercise before expiry) of options is not generally desirable. If an option has become profitable, with the one exception previously mentioned, the profit should not be taken by exercising the option, but rather by either selling the option in the market or by hedging with the underlying. This idea will be expanded upon at a later stage.

Exercise 2.1

Consider the following option:

December FTSE 5925 call

1. What is the underlying of this option?
2. What is the strike price of this option?
3. When does this option expire?
4. Is this an option to buy or sell the underlying?
5. Is this a European-style or an American-style option?

Consider the following option:

September BP £5.00 put

1. What is the underlying of this option?
2. What is the strike price of this option?
3. When does this option expire?
4. Is this an option to buy or sell the underlying?
5. Is this a European-style or an American-style option?

Exercise 2.1: Answers

December FTSE 5925 call

1. The underlying of this option is the FTSE 100 cash index.
2. The strike price of this option is 5925.
3. This option expires at 10:30 on the third Friday of December.
4. This is this an option to buy the underlying.
5. This is a European-style option because it may only be exercised on expiry.

September BP £5.00 put

1. The underlying of this option is 1000 BP shares.
2. The strike price of this option is £5.00.
3. This option expires at 18:30 on the third Friday in September.
4. This an option to sell the underlying.
5. This is an American-style option because it may be exercised at any time.

3
Exercise and Assignment

The point has already been made that derivatives, whether options or futures, are contracts. When we trade a future, we are trading a *futures contract*. When we trade an option, we are trading an *options contract*. These contracts are transferable, they are tradable between market participants. We can buy an option from one person and sell it to a different person. We do this via the exchange and the related clearing house, such as LIFFE and LCH Clearnet. Trading is anonymous. We don't know who we have traded with and nor do we care; it is irrelevant. When we buy 5 Sept BP £6.00 puts and then sell 3 of them, we don't have two positions. We are not long of 5 puts and short of 3 puts. Rather, we have a net position of long 2 puts. There may also be a profit or loss, depending upon the prices at which we traded, but our position is simply the net result of the two trades. Furthermore, we can trade in and out of options positions as and when we want, at any time while the market is open until expiry. Options positions do not have to be held until expiry. We may buy some options this morning and sell them an hour later ("intra-day" trading). Or we may buy some options today and sell them tomorrow or next week or next month, any time until expiry. The following section considers what happens if we hold an option position all the way to expiry; the mechanics and consequences of *exercise* and *assignment*.

The owner of an option may exercise their right to buy (in the case of a call) or sell (in the case of a put) the underlying at the option's strike price.

For example, the owner of a September BP £7.00 call may exercise their right to buy (because this is a call) 1000 BP shares (the underlying) at a price of £7.00 (the strike price).

Clearly, the owner of this option will only exercise their right to buy BP shares at £7.00 if a profit results. In other words, in this example, the option will only be exercised if the BP share price is above £7.00. The owner of the option will not (logically!) exercise their right to buy BP shares at £7.00 if the share price is below

£7.00 *because they don't have to*. Remember, the price that was paid for the option gave the option buyer the right *but not the obligation* to buy BP shares at £7.00.

Ultimately, if September expiry is reached with the share price below £7.00, then the option will be allowed to *expire worthless*.

In the event that the owner of a September BP £7.00 call does decide to exercise their call, then someone who is short of these calls will be *assigned*. They will be compelled to sell 1000 BP shares at £7.00 – regardless of the current price of BP.

Exercise 3.1

Given that the prevailing price of Lloyds TSB shares is £6.50, which of the following options could be exercised, and which allowed to expire worthless?

1. £6.00 call
2. £5.50 call
3. £7.00 call
4. £7.00 put
5. £6.00 put

Exercise 3.1: Answers

1. £6.00 call could be exercised, because the underlying is trading £0.50 *above* the option's strike.
2. £5.50 call could be exercised, because the underlying is trading £1.00 *above* the option's strike.
3. £7.00 call would be allowed to expire worthless; why choose to buy the underlying at £7.00 when it can be bought at £6.50 in the open market?
4. £7.00 put could be exercised, because the underlying is trading £0.50 *below* the option's strike.
5. £6.00 put would be allowed to expire worthless; why choose to sell the underlying at £6.00 when it can be sold at £6.50 in the open market?

A call conveys the right to buy the underlying, so the exercise of a call will result in a *long* position in the underlying. For example, exercising one LIFFE BP £6.00 call will result in a position of long 1000 BP shares (remember that one LIFFE stock option equates to 1000 of the underlying shares).

In the event of a call being exercised, someone who is short of these calls will be assigned. Since a call conveys the right to buy the underlying, *assignment* of a short call will result in a *short* position in the underlying. For example, assignment on one LIFFE BP £6.00 call will result in a position of short 1000 BP shares.

A put conveys the right to sell the underlying, so the exercise of a put will result in a short position in the underlying. For example, exercising one LIFFE Lloyds TSB £7.00 put will result in a position of short 1000 Lloyds TSB shares.

In the event of a put being exercised, someone who is short of these puts will be assigned. Since a put conveys the right to sell the underlying, *assignment* of a short put will result in a *long* position in the underlying. For example, assignment on one LIFFE Lloyds TSB £7.00 put will result in a position of long 1000 Lloyds TSB shares.

A simple way of understanding the above is as follows.

- A call conveys the right to buy, so it may be represented by a *plus* sign.
- A put conveys the right to sell, so it may be represented by a *minus* sign.
- Long may be represented by a *plus* sign.
- Short may be represented by a *minus* sign.

Consider the four possibilities:

LONG CALL $= +$(multiplied by) $+ = $ A LONG POSITION

SHORT CALL $= -$(multiplied by) $+ = $ A SHORT POSITION

LONG PUT $= +$(multiplied by) $- = $ A SHORT POSITION

SHORT PUT $= -$(multiplied by) $- = $ A LONG POSITION

The exercise of a long call position will result in a long underlying position. Therefore, being long calls is similar to being long the underlying. For example, being long BP calls is like being long BP shares. Being long BP calls is a proxy for being long the shares, an alternative to being long the shares.

Being assigned upon a short call position will result in a short underlying position. So being short calls is similar to being short the underlying stock. For example, being short BP calls is like being short BP shares.

The exercise of a long put position will result in a short underlying position. Therefore, being long puts is similar to being short the underlying. For example, being long BP puts is like being short BP shares. Being long BP puts is a proxy for being short the shares, an alternative to being short the shares.

Being assigned upon a short put position will result in a long underlying position. So being short puts is similar to being long the underlying stock. For example, being short BP puts is like being long BP shares.

Exercise 3.2

1. We exercise 5 June BP £5.50 calls at the close on Tuesday. What will be our resulting position in BP shares on Wednesday morning?
2. We exercise 8 June BP £7.00 puts at the close on Tuesday. What will be our resulting position in BP shares on Wednesday morning?
3. We are short of 15 September Lloyds TSB £6.00 calls that are exercised, and on which we are therefore assigned; what is our resulting position in Lloyds TSB?
4. We are short of 7 September Lloyds TSB £7.50 puts that are exercised, and on which we are therefore assigned; what is our resulting position in Lloyds TSB?

Exercise 3.2: Answers

1. Long 5000 BP shares at £5.50 (because each of our 5 calls gave us the right to buy 1000 BP shares at a price of £5.50).
2. Short 8000 BP shares at £7.00 (because each of our 8 puts gave us the right to sell 1000 BP shares at a price of £7.00).
3. Short 15 000 Lloyds TSB shares at £6.00 (because each of the 15 calls that we sold gave someone else the right to buy 1000 Lloyds TSB shares from us at a price of £6.00).
4. Long 7000 Lloyds TSB shares at £7.50 (because each of the 7 puts that we sold gave someone else the right to sell us 1000 Lloyds TSB shares at a price of £7.50).

THE PRACTICALITIES OF EXERCISE AND ASSIGNMENT

For reasons that will be explained at a later stage, it is unlikely (though not inconceivable) that an option will be exercised before expiry. However, in the unlikely event that we do want to exercise some options, we simply need to contact our broker to request that they exercise the relevant options on our behalf. If we own exercisable options upon expiry, they will normally be *exercised automatically* on our behalf, but we need to check with our broker as different exchanges and clearing houses have different rules.

From the short option perspective, our broker will inform us if we are assigned upon some options. Again, this is unlikely (though not inconceivable) to happen before expiry.

Exercise 3.3: Bringing the Basics Together

Consider the following detail taken from the contract specification for the LIFFE BP option contract (correct at time of publishing; check on LIFFE website, www.liffe.com).

Unit of trading: One option normally equals rights over 1000 shares
Quotation: Pence per share
Last trading day: 16:30 on third Friday in expiry month
Exercise: American style

Given the above information, consider the following option:

LIFFE BP March £5.00 call

1. Does this option convey the right to buy or sell BP?
2. At what price?
3. Until when?

4. Can this option be exercised at any time, or only at expiry?
5. Who has the right to exercise; the option buyer or seller?
6. If the buyer exercises this option, what position will result?

Exercise 3.3: Answers

1. The option conveys the right to buy since it is a call.
2. At the strike price of £5.00.
3. Until the (March) expiry time/date which is 18:30 on the third Friday in March.
4. This option may be exercised at any time until expiry since it is American style.
5. The option buyer has the right to exercise the option.
6. If the option buyer exercises the call, a position of long 1000 BP shares will result, because the buyer (owner) of one LIFFE BP March £5.00 call has the right to buy 1000 BP shares at £5.00.

SUMMARY OF CHAPTERS 1, 2 AND 3

- Options convey the right but not the obligation to buy or sell something (the "underlying").
- Calls convey the right (but not the obligation) to buy the underlying.
- Puts convey the right (but not the obligation) to sell the underlying.
- Options may be bought or sold – they are transferable.
- Options may be traded on a recognised exchange such as LIFFE or directly between counterparties ("over-the-counter").
- The owner of an option may exercise their right to buy (in the case of a call) or sell (in the case of a put).
- The mirror image of exercise is known as assignment.

4
Option Uses

The ways in which options may be used were briefly outlined in the preface to this book. These possible uses will be expanded upon in this chapter but first it is worth considering the evolution of options.

Many people conceive of options as a relatively recent phenomenon; complex financial instruments traded by sophisticated traders in high-tech dealing rooms. In fact, options have been around for a very long time. It is likely that options have been traded since man first assigned values and prices to goods and assets; indeed, there is evidence that grain and metal options were traded by the Phoenicians as early as the second millennium BC. The driver behind this early option use was almost certainly hedging, a desire to guard against adverse price movements. Farmers have always been exposed to fluctuating crop prices; derivatives such as grain options developed as a way of managing this risk.

While hedging may be viewed as the "correct" or "true" use of options, the reason why options were "invented", it is nonetheless true that options also offer tempting opportunities to speculators. In his book entitled *Politics*, Aristotle tells the story of Thales, the first known Greek philosopher, mathematician and scientist (thought, incidentally, to be the teacher of the better known Pythagoras). Thales is said to have anticipated a bumper olive harvest and therefore decided to take out options on all the olive presses in the region, which he was then able to rent out at highly profitable rates. This happy conjunction of philosophical and financial acumen is echoed in the modern day successes of uber-speculators such as George Soros.

Post-Renaissance, there are plentiful examples of option use, both speculative and protective. There is written evidence of Dutch tulip-bulb traders and Japanese rice traders using options as speculative instruments during the 17th century, while currency options (based upon the French franc) were used for hedging purposes during the American Civil War. That said, it was in the early 1970s that option use really took off. This was a time of market deregulation, oil price shocks and, crucially, technological advance. As we will see in a later chapter, you don't need a computer to trade options – but it helps. IT developments in the early 1970s allowed academics such as Black, Scholes and Merton to come up with the first option pricing models, work that merited a subsequent "Nobel" Prize in Economics (Swedish Riksbank Prize in Economic Sciences, 1997). Interest in option trading grew, with the Chicago Board Options Exchange (CBOE) opening in 1973 and LIFFE starting option trading in London in 1985.

Today, options are traded on a bewildering array of assets across the globe. The US exchanges continue to dominate, with LIFFE and Eurex leading the way in Europe. OTC options (i.e. non-exchange traded) also trade in vast size and are a vital component of many structured products.

So how are options used? What were options "invented" for?

The origins of modern option markets lay in "hedging". Early examples of option use tended to relate to agriculture, an undertaking in which a key area of uncertainty is the price of a crop at harvest time. Derivatives evolved as a method of either fixing that price (via futures/forwards) or guaranteeing a minimum price (via options). It is no coincidence that the first major derivatives market, the Chicago Board of Trade (CBOT), grew up in a city on the edge of the Great Plains, the "bread basket of America". With this in mind, and before we move on to equity options, consider how a farmer might use commodity futures and options to remove price risk; to "hedge" himself.

USING OPTIONS TO HEDGE: AN INTUITIVE EXAMPLE

Consider a wheat farmer. At the beginning of the year, the farmer has a good idea of his costs; rent, seed, machinery, fertilisers and so on. What he doesn't know is the price that he will receive for his crop when he harvests in September. A high price will be good for the farmer, a low price bad. Clearly, the farmer is exposed to the price of wheat falling between sowing the crop and harvest; he is exposed to "price risk".

What are the farmer's choices? Do nothing! Simply hope for the best, hope that the wheat price rises. In doing this, whether he knows it or not, the farmer is "taking a view". Specifically, he is taking a "punt" on the wheat price staying at its current level or rising. And "punting" is not the farmer's business. If he gets it wrong and the wheat price falls significantly, he may find himself out of business. By the very nature of his business, our farmer is exposed; he really should hedge, but how?

He could sell his wheat "forward". That is, he could find someone to buy his wheat for delivery at harvest time. The price is agreed today but delivery doesn't take place until September. He has sold his wheat forward. The counterparty has bought wheat forward. The written agreement exchanged between the two parties is a "forward contract". Such agreements are common in the farming world, both OTC as in the above example, or traded on exchanges like the CBOT and LIFFE. A forward contract traded on an exchange is known as a "futures" contract.

Here, let's assume that the farmer sells his wheat forward at a price of £160 per tonne.

By selling his wheat forward, the farmer has eliminated price risk but he has also eliminated any chance of benefiting from the wheat price rising between now and September. He has "locked in" the price (£160 per tonne) that he will receive for his crop. Now, in this example, it could be argued that this is not a serious problem. The farmer has protected himself against a fall in wheat prices and, if wheat prices rise, it represents an opportunity cost rather than an actual, realised cost. However, humans are emotional beings and we can expect our farmer to be less than pleased if the wheat price rises significantly and he is unable to benefit. How can our farmer protect himself against falling wheat prices while retaining his potential to profit from rising wheat prices? The answer, by using options.

Rather than contracting to sell his wheat forward, our farmer could make a contract to sell his wheat if he needs to. He can participate in a contract in which he has the choice, but not the obligation, to sell his wheat at a certain price. He can buy a put option. He can buy the option directly from a grain merchant, or on an exchange such as LIFFE.

Here, let's assume that the farmer buys a September wheat £160 put at a price of £10.00. This option gives the farmer the right, but not the obligation, to sell (because it is a put) his wheat (the underlying) at a price of £160 per tonne (the strike price) at any time up until September (the expiry date).

So if the wheat price falls to, say, £115 per tonne, the farmer is protected because he will exercise his right to sell his wheat at £160 per tonne. He originally paid a price of £10.00 for the option, so the net price at which he has sold his wheat is £150 per tonne, significantly better than the prevailing price of £115 per tonne.

If, on the other hand, the wheat price rises to £200 per tonne, the farmer will allow his £160 put to expire worthless and instead sell his wheat in the open market at the prevailing price of £200 per tonne. As before, he originally paid a price of £10.00 for the option, so the net price at which he has sold his wheat is £190 per tonne, significantly better than if he had originally sold his wheat forward and "locked in" at £160 per tonne.

The farmer has protected himself against a fall in wheat prices while retaining the ability to benefit from rising wheat prices. He has "had his cake and eaten it" – at a cost. Remember, the option originally cost £10.00. It is only worth paying this cost if the farmer believes that there is a chance of the wheat price rising by at least £10.00!

To understand the validity of this statement, consider what would happen if the wheat price remained unchanged between now and harvest.

Remember, the farmer has bought a September wheat £160 put at a price of £10.00. If the wheat price remains unchanged at £160 per tonne between now and September, then the option will expire worthless. The £10.00 premium paid for the option has been "wasted". The farmer would have been better off doing nothing, right? Wrong! The farmer has been protected against a fall in the wheat price. He has been "insured". Do we complain when our house insurance expires worthless? Do we consider the insurance premium to have been wasted? Do we wish that we had had the chance to make a claim? No, no and no again. In this example, the £10 premium paid for the option is like an insurance policy, protecting the farmer against downside price risk. The farmer doesn't want the wheat price to fall, he doesn't want to use his policy. Rather, he wants something good to happen elsewhere; specifically, he wants the wheat price to rise so that he can sell his wheat at harvest time at a better price than the price prevailing today. As long as the wheat price rises by more than £10.00 between now and harvest, the farmer will be in a better net position.

Bearing the above example in mind, the hedging process for a "natural long" such as a farmer may be formalised into a simple decision tree as follows.

Q1. Do we want or need downside protection?

A1. No. DO NOTHING but this implies a definite belief that the market will *not* fall
A1. Yes. Go to Q2.

Q2. What is our market view?

A2. Bullish: BUY PUTS
A2. Bearish: SELL FORWARD/FUTURE
A2. Neutral: BUY PUT & SELL CALL (collectively known as a "FENCE" or "COLLAR", explained in detail at a later stage)

Figure 4.1   Hedging a long underlying position; decision tree

Having considered how a farmer might hedge with options, let's consider how this might translate into the world of equities and equity indices. Private investors with positions in individual stocks can protect those positions very effectively by buying options. Specifically, a long stock position can be protected by buying puts and a short stock position (whether through stock futures, CFDs, etc.) can be protected by buying calls. At a professional level, the same principles can be applied to money under management as the following (hypothetical) exercise illustrates.

Exercise 4.1: Hedging an Equity Portfolio

We own a portfolio of FTSE 100 equities.

1. Is our exposure to the upside or downside? In other words, do we want UK share prices to rise or fall

We are concerned that UK share prices may fall in the next quarter but do not wish to simply sell our portfolio of equities (for various reasons such as fees, tax implications, etc.).

2. How could we protect our share portfolio with FTSE 100 futures?
3. If we sell FTSE 100 futures to protect our share portfolio, do we still have upside profit potential?
4. Using FTSE 100 options, how could we protect our share portfolio *and* retain our upside potential?
5. If we buy FTSE 100 puts to protect our share portfolio, which way do we want UK share prices to move in the next 3 months?
6. If, for example, we buy the 3 month 5850 puts at a price of 103 to protect our share portfolio, this implies a belief that share prices will rise by at least how much over the next 3 months?

A key question that has not yet been addressed is *which* particular put we should buy. This question will be addressed immediately after the answers to this exercise.

Exercise 4.1: Answers

1. Our exposure is to the downside. We want UK share prices to rise and are exposed to UK share prices falling.
2. We could protect our share portfolio by selling the appropriate number of FTSE 100 futures. Any losses on our physical share portfolio as a result of falling share prices should be offset by profit on our short FTSE futures trade. Note the use of the word "should". Specific shares are unlikely to be correlated exactly to the FTSE 100 Index. Nonetheless, for a basket of shares, there is likely to be a correlation with the index.
3. No, if we sell FTSE 100 futures to protect our share portfolio, then we are locked in. If share prices rise, then the resulting profits on our physical share portfolio are likely to be offset by a loss on our short FTSE futures trade.
4. We could protect our share portfolio *and* retain our upside potential by buying FTSE 100 puts. In the event that UK share prices fall, we may exercise our right to sell the FTSE 100 Index. Conversely, in the event that UK share prices rise, we will allow our puts to expire worthless and, if we so wish, sell our physical shares at the higher prevailing prices.
5. If we buy FTSE 100 puts to protect our share portfolio, we want UK share prices to *rise* in the next 3 months. The puts are there for protection; they are insurance policies to protect us against an undesirable event. It may seem counterintuitive but, just like an insurance policy, we want the puts to expire worthless since this implies that share prices haven't fallen significantly.
6. If we buy the 3 month 5850 puts at a price of 103 to protect our share portfolio, this implies a belief that share prices will rise by at least 103 index points over the next 3 months. In other words, we believe that the FTSE 100 Index will rise to at least 6103 (the current price of 6000 plus the put premium of 103) over the next 3 months.

Table 4.1 LIFFE 3 month FTSE 100 option prices (LIFFE 3 month
FTSE 100 future = 6000)

Call Prices	Strike Prices	Put Prices
284	**5800**	89
250	**5850**	103
217	**5900**	119
185	**5950**	136
155	**6000**	155

Notes: Strike prices are listed in bold down the middle of the table.

There are more strike prices than those shown, but the table focuses upon those
strikes closest to the prevailing underlying futures price of 6000.

The prices of the calls are shown in the left-hand column, and the prices of the
puts are shown in the right-hand column. During the trading day, these prices
would be moving around and there would be a bid/offer spread; here mid-prices
are used for the sake of simplicity.

Each "tick" is worth £10.00. The cost of one 5800 put is 89 "ticks" with a
monetary equivalent of £890.

Finally, let's consider the question of which particular puts should be bought. With
reference to the put prices in Table 4.1, the choices are clear. The 6000 put may be
bought for 155, the 5950 put for 136 and so on down to the 5800 put which my be
bought for 89. The put prices become progressively cheaper as the strikes become
progressively lower. This seems logical since the 6000 put conveys the right to sell at
6000 and the 5800 put conveys the right to sell at the lower price of 5800. It therefore
makes sense that the 6000 put costs more than the 5950 put, which in turn costs more
than the 5900 put and so on. In terms of choosing a specific put to hedge the portfolio,
the higher the strike and the higher the level of protection, the higher the cost of the
option, and vice versa. The choice of specific put therefore depends primarily on two
factors: the level at which protection is required/desired and the amount that we are
prepared to pay. "You pays your money and takes your choice."

A further potential factor in this decision is our market view. For example, if we
feel that the market is unlikely to fall significantly but we protect our portfolio as a
matter of good practice, then we may choose to buy a lower put (such as the 5800
put) for a lower price. It is there to "insure" against an unlikely event. An everyday
comparison might be agreeing to pay a larger excess on our car insurance in order to
pay a lower premium. We consider it highly unlikely that we will make a claim and
so are prepared to take a greater risk to secure a lower up-front cost.

Futures and options can be used highly effectively to hedge any underlying position,
whether it be an equity portfolio, a single stock holding or a farmer's crop. Indeed,
as already stated, derivatives were invented for that very purpose.

The simplest way of using derivatives to hedge is to trade the appropriate fu-
tures/forwards, but in removing risk, profit potential is also removed. The price is
"locked in". The only way to remove price risk while retaining profit potential is

to buy options. Note that protection cannot be achieved by selling options. Selling options may bring in some cash, it may enhance yield, but it also increases risk. In everyday life, we buy insurance to protect ourselves, selling insurance to others would bring in some cash but also expose us to significant risk. By buying options to hedge an existing underlying position, protection is achieved and profit potential retained, but *at a cost*. Our willingness to pay that cost will depend upon our attitude to risk and our view of the market.

These themes will be expanded upon in a later chapter on option spreads; specifically, the sections on the "Fence" or "Collar".

Having considered how options may be used for hedging purposes, let's now consider the other main use of options – *speculation*.

USING OPTIONS TO SPECULATE

Speculation may be defined as taking a risk in the hope or expectation of making a profit. In everyday terms, speculation is akin to gambling. Speculators risk some money in the hope of making some money. The idea is to limit risk while maximising potential profit. This "risk/reward" relationship is fundamental to all forms of trading.

Derivatives in general are ideally suited to speculation for a number of reasons. Trading derivatives is more capitally efficient than physical trading due to the use of margin and marking-to-market. In turn, this capital efficiency allows for gearing or leverage, for greater exposure to the market. An example of this follows.

Trading derivatives may also have tax advantages over physical trading. For example, stamp duty of 0.5% is payable when buying UK equities but is not payable when buying UK equity derivatives.

Derivatives may allow us access to markets that would otherwise be inaccessible. A good example is the FTSE 100 Index. It would be highly impractical and expensive to trade the cash FTSE 100 Index. We would need to buy all of the shares in the index in exactly the right amount, a time consuming and costly business. In contrast, trading FTSE 100 Index derivatives is a much simpler and less costly proposition.

Trading derivatives allows us to go short as well as long, a choice that physical trading doesn't allow. We cannot go short of physical shares. We cannot sell physical shares that we do not own. We can, however, go short of equity derivatives, allowing us to exploit bearish as well as bullish views upon a share price.

We can see that trading derivatives, whether futures or options, has several significant advantages over cash or physical trading. The following example illustrates these advantages, as well as the additional advantages of trading options over futures.

Let's assume that we are speculators with trading capital of £5000.

We believe that shares in XYZ Ltd are about to rise in value. We are bullish. Shares in XYZ Ltd are currently trading at a price of £5.00 on the London Stock Exchange. If we buy 1000 XYZ shares on the LSE, we will have to come up with £5000 (i.e. 1000 × £5.00), the full value of the shares. Further, we will have to pay £25 (i.e.

0.5% of £5000) in stamp duty. Buying 1000 physical shares will use up all of our trading capital. What are the alternatives?

We could buy XYZ stock futures on an exchange such as LIFFE. On LIFFE, one "universal stock future" equates to 1000 shares. The price of XYZ stock futures will be similar to that of XYZ shares on the LSE, any difference being a function of interest rates and dividends where applicable.

The key advantage of buying the stock futures rather than the physical shares is that we don't have to come up with the full value of the shares. Rather, we have to come up with the "initial margin" on the futures trade, which will typically equate to about 10% of the total value. Each XYZ stock future represents 1000 XYZ shares, the price of which is £5.00. The nominal value of each XYZ stock future is therefore £5000. If the initial margin required for each stock future is 10% of the nominal value, then we will need to provide £500 of initial margin for every XYZ stock future that we buy. Since we have £5000 of trading capital, we can therefore afford to buy 10 XYZ stock futures, giving us exposure to 10 000 XYZ shares.

If, as we expect, the price of XYZ rises, we will make 10 times more by trading the futures than if we had bought the physical shares. Of course, if we are wrong and XYZ falls, we can also lose 10 times as much. But speculators are looking to back their own judgement, and the gearing that futures afford is highly attractive to such market users.

A further alternative to buying either the physical shares or stock futures would be to buy some call options. Other things being equal, as the underlying share price rises, the value of calls will also rise. In this sense, buying calls is a proxy for buying the underlying share; being long calls is like being long the underlying. In this case, let's assume that we buy 3 month XYZ £5.00 calls at a price of 10 ticks (equivalent to £100) per contract. Each £5.00 call costs £100 so we can afford to buy 50 of them with our trading capital of £5000. Each of the 50 calls gives us the right to buy 1000 shares at the strike price of £5.00, thus giving us the chance to be long of 50 000 shares, five times as many shares as the futures allow and 50 times the number of physical shares that we could buy. The potential for gearing is clear.

If, as we expect, the price of XYZ rises, we have the potential to be long 50 times more shares by trading the options than if we had bought the physical shares, and long five times more shares than if we had bought XYZ stock futures.

Furthermore, if we are wrong and the price of XYZ falls, we can only lose the premium that we have paid for the calls, in this case £5000. Contrast this with the futures where we have achieved gearing at the expense of commensurately large potential losses. Table 4.2 summarises the three choices considered above.

Note: All trading costs including stamp duty have been ignored for the sake of simplicity. For the same reason, any difference in price between the physical shares and stock futures has also been ignored. Neither of these factors is significant to the comparisons made.

Table 4.2 Physical vs futures vs options

	Initial Outlay	Exposure to XYZ Shares	Maximum Loss
Buy 1000 physical XYZ shares @ £5.00	£5000 (full cash value)	Long 1000	£5000
Buy 10 XYZ stock futures @ £5.00	£5000 (initial margin)	Long 10 000	£50 000
Buy 50 XYZ £5.00 calls @ 10 (i.e. £10) per contract	£5000 (premium)	Long 50 000	£5000

We can see that, given a finite amount of trading capital, buying the calls is the most capitally efficient choice of trade. With just £5000 of trading capital, we can buy 50 calls giving us the right (but not the obligation) to buy 50 000 shares.

We can also see that buying the calls offers the best risk/reward. If we buy 1000 physical XYZ shares at a price of £5.00 per share, we can lose £5000 (if the share price falls to zero) and, in theory at least, we have unlimited potential profit to the upside. More realistically, if the price of XYZ doubles to £10.00, we will double our initial investment, a return of 100%.

If we buy 10 XYZ stock futures at a price of £5.00 per contract, we can lose £50 000 (if the share price falls to zero) and again, in theory at least, we have unlimited potential profit to the upside. More realistically, if the price of XYZ doubles to £10.00, we will make a return of 1000% (10 times) on our initial outlay (initial margin) of £5000.

If we buy 50 3 month XYZ £5.00 calls at a price of 10 ticks (equivalent to £100) per contract, we can lose £5000 (if the share price is at or below £5.00 upon expiry) and, in theory at least, we have unlimited potential profit to the upside. More realistically, if the price of XYZ doubles to £10.00, we will make a return of 4900% (49 times) on our initial outlay (option premium) of £5000. In the event that the price of XYZ doubles to £10.00, the £5.00 calls will be worth at least £5.00 (the difference between the current share price of £10.00 and the strike price of £5.00). We originally paid £0.10 for the calls, so our profit will be at least £4.90 (the value of the call less the price originally paid), giving a return of at least 49 times the original "stake".

In summary, buying the calls offers the greatest leverage and the best risk/reward. So where is the catch? What works against us when we buy options but not when we buy futures or physical? The answer is *time*. As we will see in a subsequent chapter, options "erode", they lose value due to the passage of time. In the above comparison, we can see that, in the event of a large rise or fall in the price of XYZ, buying the options was the best choice in terms of both gearing and risk/reward. But what if nothing happened during the 3 months in question? What if the price of XYZ shares stayed at £5.00 all the way to the options' expiry 3 months hence?

In such circumstances, the physical and futures trades would be "flat"; there would be neither profit nor loss. The options, however, would expire worthless in such circumstances; we would lose our investment of £5000.

We can see the basic dynamic at work here. Buying options gives us an attractive risk/reward – but time works against us. Unsurprisingly, as we shall see at a later stage, the dynamic of selling options is a mirror image of this relationship. Having examined the basic dynamics at work when buying options, it is worth noting some further advantages that options offer over physical or futures trading.

Professional speculators employ "stop-loss orders", commonly known as "stops". What is a "stop"? Consider the following example.

As before, we are speculators in XYZ shares. We believe that the price of XYZ will rise so we buy 10 XYZ futures at a price of £5.00. Our risk is clearly to the downside. If XYZ falls in price to zero, we will lose £50 000 (10 lots × 1000 XYZ shares × £5.00). To protect ourselves against such damaging losses, we place a "stop" order in the market. For example, we instruct our broker to sell our 10 XYZ futures "at market" (i.e. the first available price) if the price falls to £4.90. We have bought 10 XYZ futures in the expectation that the price of XYZ will rise. However, to protect ourselves against excessive losses to the downside in the event that our view is wrong, we place a "stop" to sell our futures at £4.90. Should the price of XYZ futures fall to £4.90, our broker will close our position by selling our 10 XYZ futures at the best price available at that moment.

All intelligent speculators use "stops". Those that do not tend to sustain crippling losses and go out of business. The problem with using stops, a necessary precaution in potentially volatile markets, is that traders may get "stopped out". Again, this is best illustrated with an example.

As before, we buy 10 XYZ futures at £5.00 because we believe that the price of XYZ will rise. At the same time, we place a "stop" to sell the 10 XYZ futures at £4.90, should the price fall to that level. The XYZ futures price now falls to £4.90, causing our broker to close our position by selling 10 XYZ futures at £4.90, as instructed. We have been "stopped out" at £4.90. We have taken a loss of £1000 (i.e. £0.10 × 10 lots × 1000 shares) and we no longer have a position. Now, to our frustration, the price of XYZ starts to rise, exactly as we predicted. The problem is that we no longer have a position because we were stopped out when the market dipped, albeit only briefly, to £4.90. Our view was ultimately correct, but we had not bargained for a short-term dip in the market.

Remember, all professional traders use stops; indeed, it could be argued that all traders should use stops, whether professional or not. But markets tend not to move in straight lines. There are often short-term price corrections, and this "noise" (traders' name for such short-term fluctuations around the underlying trend) is a real problem. We can be right about the underlying market trend yet be hurt by the "noise".

Options remove the need for stops. The stop is built in since we can only ever lose what we pay for the option. If, in the above example, we buy some calls instead of buying futures, we don't need to place a stop because we can only ever lose the option premium paid. For example, we could buy some £5.00 calls at a price of 10 (i.e. £0.10) per contract, in the knowledge that they are likely to increase in price if, as expected, the price of XYZ rises. If, as before, the price of XYZ falls to £4.90, the value of our calls is likely to fall to about 6 (i.e. £0.06). This represents a loss but, critically and in direct contrast to the futures position, we know that we can only ever lose another 6 ticks per contract. We don't need to sell the calls, we don't need to close our position, we don't get stopped out. If, as before, the price of XYZ now rises, our calls will start to gain value, our losses will reduce and we may well move into profit. Buying options rather than buying futures allows us to stay in the position, to ride out the short-term fluctuations. In summary, you don't get stopped out with options, a further advantage over other speculative instruments.

Another advantage of using options over futures or physical is *exact tailoring*. Options offer many more ways to exploit a particular view than the alternatives. Consider the following question.

Can we use futures or physical to exploit a view on the speed of moves? For example, what should we do with XYZ shares if we think that they will appreciate quickly in value? Buy them of course. And what should we do with XYZ shares if we think that they will appreciate slowly in value? Same answer; buy them! Regardless of our view on the speed of a move, the answer is the same. And yet traders spend valuable time and resources on analysing information and charts to try to make precise predictions about price behaviour, only to employ a sledgehammer (futures or physical) to exploit that precise view. Options, by contrast, allow us to exploit every last detail of a particular view, whether it relates to the speed, timing or extent of an anticipated move. Options are like a scalpel; they allow us to be precise, to optimise returns from a given market view. Indeed, as we shall see later, for any given view, there is an option strategy that is "correct", an option strategy that will optimise our returns in the event that we are proved correct.

Trading options have one final advantage over futures or physical trading. Can we use futures or physical to exploit a view that the market will stay where it is for, say, the next 3 months? No we cannot. If our view is that the price of XYZ will stay exactly where it is for the next 3 months, then we can neither buy nor sell XYZ. What we can do is use options to exploit our view. Specifically, we can sell options to exploit such a view highly effectively, with the crucial rider that there are "good" and "bad" ways of doing this which we will consider at length in a later chapter.

USING OPTIONS TO SPECULATE: SUMMARY

Despite the fact that options were "invented" as hedging tools, the vast majority of option trading in practice is speculative. Traders have long since discovered that options are ideally suited to speculation. When we buy an option, we can only lose the premium paid. Our maximum loss is known from the moment we trade. Our risk is known exactly, a comfortable position for any trader. Broadly speaking, because we know our maximum loss, we can afford to buy more options than we would either futures or physical. We can gain more exposure to the market; we can gear up – an attractive proposition for speculators. The bad news is that time works against us when we buy options. If the underlying market doesn't move, if nothing happens during the life of our options, they will lose value over time and expire worthless.

Options offer further key advantages for speculators over trading physical or futures:

- We don't need to employ "stops" when we speculate with options.
- We can use options to exploit a view that the market will remain unchanged over a given period.
- We can be far more precise in our trading with options; we can optimise returns on any given view.

We will return to this subject at a later stage when we consider option strategy.

Note: The next two chapters deal with the pricing and valuation of options. We will look at this subject from two perspectives:

- We will consider how option prices may be broken down into their constituent parts.
- We will then consider how those option prices were arrived at in the first place.

Along the way, some key option language will be introduced and explained.

5
Option Price and Value

GLOSSARY

Arbitrage: The exploitation of anomalies in pricing between different markets and instruments

Settlement price: The price at which an instrument closes at the end of the trading session

Option prices may be broken down into two parts; *intrinsic value* and *time value* (USA = *extrinsic value*).

Depending upon the specific circumstances, an option price may consist only of intrinsic value, it may consist only of time value or it may consist of both intrinsic and time value.

Intrinsic value is the value of an option if it were exercised now. In other words, it is the difference between the option's strike price and the prevailing price of the underlying.

EXAMPLES OF INTRINSIC VALUE

Stock XYZ is trading at £5.00.

Consider the XYZ £4.50 call. The XYZ £4.50 call confers the right to *buy* XYZ shares at £4.50. If this right is exercised, then the shares bought for £4.50 can be sold on the open market at the prevailing price of £5.00; a difference of £0.50. This £0.50, this difference between the strike price (£4.50) and the prevailing share price (£5.00), is the intrinsic value of the call:

INTRINSIC VALUE OF CALL = UNDERLYING PRICE MINUS STRIKE PRICE

Consider the XYZ £6.00 put. The XYZ £6.00 put confers the right to *sell* XYZ shares at £6.00. If this right is exercised, then the shares sold at £6.00 can be bought back on the open market at the prevailing price of £5.00; a difference of £1.00. This £1.00, the difference between the strike price (£6.00) and the prevailing share price (£5.00), is the intrinsic value of the put:

INTRINSIC VALUE OF PUT = STRIKE PRICE MINUS UNDERLYING PRICE

Exercise 5.1: Identifying Intrinsic Value

Stock XYZ is trading at £5.00. What is the intrinsic value of the:

1. £4.75 call?
2. £4.25 call?
3. £5.25 call?
4. £5.25 put?
5. £5.75 put?
6. £4.00 put?

Exercise 5.1: Answers

1. £0.25 (the prevailing share price of £5.00 less the option's strike price of £4.75)
2. £0.75 (the prevailing share price of £5.00 less the option's strike price of £4.25)
3. Zero! Note that the lower limit of intrinsic value is zero; intrinsic value cannot be negative (see note below).
4. £0.25 (the option's strike price of £5.25 less the prevailing share price of £5.00)
5. £0.75 (the option's strike price of £5.75 less the prevailing share price of £5.00)
6. Zero! Note that the lower limit of intrinsic value is zero; intrinsic value cannot be negative (see note below)

Note: "The lower limit of intrinsic value is zero; intrinsic value cannot be negative." Why is this the case? Remember, options convey the right *but not the obligation* to buy (call) or sell (put). Logic therefore dictates that an option will only be exercised if it has some intrinsic value. For example, if stock XYZ were trading at £5.00, we would not exercise the £4.00 put *because we don't have to*. If we want to sell the shares, it is better to sell them on the open market at the prevailing share price of £5.00 rather than exercise our right to sell them at the option's strike price of £4.00. Simple common sense.

Intrinsic value is what an option is worth if it were exercised right now. It is, at any particular time, a mathematical fact, the simple difference between the option strike price and the underlying share price.

In most cases, intrinsic value will only account for *part* of an option's price. The remainder of the option's price is the option's *time value*. Simply, time value is everything that is *not* intrinsic value. This is best illustrated with the use of some historical option prices. The inter-relationships between intrinsic value and time value are easiest to see with a futures-based option such as LIFFE coffee. The same relationships may be observed in stock option prices, though with a couple of additional complications. For that reason, we will first consider some LIFFE coffee and LIFFE cocoa option prices before looking at some LIFFE FTSE option prices.

Table 5.1   LIFFE July coffee option prices at close on 25 February 2008 (LIFFE July coffee future = 2601)

Call Prices	Strike Prices	Put Prices
248	**2500**	147
222	**2550**	171
199	**2600**	198
179	**2650**	228
160	**2700**	259

Notes: Strike prices are listed down the middle of the table.

There are more strike prices than those shown, but the table focuses upon those strikes closest to the prevailing underlying futures price of 2601.

The prices of the calls are shown in the left-hand column, and the prices of the puts are shown in the right-hand column. During the trading day, these prices would be moving around and there would be a bid/offer spread; here mid-prices are used for the sake of simplicity.

The underlying of one LIFFE July coffee option is one LIFFE July coffee future.

On the LIFFE market, coffee is quoted in US dollars per tonne.

Each "tick" was worth $5.

EXAMPLES OF INTRINSIC VALUE AND TIME VALUE FROM TABLE 5.1

1. On the day in question the July future closed at 2601. The July 2500 call therefore had 101 ticks of intrinsic value (2601 − 2500). On the day in question the July 2500 call closed at a price of 248. 101 ticks of this price were accounted for by intrinsic value. The remaining 147 ticks (i.e. 248 − 101) represented the option's time value.
2. On the day in question the July future closed at 2601. The July 2550 call therefore had 51 ticks of intrinsic value (i.e. 2601 − 2550). On the day in question the July 2550 call closed at a price of 222. 51 ticks of this price were accounted for by intrinsic value. The remaining 171 ticks (i.e. 222 − 51) represented the option's time value.
3. On the day in question the July future closed at 2601. The July 2650 call therefore had no intrinsic value. (Why exercise the right to buy at 2650 when you could buy in the open market at 2601?) On the day in question the July 2650 call closed at a price of 179. This entire price was accounted for by time value.
4. On the day in question the July future closed at 2601. The July 2650 put therefore had 49 ticks of intrinsic value (i.e. 2650 − 2601). On the day in question the July 2650 put closed at a price of 228. 49 ticks of this price were accounted for by

intrinsic value. The remaining 179 ticks (i.e. 228 − 49) represented the option's time value.

5. On the day in question the July future closed at 2601. The July 2700 put therefore had 99 ticks of intrinsic value (i.e. 2700 − 2601). On the day in question the July 2700 put closed at a price of 259. 99 ticks of this price were accounted for by intrinsic value. The remaining 160 ticks (i.e. 259 − 99) represented the option's time value.

6. On the day in question the July future closed at 2601. The July 2500 put therefore had no intrinsic value. (Why exercise the right to sell at 2500 when you could sell in the open market at 2601?) On the day in question the July 2500 put closed at a price of 147. This entire price was accounted for by time value.

Exercise 5.2: Identifying Intrinsic Value and Time Value using Table 5.2

1. On the day in question the July future closed at 1354. The July 1300 call closed at a price of 124. How much of this price was accounted for by intrinsic value? How much of this price was accounted for by time value? What was the price of the July 1300 put at this time?

2. On the day in question the July future closed at 1354. The July 1350 call closed at a price of 101. How much of this price was accounted for by intrinsic value? How much of this price was accounted for by time value? What was the price of the July 1350 put at this time?

3. On the day in question the July future closed at 1354. The July 1375 put closed at a price of 112. How much of this price was accounted for by intrinsic value?

Table 5.2 LIFFE July cocoa option prices at close on 25 February 2008 (LIFFE July cocoa future = 1354)

Call Prices	Strike Prices	Put Prices
124	**1300**	70
111	**1325**	82
101	**1350**	97
91	**1375**	112
82	**1400**	128

Notes: Strike prices are listed down the middle of the table.

There are more strike prices than those shown, but the table focuses upon those strikes closest to the prevailing underlying futures price of 1354.

The prices of the calls are shown in the left-hand column, and the prices of the puts are shown in the right-hand column. During the trading day, these prices would be moving around and there would be a bid/offer spread; here mid-prices are used for the sake of simplicity.

The underlying of one LIFFE July cocoa option is one LIFFE July cocoa future.

On the LIFFE market, cocoa is quoted in pounds sterling per tonne.

Each "tick" is worth £10.

How much of this price was accounted for by time value? What was the price of the July 1375 call at this time?

4. On the day in question the July future closed at 1354. The July 1400 put closed at a price of 128. How much of this price was accounted for by intrinsic value? How much of this price was accounted for by time value? What was the price of the July 1400 call at this time?

Exercise 5.2: Answers

1. On the day in question the July future closed at 1354. The July 1300 call closed at a price of 124. 54 ticks of this price (i.e. 1354 − 1300) were accounted for by intrinsic value. 70 ticks of this price (i.e. 124 − 54) were accounted for by time value. The price of the July 1300 put at this time was also 70 ticks. Note that the 1300 put and 1300 call had the *same amount of time value.*

2. On the day in question the July future closed at 1354. The July 1350 call closed at a price of 101. 4 ticks of this price (i.e. 1354 − 1350) were accounted for by intrinsic value. 97 ticks of this price (i.e. 101 − 4) were accounted for by time value. The price of the July 1350 put at this time was also 97 ticks. Note that the 1350 put and 1350 call had the *same amount of time value.*

3. On the day in question the July future closed at 1354. The July 1375 put closed at a price of 112. 21 ticks of this price (i.e. 1375 − 1354) were accounted for by intrinsic value. 91 ticks of this price (i.e. 112 − 21) were accounted for by time value. The price of the July 1375 call at this time was also 91 ticks. Note that the 1375 put and 1375 call had the *same amount of time value.*

4. On the day in question the July future closed at 1354. The July 1400 put closed at a price of 128. 46 ticks of this price (i.e. 1400 − 1354) were accounted for by intrinsic value. 82 ticks of this price (i.e. 128 − 82) were accounted for by time value. The price of the July 1400 call at this time was also 82 ticks. Note that the 1400 put and 1400 call had the *same amount of time value.*

From the answers to the above exercise, it may be seen that calls and puts with the same strike price and the same expiry have the same amount of time value. For example, the July 1300 call and the July 1300 put had 70 ticks of time value. The only difference in the price of the two options was that the call had intrinsic value while the put did not.

As a further example, the July 1400 call and the July 1400 put both had 82 ticks of time value. The only difference in the price of the two options was that the put had some intrinsic value while the call did not.

This relationship may be observed in *all* option prices. It is called "put/call parity". In relation to single stock options, there are specific circumstances in which this relationship may *not* apply, such as when a significant dividend is payable. This is explored in a subsequent chapter. Such circumstances aside, put/call parity may be observed in *all* option prices. The existence of put/call parity is important for various reasons. Exercise 5.3 shows how put/call parity can be used to calculate option prices.

Later chapters will show how put/call parity offers both arbitrage opportunities and enhanced flexibility in option trading.

Exercise 5.3: Using Put/Call Parity

XYZ future = 1300
Fill in the missing XYZ option prices
Remember, option price = intrinsic value + time value
Intrinsic value is the value of the option if exercised right now
The time value of calls and puts of the same strike and expiry is equal

Call Prices	Strike Prices	Put Prices
	1150	35
	1200	45
	1250	60
	1300	80
62	1350	
47	1400	
37	1450	
29	1500	

Exercise 5.3: Answers

Key: IV = intrinsic value, TV = time value

Call Prices	Strike Prices	Put Prices
185 (150 IV + 35 TV)	1150	35
145 (100 IV + 45 TV)	1200	45
110 (50 IV + 60 TV)	1250	60
80 (0 IV + 80 TV)	1300	80
62	1350	112 (50 IV + 62 TV)
47	1400	147 (100 IV + 47 TV)
37	1450	187 (150 IV + 37 TV)
29	1500	229 (200 IV + 29 TV)

Notes to the answers above:

Consider the 1150 call
It has 150 ticks of intrinsic value (underlying price of 1300 less strike price of 1150).
  It also has 35 ticks of time value (the same as the corresponding put). The 1150
  call is therefore worth 185 ticks (intrinsic value of 150 plus time value of 35).

Consider the 1500 put

It has 200 ticks of intrinsic value (strike price of 1500 less underlying price of 1300).
It also has 29 ticks of time value (the same as the corresponding call). The 1500
put is therefore worth 229 ticks (intrinsic value of 200 plus time value of 29).

Consider the 1300 call

It has no intrinsic value (underlying price of 1300 *equals* the strike price of 1300).
It has 80 ticks of time value (the same as the corresponding put). The 1300 call is
therefore worth 80 ticks, *all* of which is time value.

As previously stated, put/call parity applies to all options, with one or two very
specific exceptions. Put/call parity is easiest to observe:

1. In the settlement or closing prices. During the day, there will be bid/offer spreads
   on option prices, a fact that may disguise or temporarily distort put/call parity. For
   that reason, put/call parity is best observed in settlement prices.
2. In options that are "margined" rather than "premium-paid". There are two ways
   in which option premiums may be paid/received (see the following).

Some options, such as LIFFE commodity options, are *margined*. That is to say, option
buyers only pay a small percentage of the option premium upfront (roughly 10% as
a rule of thumb, but check on a specific basis), with the option then "marked-to-
market" on a daily basis. If the option increases in value, money will flow *into* the
option buyer's trading account. If the option decreases in value, money will flow *out
of* the option buyer's trading account. Other options, such as LIFFE equity and index
options, are "premium-paid". That is to say, the *whole* option premium is paid at the
time of trading. Premium is paid "upfront".

As previously stated, put/call parity is best observed in margined options on futures.
Equity and index options tend not to be margined; equity and index options on LIFFE
and most other exchanges tend to be premium paid. For that reason, while put/call
parity does apply to equity options, it is sometimes disguised by minor interest rate
considerations. Consider Table 5.3.

Table 5.3 LIFFE 3 month FTSE 100 option prices (LIFFE 3 month
FTSE 100 future = 6000. 3 month (£) interest rate = 6% p.a.)

Call Prices	Strike Prices	Put Prices
217	5900	119
185	5950	136
155	6000	155
130	6050	179
110	6100	208

The "at-the-money" (i.e. the 6000 strike) calls and puts are the same price. Both call and put have 155 ticks of time value. Neither option has any intrinsic value. Put/call parity is evident.

Now consider the 5900 calls and puts. With the future at 6000, the 5900 call has 100 ticks of intrinsic value (i.e. 6000 − 5900) and 119 ticks of time value (the value of the corresponding put). The value of the 5900 call should be $100 + 119 = 219$. In fact, it is priced not at 219 but at 217. Why the difference?

Take a deep breath and consider the following. By trading the appropriate amount of FTSE futures, we can turn the 5900 call into the 5900 put and vice versa. In fact, as a professional options trader, I don't care whether I own the 5900 call or the 5900 put because I can use the underlying future to turn one into the other; to *synthesize* one from the other. This process, the subject of "synthetics", will be considered in detail in a later chapter. At this stage, we simply need to accept that, by using futures, we can turn calls into puts and vice versa. We are therefore ambivalent as to whether we trade calls or puts of the same strike and series. Given this ambivalence, what would you rather own; the 5900 call for 217 or the 5900 put for 119? Clearly the latter since it is nearly 100 ticks cheaper. We can put these 100 ticks in the bank and earn interest at 6% p.a. for the next 3 months. This equates to about 1.5 ticks.

Now reconsider put/call parity in the 5900 calls and puts. As previously stated, the 5900 call is 2 ticks cheaper than it "should be" relative to the 5900 put. The difference is the interest rate advantage/disadvantage previously mentioned. The 5900 call is 2 ticks cheaper than put/call parity would suggest because it is less attractive to own than the 5900 put from a cost-of-carry perspective.

Further, if the 5900 call and put were the same price, arbitrage traders would sell the "expensive" call, buy the "cheaper" put, buy the appropriate number of futures and invest the cash difference in the two option premiums to make a pure arbitrage profit.

In summary, the absence of put/call parity in such cases is a function of cash-flow advantages of one option over another. When cost-of-carry is taken into account, put/call parity may still be seen to exist.

6
"Moneyness"

This chapter deals with some key everyday option language; the lingua franca of the options market. Specifically, we will consider the terms "in-the-money", "at-the-money" and "out-of-the-money". "The money", in all of these cases, refers to the prevailing price of the underlying share or index, hence the chapter title of "moneyness". Consider the set of prices in Table 6.1.

Note that the underlying FTSE future is trading at 6000. The "*at*-the-money" options are those with strike prices closest to this underlying price. In this case, then, the at-the-money options are the 6000 calls and puts. If the futures price was between two strikes, at 6022 for example, then the at-the-moneys would be both the 6000 and the 6050 calls and puts. In summary, the at-the-money options are those with strikes closest to the current price of the underlying.

"In-the-money" options are those that currently have intrinsic value. In-the-moneys are options that we would choose to exercise if they were expiring right now. From Table 6.1, the in-the- money calls are the 5900 calls and the 5950 calls. The in-the-

Table 6.1   LIFFE 3 month FTSE 100 option prices
(LIFFE 3 month FTSE 100 future = 6000)

Call Prices	Strike Prices	Put Prices
217	**5900**	119
185	**5950**	136
155	**6000**	155
130	**6050**	179
110	**6100**	208

money puts are the 6050 puts and the 6100 puts. All of these options, the 5900 and 5950 calls and the 6100 and 6050 puts, are exercisable with the future at 6000.

We talk about "deep" in-the-money options (options with lots of intrinsic value), "deeper" in-the-money options (options with more intrinsic value) and "deepest" in-the-money options (options with the most intrinsic value).

The opposite of in-the-money is "out-of-the-money". Out-of-the-money options are those that currently have no intrinsic value. Out-of-the-moneys are options that we would *not* choose to exercise if they were expiring right now. From Table 6.1, the out-of-the-money calls are the 6050 calls and the 6100 calls. The out-of-the-money puts are the 5950 puts and the 5900 puts. None of these options, the 5900 and 5950 puts and the 6050 and 6100 calls, are exercisable with the future at 6000.

We talk about "far" out-of-the-money options (options a long way away from the current underlying), "further" out-of-the-money options (options further away from the current underlying) and "furthest" out-of-the-money options (options furthest from the current underlying).

Let's apply these terms to the options in Table 6.2.

All regular option market participants, whether traders or brokers, will understand these terms. They are part of the everyday language of any options market. Consider the following exercise.

Table 6.2   LIFFE 3 month FTSE 100 option prices
(LIFFE 3 month FTSE 100 future = 6000)

Call Prices	Strike Prices	Put Prices
IN 217	**5900**	119 OUT
IN 185	**5950**	136 OUT
AT 155	**6000**	155 AT
OUT 130	**6050**	179 IN
OUT 110	**6100**	208 IN

Exercise 6.1: Moneyness

Consider the following table of stock option prices. Given that the underlying stock is trading at £2.11, identify:

1. The at-the-money options
2. The deepest in-the-money call
3. The furthest out-of-the money put
4. The deepest in-the-money put
5. The furthest out-of-the-money call

Call Prices	Strike Prices	Put Prices
0.24	**1.90**	0.05
0.17	**2.00**	0.07
0.11	**2.10**	0.10
0.07	**2.20**	0.15
0.04	**2.30**	0.22
0.02	**2.40**	0.30

Exercise 6.1: Answers

1. The at-the-money options are the £2.10 calls and puts (those with a strike price closest to the current stock price of £2.11).
2. The deepest in-the-money call is the £1.90 call (the call with the greatest intrinsic value and therefore the most expensive).
3. The furthest out-of-the-money put is the £1.90 put (the put furthest away from the current stock price and therefore the cheapest).
4. The deepest in-the-money put is the £2.40 put (the put with the greatest intrinsic value and therefore the most expensive).
5. The furthest out-of-the-money call is the £2.40 call (the call furthest away from the current stock price and therefore the cheapest).

SUMMARY OF CHAPTERS 5 AND 6

Option prices may be broken down into intrinsic value and time value.

Intrinsic value is the value of an option if it were exercised right now. It is, at any particular point in time, a mathematical fact.

Time value is everything that is *not* intrinsic value. It compensates option sellers against the chance of the option gaining intrinsic value. As we will see next, time value is determined by a number of factors, only one of which is time.

Some options (out-of-the-moneys) have no intrinsic value; their value is all time value.

Some options (in-the-moneys) have significant intrinsic value as well as some time value.

On expiry, options have no further time value; they either do or do not have intrinsic value.

Having broken options down into their constituent parts, let's now consider how option prices are arrived at in the first place.

7
Pricing Options

GLOSSARY

(Option) market-maker: Market professional specialising in the provision of two-way prices in options.
Cost-of-carry: The interest rate cost of holding a long stock position.

As discussed in Chapter 4, options are by no means a modern-day invention. From Phoenician grain traders to Yankee and Confederate financiers, options have played a key role in the management of price risk. In short, options have been around for a very long time. However, it was only as recently as 1973 that the first accurate method of valuing and pricing options was invented. Robert Merton, an American economist, enhanced the work of two fellow academics, Fischer Black and Myron Scholes, to come up with the first "option pricing model"; the ubiquitous "Black & Scholes". The significance of this pioneering mathematical work was subsequently recognised in 1997 by the award of a "Nobel Prize", a fact that underlines both its value and its complexity. All of which begs a question. If the first method of accurately pricing options was not developed until 1973, how were options valued before that? How were options evaluated by Thales or the advisers to General Lee? The best way to answer this is with another question, a little closer to home (or home contents!).

Remember the everyday example of a put option from Chapter 1? How do we price our home insurance? Presumably, we contact a number of insurance companies and choose the cheapest and/or most suitable policy. We make a comparison between the various providers; we make a relative judgement. But what about the cost in absolute terms? What would we do if we were quoted a premium of £10.00? We would buy the policy because it is obviously cheap. What about if we were quoted a premium of £5000? We would *not* buy the policy because it is equally obviously too expensive. The extremes of price are easy to deal with. But what about the real world? What about when the price is somewhere between these extremes of price? How do we judge whether or not the policy is good value? How do we decide whether or not the price is right? The answer is that we would take three key factors into consideration, whether explicitly or intuitively.

First, we would consider the *underlying value* at risk. The greater the amount at risk, the more we are prepared to pay to insure it.

Second, we would consider the *probability*, the likelihood of needing to make a claim. The greater the probability of needing to make a claim, the more we are prepared to pay to insure against it.

Third, we would consider *time*; what period is the insurance for? In the case of insurance, the period is normally standardised at 1 year, but it is clear that, if insurance were required for a longer period, it would be more expensive.

When Merton, Black and Scholes came up with their Nobel Prize winning work of 1973, they considered exactly the same three factors to be relevant, with the addition of a fourth factor, interest rates, to take account of the cost-of-carry of options. Further, the everyday concept of probability was adapted to the option-world equivalent of volatility.

The original work of Merton, Black and Scholes has since been adapted and tweaked by countless economists and mathematicians. There is now a bewildering range of variations of the original Black–Scholes model. Nonetheless, a quarter of a century on, Black–Scholes still provides the basis of option pricing throughout the derivatives markets.

Across the markets and across the various asset classes traded today, option prices are a function of four variables:

1. Underlying price in relation to the option strike price
2. Time to expiry
3. Interest rates
4. Volatility

These are the factors that determine the prices of options on commodities, interest rates, bonds and so on. For stock options, options based on physical equities, we need to add a fifth factor; dividends. Detail on the effect of dividends is included in pricing factor 1, the underlying.

We will consider each of these pricing factors in turn and see how they affect the prices of options. Before doing that, it is important to point out that, in practice, we simply get our prices from the market. We contact our broker and ask for a price. The price we get back is the market price, the result of supply and demand from all of the various market participants. We don't need to calculate our own option prices; that is the job of market professionals such as option market-makers, but we do need to understand how the four pricing factors impact option prices. We can look at these pricing factors on two levels.

First, we can simply learn how each of the factors affects option prices and accept it as fact, as received wisdom. We can be aware of the general relationships, the general rules noted below.

Second, we can dig a little deeper, drill down into the maths and understand how and *why* each of the pricing factors affects option prices.

For many option users, particularly those new to the market, the former will suffice. For more experienced, more sophisticated participants, the latter, deeper understanding is desirable, if not necessary. With this in mind, consider each of the four pricing variables to the appropriate level.

PRICING FACTOR 1: UNDERLYING VALUE

Options convey the right but not the obligation to buy or sell at a fixed price; the strike price. Specifically, calls convey the right to buy the underlying at a fixed price. This right to buy at a fixed price becomes *more* valuable as the underlying price *rises*, as in the following example.

XYZ share price is £4.00. Consider the XYZ £5.00 call. The call is currently £1.00 out-of-the-money. As the XYZ share price starts to rise towards £5.00, the £5.00 call has a better chance of becoming in-the-money. If the share price rises above £5.00, then the £5.00 call will indeed be in-the-money; it will have intrinsic value. The more the share price rises, the more intrinsic value the call will gain and the higher its price as a result.

This leads us to a general rule. All other things being equal, *as the underlying rises, the value of calls rises*.

Remember, calls convey the right to buy the underlying at a fixed price. This right to buy at a fixed price becomes *less* valuable as the underlying price *falls*, as in the following example.

XYZ share price is £4.00. Consider the XYZ £3.00 call. The call is currently £1.00 in-the-money. It has £1.00 of intrinsic value. As the XYZ share price starts to fall towards £3.00, the £3.00 call has less and less intrinsic value. As the share price falls below £3.00, the call ceases to be in-the-money and becomes out-of-the-money. And as the XYZ share price falls towards zero, the £3.00 call has less and less chance of being in-the-money by expiry and therefore has a lower and lower price.

This leads us to extend our general rule. All other things being equal, *as the underlying falls, the value of calls falls*.

Having considered the effect of the underlying upon calls, let's now turn our attention to puts.

Puts convey the right to sell the underlying at a fixed price. This right to sell at a fixed price becomes *more* valuable as the underlying price *falls*, as in the following example.

XYZ share price is £4.00. Consider the XYZ £3.00 put. The put is currently £1.00 out-of-the-money. As the XYZ share price starts to fall towards £3.00, the £3.00 put has a better chance of becoming in-the-money. If the share price falls below £3.00, then the £3.00 put will indeed be in-the-money; it will have intrinsic value. The more the share price falls, the more intrinsic value the put will gain and the higher its price as a result.

This again leads us to a general rule. All other things being equal, *as the underlying falls, the value of puts rises.*

Remember, puts convey the right to sell the underlying at a fixed price. This right to sell at a fixed price becomes *less* valuable as the underlying price *rises*, as in the following example.

XYZ share price is £4.00. Consider the XYZ £5.00 put. The put is currently £1.00 in-the-money. It has £1.00 of intrinsic value. As the XYZ share price starts to rise towards £5.00, the £5.00 put has less and less intrinsic value. As the share price rises above £5.00, the put ceases to be in-the-money and becomes out-of-the-money. And as the XYZ share price rises ever higher, the £5.00 put has less and less chance of being in-the-money by expiry and therefore has a lower and lower price.

This leads us to further extend our general rule. All other things being equal, *as the underlying rises, the value of puts falls.*

Let's summarise the effect of the underlying upon the price of options:

- All other things being equal, as the underlying rises, the value of calls rises and the value of puts falls.
- All other things being equal, as the underlying falls, the value of puts rises and the value of calls falls.

If we want to refine these general rules, if we wish to quantify the extent to which a move in the price of the underlying will affect option prices, then we need to understand *delta*, the subject of a later chapter.

Having seen how a move in the underlying affects option prices, let's now consider which underlying price should be used to price options. The importance of this point is not immediately obvious. For example, if we are trading BP options, surely the relevant underlying is the BP share price, right? Yes and no. In fact, the correct underlying price will depend upon the tenor of the options. With the exception of deep in-the-money options, if it is 6 month BP options that are under consideration, then the 6 month BP forward price should be used for pricing purposes. The 6 month BP forward and the current ("spot") BP share price, while closely related to one another, are unlikely to be the same price. We would expect the 6 month forward price to be higher than the spot price because of interest rates, the cost-of-carry. Simply put, if the spot and forward prices were the same, then arbitrageurs would short the physical stock, buy the forward against it and pocket the interest on the cash proceeds of the short stock trade. The forward purchase is cash efficient in relation to the spot trade.

Remember, forward/futures prices are not predictions. Rather, forward prices reflect the cost-of-carry of the stock for the relevant period. The calculation of the "fair value" of a forward or futures price is as follows:

FORWARD PRICE = CURRENT PRICE + INTEREST − DIVIDEND

(if applicable)

Example 1 (no dividends): Current XYZ share price = £5.00
Interest rates = 4% p.a.
No dividend is payable

3 month XYZ forward = £5.00 + (£5.00 × 4% × 0.25 yrs) = £5.05
6 month XYZ forward = £5.00 + (£5.00 × 4% × 0.50 yrs) = £5.10
9 month XYZ forward = £5.00 + (£5.00 × 4% × 0.75 yrs) = £5.15
1 year XYZ forward = £5.00 + (£5.00 × 4% × 1.00 yrs) = £5.20

Note the "term structure" of the forwards market. The longer the timeframe, the greater the fair value of the forward price. Now let's introduce a dividend to this calculation.

Example 2: Current XYZ share price = £5.00
Interest rates = 4% p.a.
Dividend of £0.30 is payable
XYZ goes "ex-div" in 4 months' time

3 month XYZ forward = £5.00 + (£5.00 × 4% × 0.25 yrs) = £5.05
6 month XYZ forward = £5.00 + (£5.00 × 4% × 0.50 yrs) − £0.30 div = £4.80
9 month XYZ forward = £5.00 + (£5.00 × 4% × 0.75 yrs) − £0.30 div = £4.85
1 year XYZ forward = £5.00 + (£5.00 × 4% × 1.00 yrs) − £0.30 div = £4.90

Note that the dividend doesn't affect the 3 month forward since the stock doesn't go "ex-div" until 4 months' time. The dividend does affect the subsequent forwards in which the increasing effect of the cost-of-carry is again visible.

In terms of valuing and pricing options, with the key exception of deep in-the-money options, the rule is simple. Apply the forward price for the same tenor as the options. For 3 month options, use the 3 month forward. For 9 month options, use the 9 month forward and so on. This is easy to do with index options because index futures are widely understood and traded. Single stock futures, while listed on various exchanges such as LIFFE, are far less popular and less widely used. Nonetheless, if we are looking to value or price 6 month BP options, then we should be using the 6 month BP forward or futures price as our basis.

This simple rule may be applied with certainty to options where a future is the underlying, such as commodity and interest-rate options traded on exchanges such as LIFFE. The rule may also be applied with certainty to all European-style options; options that may only be exercised upon expiry. However, single stock options traded on exchanges such as LIFFE tend to be American style; they may be exercised at any time up to expiry. Further, the underlying of such options is not the stock future or forward, but rather the physical shares themselves. Why is this important? Consider the following example.

Current ABC Ltd share price = £10.00
6 month ABC forward price = £10.50

Consider the £11.00 call and put. Let's assume that this stock doesn't tend to move around a great deal and, as a result, the £11.00 call is trading at just £0.01. Bearing put/call parity in mind, what should the price of the £11.00 put be? We know that the price of the £11.00 put should be the sum of its intrinsic value and the time value of the corresponding call. But how much intrinsic value does the £11.00 put have? If we use the 6 month stock forward of £10.50 as the underlying reference price, then the £11.00 put has £0.50 of intrinsic value. Adding £0.01, the value of the £11.00 call to this intrinsic value gives us a price for the £11.00 put of £0.51. But what would these £11.00 puts be worth if we exercised them right now? Exercising the £11.00 put now would result in our being short of ABC shares at £11.00. We could buy these shares back in the open market at the prevailing spot price of £10.00 and make a £1.00 profit! The £11.00 puts must therefore be worth at least £1.00.

This explains the ambivalent ("yes and no") response to the earlier question about which underlying price should be used to price single stock options. Both the spot share price and the stock forward should be taken into account when pricing single stock options. Whichever delivers the greater amount of intrinsic value is the one that should be used. This is important because, in practice, given that stock options may be exercised at any time, *an American-style option (i.e. an option that can be exercised before expiry) can never be worth less than its intrinsic value.* Consider the following example and exercise.

Current ABC Ltd "spot" share price = £10.00
6 month ABC forward price = £10.50

The minimum value of the 6 month £9.00 call is £1.50 (forward price less strike)
The minimum value of the 6 month £8.50 call is £2.00 (forward price less strike)
The minimum value of the 6 month £11.00 put is £1.00 (strike less spot price)
The minimum value of the 6 month £11.50 put is £1.50 (strike less spot price)

Exercise 7.1: Pricing Options

Current XYZ Ltd "spot" share price = £5.00
6 month XYZ forward price = £5.25

1. What is the minimum value of the 3 month £4.00 call?
2. What is the minimum value of the 3 month £4.25 call?
3. What is the minimum value of the 3 month £6.00 put?
4. What is the minimum value of the 3 month £6.25 put?

Exercise 7.1: Answers

1. The minimum value of the 3 month £4.00 call is £1.25 (forward price less strike).
2. The minimum value of the 3 month £4.25 call is £1.00 (forward price less strike).
3. The minimum value of the 3 month £6.00 put is £1.00 (strike less spot price).
4. The minimum value of the 3 month £6.25 put is £1.25 (strike less spot price).

Let's now summarise the effect of the underlying on the price of options. The most important general point is that, other things being equal, calls rise in value as the underlying rises and fall in value as the underlying falls. Puts rise in value as the underlying falls and fall in value as the underlying rises. The stock forward/futures price will tend to move broadly in line with the physical share price, so it doesn't really matter which price we follow, as long as we are aware of the relationship of option prices to the underlying.

However, this distinction, the distinction between spot and forward share prices, becomes important if we want to start valuing or pricing options ourselves. Of course, we don't need to do this – we can simply call our broker and ask for the current market price.

PRICING FACTOR 2: TIME

Options are decaying assets; they lose value due to the passage of time. As a general rule, *other things being equal, an option will be worth less tomorrow than it is worth today*. This process is known as "time decay" or "erosion". Why do options erode? The easiest way to answer this is to look at the effect of time from a different perspective.

Remember the intuitive example of a put option from Chapter 1? Insurance was the chosen comparison. What will cost more; insuring your home for one year or for 10 years? Clearly, 10 years' insurance will be significantly more expensive. There is more time in which you may need to make a claim. The same logic may be applied to options. Consider an out-of-the-money call, specifically a £6.00 call. All other things being equal (same volatilities, same interest rates, same underlying prices), what will cost more, a 1 month £6.00 call or a 2 month £6.00 call? Clearly, the 2 month option will be more expensive because there is more time for the underlying to go up through £6.00. If an option has more chance of gaining intrinsic value, more chance of "succeeding", then it must have a greater value, just as an insurance policy that has more chance of being claimed upon must command a greater premium.

So, an option that is worth 90 today will, other things being equal, be worth a bit less tomorrow. Exactly how much less? To quantify the extent to which an option will erode, we need to understand *theta*, the subject of a later chapter.

The rate at which an option decays is not linear. That is to say, an option that is worth 90 ticks today with 90 days to expiry will *not* decay at a rate of 1 tick per day. Rather, the option will erode by less than a tick per day at the moment, with the rate of decay accelerating as expiry approaches.

General rule: other things being equal, shorter-dated options erode at a faster rate than longer-dated options.

In terms of moneyness, it is at-the-money options that erode at the fastest rate. This is because, quite simply, at-the-money options have the most time value. Other options in a series may be more expensive because of intrinsic value, but intrinsic

Table 7.1   LIFFE 3 month FTSE 100 option prices
(LIFFE 3 month FTSE 100 future = 6000)

Call Prices	Strike Prices	Put Prices
217	**5900**	119
185	**5950**	136
155	**6000**	155
130	**6050**	179
110	**6100**	208

value is unaffected by time; it is at any particular moment a mathematical fact. To reinforce this idea, consider the following example.

Consider the prices in Table 7.1. The most expensive call is the 5900 call, priced at 217. With the underlying future trading at 6000, this call has 100 ticks of intrinsic value. Remember, intrinsic value is unaffected by time, it is a mathematical fact. Only 117 ticks of the price represent time value and are affected by the passage of time.

The most expensive put is the 6100 call, priced at 208. With the underlying future trading at 6000, this put has 100 ticks of intrinsic value, value that is unaffected by time. Only 108 ticks of the price represent time value and are affected by the passage of time.

Compare this with the at-the-money options, the 6000 calls and puts. Both of these options are priced at 155, *all* of the price representing time value and therefore affected by the passage of time.

In summary, the at-the-money options, while not the most expensive options in terms of absolute price, have the greatest amount of time value. The at-the-moneys have the greatest amount of time value to lose between now and expiry and therefore erode at the fastest rate.

PRICING FACTOR 3: INTEREST RATES

Interest rates are the least important of the four factors affecting the price of an option. Of course, interest rates are hugely important in a wider, economic sense, but in terms of their specific impact on option prices, interest rates are of limited concern. That said, there are relationships between option prices and interest rates, relationships which we can again approach on two levels. Given the limited impact of interest rates in this context, we may choose simply to take the relationship as read, or we may choose to delve deeper and understand the reasoning behind the relationship.

Interest rates may affect stock option prices in two ways:

1. Any change in interest rates will change the forward or futures price of the share, which in turn will impact the value of the options.
2. Any change in interest rates will affect the cost-of-carry of the option premium itself.

Depending upon the specific option(s) under consideration, these two effects may work together or in opposite directions. Either way, it is important to reiterate that, in practice, interest rates are the least important of the option pricing factors. Let's consider each of the two effects in turn:

1. Remember, buying calls is an alternative to buying the underlying. Buying BP calls is an alternative to buying BP shares. Which is the cash efficient choice? Buying the physical shares requires payment of the full cash value of the shares whereas buying the calls requires payment of the option premium, a significantly smaller amount. If we want to be long the underlying, buying calls is more cash efficient than buying the underlying shares. How much more efficient? The answer depends upon interest rates. The higher the prevailing rates of interest, the greater the cash efficiency of buying calls over buying stock. It therefore follows that as interest rates rise, we are prepared to pay more for calls because their relative cash efficiency increases. As interest rates rise, the value of calls also rises, and vice versa.

   Buying puts is an alternative to selling the underlying. Buying BP puts is an alternative to shorting BP shares. Which will result in the greater cash inflow? Clearly, buying puts will cost money whereas selling stock will result in a cash inflow. As interest rates increase, selling the stock becomes increasingly attractive and buying puts less attractive. It therefore follows that as interest rates rise, put prices fall, and vice versa.

   Interest rates impact stock option prices in this way because stock options are physically deliverable; the underlying is the physical share itself. Interest rates affect stock forward or futures prices and in turn affect stock option prices. This is *not* the case with all options. Specifically, options on futures (such as LIFFE commodity options, interest rate options, etc.) are not affected in this way.

2. As interest rates rise, the cost-of-carry of option premiums also rises. To compensate for this, as interest rates rise, option premiums (for both calls and puts) fall. As interest rates fall, option premiums (for both calls and puts) rise. *All* options, whether based on physical shares or on futures, are affected in this way.

We can see from the above that interest rates may affect option prices in two ways. The general rules are as follows:

General rule in relation to physically deliverable stock options: as interest rates rise, the value of calls rise and put prices fall; as interest rates fall, the value of puts rise and call prices fall.

   General rule in relation to all options: as interest rates rise, the value of all options (calls and puts) falls; as interest rates fall, the value of all options (calls and puts) rises.

Having considered the detail, it is worth noting that, in practice, interest rates tend to change by small amounts at irregular intervals. Sterling rates, for example, tend not to change by more than a quarter per cent a month, except in extreme circumstances such as bank failures and credit crises. In such worrying circumstances, as significant as interest rates might become, I would suggest that our main focus would be on more important factors such as the underlying and volatility!

In the event that we are going to use a pricing model, our choice of exact rate used is not particularly significant. The risk-free rate for the appropriate currency should provide sufficient real-world accuracy. For example, if we are looking to price or evaluate BP options on LIFFE, then the sterling base rate may be used. If we are looking to price or evaluate GM options in the USA, then the dollar Fed funds rate may be used.

In summary, then, interest rates are the least important of the option pricing factors but, in practice, a pricing model will require the input of the relevant interest rate. Interest rates also play a crucial role in decisions relating to the early exercise of in-the-money puts, a subject covered in a subsequent chapter.

PRICING FACTOR 4: VOLATILITY

Volatility plays a crucial role in the pricing of options. So what is it? What does "volatility" mean? Broadly speaking, volatility is a measure of *how much* a market is moving around and *how fast* it is moving around. Is the price highly volatile, fluctuating sharply up and down with high highs and low lows? Or is the price relatively calm, trading within a narrow range? These are the questions that volatility seeks to address.

Why is volatility so important? To understand this, think back to the everyday comparison of put options to insurance. Intuitively, volatility may be likened to probability. There are significant similarities between volatility and probability on both an intuitive and a technical, mathematical level. Consider the way in which probability impacts the price of insurance. The higher the likelihood of a claim, the higher the cost of the insurance and vice versa. Hence, a teenaged driver pays significantly more for their insurance than a 40-something because, statistically (and unfortunately), they are more likely to have an accident.

To understand the significance of probability in this context, consider the role of actuaries. Actuaries are professional assessors of risk, of probability, and they are generally very well paid for doing so. No insurer would offer insurance without first assessing risk; similarly, no serious option trader should trade options without first considering volatility. The key role of probability in the insurance markets may be directly compared to the key role of volatility in the option markets.

In general, then, the cost of insurance increases as the likelihood of making a claim increases. This can be compared to a general rule in the option world; *the greater the volatility in the underlying market, the greater the price of options.*

For example, if BP shares are highly volatile, the share price racing all over the place, then BP options will tend to be relatively expensive. On the other hand, if BP shares are calm, the share price trading within a narrow, well-established range, then BP options will tend to be relatively cheap.

In general, broad brushstroke terms, this is how and why volatility impacts the price of options. We could stop there at a simple, intuitive level but for those who wish to understand more, consider the following.

There are two basic types of volatility, historical and market (implied). Both are expressed as annualised percentages. This has no immediate significance. Don't be tempted to try to use this percentage number simplistically, perhaps by applying it to the price to predict an expected move. Things are, unfortunately, a little more complicated than that. For those of you new to volatility, a health warning. Volatility is a nebulous concept, underpinned by some complex maths. While it is certainly important to understand how it affects option prices and how it is therefore used, it is by no means essential to understand the nitty-gritty. With this in mind, let's consider the different types of "vol" in a little more detail.

Historical Volatility

Historical volatility relates to the price of the underlying. Specifically, it looks backwards at the price history of a share price or index. If we want a rough idea of where the share traded over the given period, we can calculate the mean or average price for that period. If we want to gauge how much the price deviated, how much it moved around over the period, we can calculate the standard deviation of the price. This standard deviation, this measure of how much the share price deviated from its mean, equates essentially to historical volatility. It is, at any particular moment, a fact, a statistic. It tells us how volatile a share was, but that is the limit of its use. It is like any historical data; it may be used as the basis of judgements about the future. However, it also has all the weaknesses of anything historical, anything backward looking. Just because something happened yesterday doesn't mean it will happen today or tomorrow. It is useful information but that is all. What is far more useful is the second type of volatility; market (implied) volatility.

Market (Implied) Volatility

Whereas historical volatility relates to the price of the underlying, market or implied volatility relates to the option prices themselves.

Market volatility is the volatility currently trading in the market. It represents the collective wisdom of the market as to how volatile the underlying will be during the forthcoming period. Market volatility will rise as the market anticipates increasingly volatile conditions and fall as the market anticipates a calmer period. As market volatility rises, options become more expensive. As market volatility falls, options become cheaper.

Market volatility needs a context. A good everyday comparison is with temperature in different locations. If we are trying to establish what is "hot", we need to know where we are talking about. "Hot" in London is not the same as "hot" in Riyadh. "Cold" in Paris is not the same as "cold" in Siberia. The same applies to volatility.

"High" volatility in BP is not the same as "high" volatility in Brent Crude or Eurodollars or Microsoft. "Low" volatility in the FTSE is not the same as "low" volatility in coffee or Euribor. We need to build up an idea of what constitutes relatively high and relatively low volatility in the shares or indices in which we are interested. If we want to trade FTSE 100 Index options, we need to build up an idea of the "normal" range of market volatility in the FTSE. If market volatility in the FTSE tends to range from 10% to 30%, then we know that FTSE options are relatively cheap when volatility is in the low teens and relatively expensive when volatility is in the high 20s. This is how we use market volatility as traders. In this sense, market volatility may simply be thought of as an index of the relative cheapness or expensiveness of options.

Over the course of time, which asset class do you think has the lowest volatility? Equities, indices, bonds, commodities? Historically speaking, the lowest volatilities have been observed in short-term interest rates ("STIRs") and bonds. This makes intuitive sense. How often do interest rates change significantly? Perhaps once a month, once every few months. And by how much do rates tend to change? By a quarter per cent, a half per cent at most. Even in the most extraordinary circumstances, interest rates tend not to change by more than 1% at a time. It is therefore no surprise that in relative terms, STIRs options and bond options *tend* to display the lowest volatilities. Please note the highlighting of the word "tend". That which we have observed before may change tomorrow; there are no fixed rules here, just observations and tendencies.

What about equities and indices? What magnitude of volatilities would we expect to see in equity index option markets? I can tell you that in two decades of trading FTSE 100 options on LIFFE, market volatility rarely got far below 10%. On a practical level, this means that FTSE options are about as cheap as they ever get when market volatility falls to around 8 or 9%. Perhaps this low volatility is justified; perhaps the market is going through a particularly quiet phase. On the other hand, this may represent a great opportunity for hedgers to buy cheap "insurance" or for speculators to place a cheap "bet". Either way, we need to be aware of where volatility is trading; whether options are currently cheap or expensive.

Market volatility is also known as "implied" volatility. "Implied" by what exactly? Implied by the current option prices. We have already seen that option prices are affected by four main variables: underlying price, time, interest rates and volatility. Stock options may also be affected by dividends. At any particular moment in time, we know where the underlying is trading, we know how much time remains to expiry, we know what interest rates prevail and we know if a dividend is payable. These are all, at any particular time, facts (or accepted estimates in the case of dividends). The key variable is volatility. It is the key variable in terms of determining whether options are currently relatively cheap or expensive. Everything else is known.

Table 7.2   LIFFE December 2008 FTSE 100 option prices as at close on
18 June 2008 (LIFFE December 2008 FTSE 100 future = 5825)

Calls	Strike Price	Puts
616	5425	227
547	5525	256
483	5625	288
421	5725	324
362	5825	362
309	5925	405
259	6025	452
213	6125	504
174	6225	561

So option prices are a function of the underlying price, time, interest rates and
volatility. If we know an option's current price, where it is trading in the market, we
can turn this function around and discover the volatility implied by that option price;
the implied volatility. Consider the set of FTSE 100 Index option prices from LIFFE
shown in Table 7.2.

Are these options relatively cheap or expensive? How can we decide? We could
compare these option prices to the same prices a year ago, but the underlying future
was different then. Alternatively, we could compare these December options to the
September option prices, except that the September options expire 3 months earlier
than the December options. How can we make these sorts of judgements? The answer
is by using volatility, specifically implied volatility; the volatility implied by the option
prices. Let's add the implied volatilities to the December FTSE option prices.

Consider the at-the-money call, the 5825 call, from Table 7.3. At the close of the
LIFFE market on 18 June 2008, the December 5825 call was priced at 362. Given
that the underlying December future was trading at 5825, given that the options

Table 7.3   LIFFE December 2008 FTSE 100 option prices as at close on
18 June 2008 (LIFFE December 2008 FTSE 100 future = 5825)

Calls (Implied Vol)	Strike Price	Puts (Implied Vol)
616 (25.33%)	5425	227 (25.33%)
547 (24.64%)	5525	256 (24.64%)
483 (24.01%)	5625	288 (24.01%)
421 (23.34%)	5725	324 (23.34%)
362 (22.62%)	5825	362 (22.62%)
309 (21.97%)	5925	405 (21.97%)
259 (21.29%)	6025	452 (21.29%)
213 (20.64%)	6125	504 (20.64%)
174 (20.06%)	6225	561 (20.06%)

would expire on 19 December 2008 (the third Friday in the month as per the contract specification) and given the prevailing interest rates, this market price of 362 implied a volatility of 22.62%. Had the options been worth more than this, the volatility implied would also have been higher. Had the options been worth less than 362, the volatility implied would have been lower than 22.62%. The implied volatility gave us an exact idea of how "cheap" or "expensive" the options were at that price. If we looked back at market volatility in LIFFE FTSE options for the preceding year, we would see that the implied volatility of at-the-money options ranged from a low of about 13.5% to a high of about 33.5%. The implied volatility of the at-the-money options at the close on 18 June was 22.62%, about mid-range compared to the last 12 months. This meant in turn that options were neither particularly "cheap" nor particularly "expensive"; the price of the options was also middling.

To summarise, we can discover the implied volatility of any option as long as we know its price. This information is useful. It allows us to decide whether options are currently cheap or expensive. It allows us to compare option prices with different expiry dates. It allows us to compare options in different series. We can make broad, intuitive judgements about the value of options simply by looking at the option prices themselves but, if we want to make accurate judgements about the relative value of options, then we need to study implied vols.

Fortunately, information on implied volatility is easy to find. At the close each day, LIFFE publishes the implied volatility of every option that is traded on the exchange, along with price, deltas and various other pieces of useful information (see the "Resources" section for further detail). Any option broker worth their salt should be able to give you an idea of the implied volatility of any price in which you are interested. Brokers' websites often publish volatility information and some provide option calculators, allowing you to calculate implied volatilities for yourself. For those of you that use technical analysis (the study of charts), both historical and implied volatility are often available as studies within charting packages such as CQG or Futuresource. Market professionals fortunate enough to have Bloomberg have a wide range of volatility information and tools at their disposal.

As a rule, I tend to look at implied volatility as a sub-study to the chart of price itself. By charting implied volatility, it is very easy to see when volatility is relatively low and relatively high, allowing us to make instant decisions upon our view as to whether options are currently "cheap" or "expensive". Such decisions will clearly affect our choice of option strategy, as we will see in a subsequent chapter. Indeed, as already stated, the vast majority of my trading is now driven primarily by such considerations of volatility rather than a view on the underlying. To illustrate this point in simple terms, consider the following exercise.

Exercise 7.2: Volatility

Consider the following stock, XYZ Ltd. The price action of XYZ and at-the-money volatility of 3 month XYZ options is depicted in Figure 7.1.

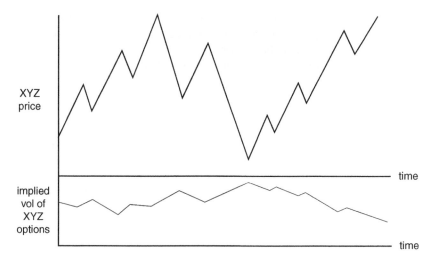

Figure 7.1   Price action of XYZ and at-the-money volatility of 3 month XYZ options

The bold line in the figure shows the share price of XYZ over the past year. The line in the lower part of the chart shows the implied volatility of 3 month at-the-money XYZ options over the past year.

1. Is implied/market volatility currently relatively high or low?
2. Are XYZ options currently relatively cheap or expensive?
3. As option users, what could we do as a result of the above?

Exercise 7.2: Answers

1. Clearly, current market volatility is low in relation to typical levels over the past year. In fact, market volatility is on its lows for the past year.
2. As a result of this low implied volatility, XYZ options are relatively cheap, as cheap as they have been for a year.
3. The key issue now is whether we think that this low volatility is justified (because we are entering a quiet period with small ranges) or whether we think that it is unjustifiably low implying that options are currently undervalued and underpriced. The implications are clear. If our judgement is that the market is currently under-pricing options, what should we do? Buy options! Buy calls if we are bullish, buy puts if we are bearish and buy both if we are unsure about direction.

At the beginning of this section, I warned that volatility can be a difficult subject to understand. Though the effect of "vol" upon option prices is fairly straightforward, the devil is in the detail. Let's summarise volatility so far.

In general terms, volatility is a measure of how much a market price is moving around. Volatility is expressed as an annualised percentage. There are two basic types of volatility: historical and implied (market).

Historical volatility relates to the past price action of the underlying. It is essentially the standard deviation of the past price data.

Market or implied volatility relates to the option prices themselves; the volatility implied by the option prices. If the market collectively believes that the underlying will be volatile over the forthcoming period, then market volatility and therefore option prices will be relatively high. If the market believes that the underlying will be calm over the forthcoming period, then market volatility and therefore option prices will be relatively low.

The relationship between option prices and market/implied volatility is simple; the higher the volatility, the more expensive the options and vice versa.

It follows that the most important use of volatility is to judge whether options are relatively cheap or expensive. This is turn helps inform our choice of option trade.

SUMMARY OF CHAPTER 7

Generically, option prices are affected by four factors: underlying price, time, interest rates and volatility. Single stock options may also be affected by dividends. The relationships between each of these factors and option prices are as follows.

Underlying Price

All other things being equal, as the underlying rises, call prices rise and put prices fall.

All other things being equal, as the underlying falls, put prices rise and call prices fall.

Time

All other things being equal, the passage of time causes option prices to fall. This process is known as "time decay" or "erosion".

Interest Rates

Interest rates may affect options in two ways, depending upon their exact nature.

1. In relation to physically deliverable stock options (other things being equal):
   As interest rates rise, the value of calls rise and put prices fall.
   As interest rates fall, the value of puts rise and call prices fall.

2. In relation to all options (other things being equal):
   As interest rates rise, the value of all options (calls and puts) falls.
   As interest rates fall, the value of all options (calls and puts) rises.

Volatility

All other things being equal, as market volatility rises, all option prices rise.
All other things being equal, as market volatility falls, all option prices fall.

Since their "invention" in 1973, pricing models such as Black–Scholes have been used to calculate accurate "fair values" for options. Pricing models require the input of the four pricing factors listed above with the possible addition of dividends where relevant in the case of single stock options. Pricing models are essentially glorified calculators; input the four (five including dividends) pricing factors and a set of option prices will drop magically out of the bottom. Pricing models are widely used across the markets by professional option users.

In terms of pricing options, volatility is the key variable since everything else is known. Volatility is the key to successful use of options.

As previously seen, we can calculate or ask for the implied volatility of any specific option at any particular moment in time. When volatility is spoken of in more general terms, such as your broker informing you that "Sep FTSE vol has risen to 25%", it is at-the-money volatility that is under discussion. By implicitly using at-the-money options as a benchmark for volatility, we avoid the need to consider "skew", the subject of the next chapter.

8
Skew

Skew is a real world phenomenon, a feature routinely observed in the majority of option markets.

What does "skew" mean in a wider context? Skew is asymmetry, imbalance. To describe something as "skewed" is to describe it as twisted, distorted, out of shape. How might this apply to options and to option markets? Let's consider how option prices *should* look in a perfectly mathematical, emotionless world.

Consider the set of option prices in Table 8.1. At this stage, they are just numbers. Consider them as such; don't think about the underlying, just think about the numbers.

First, consider the at-the-money options; the 200 strike. Both the 200 calls and the 200 puts are worth 10. Why? Why should at-the-money calls and puts always be the same price? *Because they have an equal chance of "success"*. They have an equal chance of being in-the-money upon expiry. Given that the underlying is trading at exactly 200, the 200 call has a 50% chance of being in-the-money on expiry because there is a 50% chance of the underlying going up and a 50% chance of it going down. Likewise, the 200 put has a 50% chance of being in-the-money on expiry because there is a 50% chance of the underlying going down and a 50% chance of it going up.

These equal chances of "success" manifest themselves in equal prices. Given that the underlying is at exactly 200 and that the options are exactly at-the-money, the above is mathematical fact.

Table 8.1 ZYX 3 month option prices (3 month ZYX future = 200)

Calls	Strike Prices	Puts
24	180	4
17	190	7
10	200	10
7	210	17
4	220	24

Following on from this, consider the 210 call and the 190 put. Both options are 10 out-of-the-money. Given that there is an equal chance of the underlying rising or falling by 10, the two options should again be the same price. In our perfect, mathematical world, both options are indeed worth 7.

Likewise, the 220 call and the 180 put. Both options are 20 out-of-the-money so both options have the same value, 4 ticks.

If we plotted the option prices as a distribution, we would see that they are perfectly symmetrical, reflecting the equal chances of the market rising or falling by any given amount. Now let's compare this with the real world. Consider the FTSE 100 option prices from the LIFFE market in Table 8.2.

First, consider the at-the-money options, the 5825 calls and puts. Both options are worth 362 ticks because both options are exactly at-the-money and therefore both options have an exactly 50% chance of being in the money on expiry.

Now consider the 5925 call and the 5725 puts. With the underlying future trading at 5825, both options are exactly 100 out-of-the-money. Probability theory suggests that both options have the same chance of "succeeding", of being in-the-money upon expiry. Probability theory would suggest that the calls and puts should therefore be the same price but they are not. In fact, the 5725 puts are priced at 324, 15 ticks more than the 5925 call. How could this be? Don't forget that the prices shown above are real prices, historical data from the LIFFE market. These prices are the product of supply and demand from market participants, of market users buying and selling options with cold, hard cash. Why, collectively, is the market prepared to pay significantly more for an out-of-the-money put than a commensurately out-of-the-money call?

Consider further out-of-the-money options. The 6025 call and 5625 puts are both exactly 200 out-of-the-money. The 5625 puts are priced at 288, 29 ticks more than the 6025 call.

Table 8.2   LIFFE December 2008 FTSE 100 option prices as at close on 18 June 2008 (LIFFE December 2008 FTSE 100 future = 5825)

Calls	Strike Price	Puts
616	5425	227
547	5525	256
483	5625	288
421	5725	324
362	5825	362
309	5925	405
259	6025	452
213	6125	504
174	6225	561

- The 6125 call and 5525 puts are both exactly 300 out-of-the-money. The 5525 puts are priced at 256, 43 ticks more than the 6125 call.
- The 6225 call and 5425 puts are both exactly 400 out-of-the-money. The 5425 puts are priced at 227, 53 ticks more than the 6225 call.

This disparity between the prices of options that are equidistant from the prevailing underlying price is called "skew". It is a phenomenon observed in option prices, the observation that, in the real world, option prices are asymmetrical (about the axis of the at-the-moneys); hence the name "skew".

Why does skew exist? To start answering this question, let's reconsider the LIFFE FTSE 100 option prices used in the above examples, this time with the addition of the implied volatilities.

In terms of probability, the one thing of which we can be certain is that the at-the-money options have a 50% chance of "success"; of being in-the-money upon expiry. That is because the at-the-money options convey the right to buy (calls) or sell (puts) at 5825, the exact price of the underlying and it is a fact that there is an exact 50% chance that the next move in the underlying will be up and a 50% chance that it will be down. So much for direction. But volatility is not simply about direction of underlying movement. Volatility is also about *speed* of underlying movement. In a purely mathematical, emotionless world, the expected speed of moves should be unrelated to the direction of that move. But in the real world, the expected speed of moves *is* related to the direction of that move.

Markets are simply collections of individuals, all of whom are prey to the same emotions as the rest of the world. Markets are driven by fear and greed and, from experience, there is no doubt that fear is the greater force. Where is the fear in equity markets? In other words, do market participants in general tend to be fearful of upward moves or downward moves? Clearly, it is the downside that commands the greatest concern. We have a word for a sharp downward movement in equity markets; a stock market "crash". It is revealing that we don't have a similar word to describe sharp upward moves. We talk of "rallies" and "advances" but these words simply do not resonate with the same strength as the word "crash"!

Given that the greater fear in equities resides to the downside, two key questions arise. First, in which direction do equity markets tend to move fastest, to the upside or to the downside? Second, what tends to happen to volatility when the underlying market rises in comparison to when the underlying market falls? The answers to these inter-related questions help explain the presence of skew in the option prices.

First, in terms of the direction in which equity markets tend to move fastest, we only need to look back at a chart of the FTSE or the Dow Jones or indeed any other stock index to see that equity markets tend to fall faster than they rise. Broadly speaking, equity markets tend to grind upwards and then correct sharply to the downside. The fastest movements tend to be the downward "corrections". Speaking from my own experience of the FTSE, it is certainly the case that the fastest, scariest moves have been to the downside.

Table 8.3 LIFFE December 2008 FTSE 100 option prices as at close on 18 June 2008 (LIFFE December 2008 FTSE 100 future = 5825)

Calls (Implied Vol)	Strike Price	Puts (Implied Vol)
616 (25.33%)	5425	227 (25.33%)
547 (24.64%)	5525	256 (24.64%)
483 (24.01%)	5625	288 (24.01%)
421 (23.34%)	5725	324 (23.34%)
362 (22.62%)	5825	362 (22.62%)
309 (21.97%)	5925	405 (21.97%)
259 (21.29%)	6025	452 (21.29%)
213 (20.64%)	6125	504 (20.64%)
174 (20.06%)	6225	561 (20.06%)

Second, in terms of the way in which volatility tends to respond to the market rising or falling, it may be observed that volatility in equity markets tends to rise far more as the market falls than when the market rises by a similar amount. In other words, volatility is observed to be directional. As the markets falls, fear grows and volatility rises as a consequence. When, on the other hand, the market rises, the world is as it should be and fear diminishes, with the consequence that volatility either stays the same or even falls.

Having recognised and observed this relationship between market volatility and market direction, let's reconsider the FTSE option prices from Table 8.3.

We observed that the 5725 puts (100 ticks out-of-the-money) had a higher implied volatility and therefore a higher price than the 5925 calls (also 100 ticks out-of-the-money). We further observed that the 5625 puts (200 ticks out-of-the-money) had a higher implied volatility and therefore a higher price than the 6025 calls (also 200 ticks out-of-the-money) and so on.

The reason that market participants are prepared to pay more for out-of-the-money puts than commensurately out-of-the-money calls *in equity markets* is that market participants have observed that volatility tends to rise as the equity markets fall and vice versa. The reason for this directional aspect of market volatility is that fear, the single greatest driver of increasing volatility in equity markets, is generally to the downside. In this sense, volatility may be thought of as an index of fear in the market. It is only logical that as fear rises, volatility also rises. How will this impact our trading?

Suppose that we believe that the FTSE 100 Index will fall. We could buy some FTSE puts. FTSE puts will rise in value as the FTSE falls. We also know from past experience that, as the FTSE falls, FTSE volatility will also tend to rise, further increasing the value of our FTSE puts. In a nutshell, volatility will tend to work in our favour as the underlying falls.

Now suppose we have the opposite underlying view. Suppose that we believe that the FTSE 100 Index will rise. We could buy some FTSE calls. FTSE calls will rise in value as the FTSE rises. We know from past experience that, as the FTSE rises, FTSE volatility will tend to remain unchanged or fall gently, reducing the value of our FTSE calls. In a nutshell, volatility will tend to work against us as the underlying rises.

In terms of trading equity and index options in practice, this means that we are more likely to buy puts to exploit a bearish view than buy calls to exploit a bullish view because of the observed directional nature of volatility in equities and indices.

Equity-based option prices tend to display "negative skew". That is, in equity-based markets, out-of-the-money puts tend to be more expensive than commensurately out-of-the-money calls. This is due to the fear residing to the downside in equity-based markets. Will all option markets display this pattern of skew? Is the fear to the downside in all asset classes?

Clearly not. In commodities markets, for example, where supply-side concerns tend to dominate, the sharpest moves tend to occur to the upside. As a result, market volatility tends to rise as commodities rally and fall or remain the same as commodities fall. The fear resides to the upside and as a consequence, out-of-the-money commodity calls tend to be more expensive than equally out-of-the-money commodity puts. Commodity option prices tend to be *positively skewed*.

How would this impact our trading in commodity-based options as opposed to equity-based options?

Suppose that we believe coffee will rise. We could buy some coffee calls on the LIFFE market. Coffee calls will rise in value as coffee rises in price. We know from past experience that, as the coffee price rises, volatility in coffee options will also tend to rise, in response to increasing fear in the coffee market. This will further increase the value of our coffee calls. In a nutshell, volatility will tend to work in our favour as the underlying rises.

Now suppose we have the opposite underlying view. Suppose that we believe that the coffee price will fall. We could buy some coffee puts. Coffee puts will rise in value as the price of coffee falls. We know from past experience that, as the coffee price falls, volatility in coffee options will tend to remain unchanged or fall gently, reducing the value of our coffee puts. In summary, volatility will tend to work against us as the underlying falls.

In terms of trading commodity options, in practice this means that we are more likely to buy calls to exploit a bullish view than buy puts to exploit a bearish view because of the observed directional nature of volatility in commodity options.

Please note the repeated use of the word "observed". Skew is a phenomenon that we observe in the real world; a commonly observed feature of option prices. Does this compromise the validity of skew? Does it make skew any less important? No! Skew is nearly always present in option markets and prices. How is skew best observed?

Standard practice in option markets is to look at skew graphically, as in Figures 8.1 and 8.2. Note that market/implied volatility is shown on the vertical axis and that strike prices are shown on the horizontal axis. Figure 8.1 shows the skew curve for the LIFFE FTSE 100 Index option prices used earlier in this chapter.

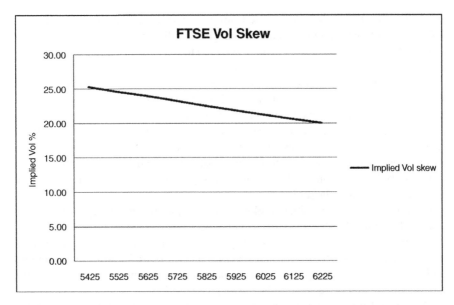

Figure 8.1   Skew curve for the LIFFE FTSE 100 Index option prices

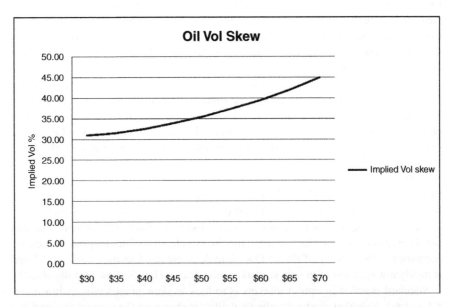

Figure 8.2   How the skew curve might usually look for a commodity such as oil

Note that the highest volatilities are for the out-of-the-money puts and that the lowest volatilities are for the out-of-the-money calls. The option prices are negatively skewed, exactly what we would expect to observe in the prices of options based upon equities. Next, consider how the skew curve might usually look for a commodity such as oil (Figure 8.2).

Note that the skew here is the opposite of the FTSE skew previously depicted. The highest volatilities are for out-of-the-money calls, the lowest for out-of-the-money puts. This is the kind of shape that we would expect to see in any commodity, whether coffee, oil, wheat or copper. In all cases, it is the supply side that is of most potential concern, the fear is to the upside, hence it is out-of-the-money calls that command the greatest volatilities.

Bear in mind that we expect to see skewed option prices. If we followed the skew in FTSE options, week after week, we would start to build up an idea of how the skew in the FTSE normally looks. What is of real interest to us as option traders is when the shape of the skew changes, when there is a deviation away from what we would normally expect to see.

A steepening of the skew curve, an exaggeration of the put skew, would indicate an increased fear of a sharp downward move. Think about what might cause such a steepening of the skew curve. What would cause out-of-the-money puts to increase in value in relation to out-of-the-money calls? Demand, of course. Market participants are prepared to spend more and more upon out-of-the-money puts, either because they are increasingly worried about a downside move or because they believe that a downside move is increasingly likely. Intuitively, people are prepared to pay more for their insurance because they are increasingly concerned about something bad happening.

How could we interpret put skew decreasing, the skew curve becoming shallower? Less demand for out-of-the-money puts, less need for downside protection, less fear to the downside. All of which is reflected in a shallower than usual skew curve.

Changes in the shape of the skew curve provide us with valuable information. Even if we never trade an option, it is surely worth knowing when the market collectively is becoming increasingly concerned or when the market is more relaxed. Think about how a fund manager or a private investor might use such information. A steepening of the skew curve may be used as a red flag, a warning that there is increasing concern in the market. In equities, that concern is almost always directional; it is fear of a downside move. It may mean, as a fund manager or an investor, that we simply reduce our exposure, cut back on our positions, just in case. It might encourage us to pay a little more attention to the news and to the charts. Or it may encourage us to hedge our book, to limit our exposure.

Monitoring the skew is easy for a professional with access to one of the major quote vendors such as CQG or Bloomberg. The skew in any particular option series may be viewed at the click of a button, then compared at regular intervals, whether daily, weekly or monthly, whatever time allows. For the private investor, brokers are

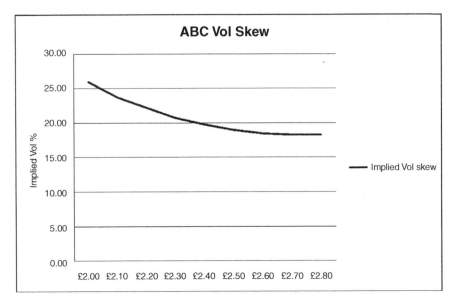

Figure 8.3   The skew in ABC option prices over a number of weeks

a good starting point for such information. Any option broker worth their salt will be able to provide general pointers on the skew in any given series.

Exercise 8.1: Interpretation of Skew

Consider Figure 8.3 depicting the skew in ABC option prices over a number of weeks.

Having observed this regular pattern of skew in ABC options for a number of weeks, the skew curve now changes as shown in Figure 8.4.

Intuitively, what is the above chart telling us? How might we use this information as hedgers (e.g. fund managers, investors with long equity portfolios, etc.)? How might we use this information as speculators?

Exercise 8.1: Answers

We can see that in Figure 8.4 the skew curve deviates significantly from both its shape and location over the preceding weeks (the line in Figure 8.3). The market's collective perception is that something has changed.

Specifically, in terms of the location of the skew curve, implied volatility has risen across the board (Figure 8.4's line is higher than Figure 8.3's). Hedgers are paying more for their protection reflecting an increased concern about adverse price movement in ABC. Speculators are paying more for options reflecting their belief that the market is becoming increasingly volatile.

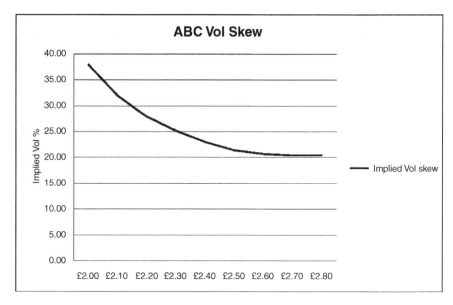

Figure 8.4 Changes in the skew curve for ABC options over a number of weeks

In terms of the shape of the skew curve, the steepening of the curve (Figure 8.4's curve is steeper than Figure 8.3's), the exaggeration of the negative skew reflects the fact that, collectively, market participants are prepared to pay more and more for out-of-the-money puts in relation to out-of-the-money calls. This further reinforces the fact that hedgers are becoming increasingly concerned about a downside move, a fall in the share price of ABC.

This information is useful to hedgers and speculators alike. Hedgers may use these observations as a warning sign, a red flag. It may simply mean that hedgers keep a closer eye upon the market. It may mean that stops are put in place or moved to more conservative levels. Or it may mean that certain positions are closed or protected with futures or options. Whatever the reaction, it is surely worth being aware that the market is showing signs of increasing concern.

Speculators may treat this as an opportunity. We know that, historically, the sharpest moves in equity markets tend to occur to the downside. For speculators who can short the market as easily as buying it, this presents an opportunity for quick profit.

SUMMARY OF CHAPTER 8

Skew is a real world phenomenon, a feature of option prices that is observed. Skew reflects the fact that calls and puts that are equally out-of-the-money may have different implied volatilities and different prices.

Skew exists because, in the real world, changes in volatility may be directional, reflecting in turn the fact that there may be more fear to the upside than the downside, or vice versa.

Equity and index options tend to be negatively skewed, with out-of-the-money puts worth more than commensurately out-of-the-money calls, reflecting that fear in equity markets tends to be greater to the downside.

Commodity options tend to be positively skewed, with out-of-the-money calls worth more than commensurately out-of-the-money puts, reflecting that fear in commodity markets tends to be greater to the upside.

Skew is generally considered in graphical form, hence the terms "vol smile", "vol smirk" and so on, market names given to the shapes of volatility skew curves.

Changes in skew may be used as indicators of increasing or decreasing fear in the market.

9
Option Pricing Revisited; the "Greeks"

Chapter 7 focused upon the various factors that influence the price of an option. Generically, option prices are influenced by four variables:

1. Underlying price in relation to the option strike price
2. Time to expiry
3. Interest rates
4. Volatility

Single stock options may also be affected by a fifth factor, dividends.

Whether we are trying to roughly price an option using our intuition or value more accurately with a pricing model, it is the four (or five) factors listed above that are key. Let's reconsider the relationships between each of these four main factors and option prices.

1. Underlying Price

All other things being equal, as the underlying rises, call prices rise and put prices fall.

All other things being equal, as the underlying falls, put prices rise and call prices fall.

2. Time

All other things being equal, the passage of time causes option prices to fall. This process is known as "time decay" or "erosion".

3. Interest Rates

Interest rates may affect options in two ways, depending upon their exact nature.

1. In relation to physically deliverable stock options (other things being equal):
    As interest rates rise, the value of calls rise and put prices fall.
    As interest rates fall, the value of puts rise and call prices fall.
2. In relation to all options (other things being equal):
    As interest rates rise, the value of all options (calls and puts) falls.
    As interest rates fall, the value of all options (calls and puts) rises.

4. Volatility

All other things being equal, as market volatility rises, all option prices rise.
All other things being equal, as market volatility falls, all option prices fall.

In broad brushstroke terms, a change in any of these four main pricing factors will affect option prices in the ways described above. But what if we want to be more precise? What if we want to quantify the effects of these pricing factors? For this, we need to understand the option sensitivities known colloquially as the "Greeks".

There are four primary Greeks, one for each of the four main pricing factors:

1. **Delta** – the relationship between the *underlying* and option prices
2. **Theta** – the relationship between *time* and option prices
3. **Rho** – the relationship between *interest rates* and option prices
4. **Vega** – the relationship between *volatility* and option prices

Collectively, delta, theta, rho and vega are known as the "Greeks" because, as is common in mathematical notation, they are often represented by Greek letters or symbols. Each of the Greeks seeks to isolate the effect of a specific pricing factor upon option prices. As a consequence, the term "all other things being equal" appears frequently. For the sake of brevity, the shorter "cet.par.", an abbreviation of the Latin term "ceteris paribus" will sometimes be used in the place of "all other things being equal". Let's consider each of the Greeks in detail.

GREEK NUMBER 1: DELTA (Δ)

Delta is the first and best known of the Greeks. This is not surprising since delta explains the relationship between the underlying and option prices. A view on the underlying is often the starting point, the driver behind the desire to trade. Many market participants will understand delta reasonably well without knowing the other Greeks quite so well.

If we wish to understand how a move in the underlying will impact our option trades, then we need to understand delta.

We know that (cet.par.) as the underlying rises, call prices rise and put prices fall. We know that (cet.par.) as the underlying falls, call prices fall and put prices rise.

(Cet.par.) as the underlying rises, call prices rise and put prices fall but by how much? (Cet.par.) as the underlying falls, call prices fall and put prices rise but by how much?

This is what delta tells us. Delta quantifies the effect of a change in the underlying upon option prices. Delta tells how much an option price should change for a given move in the underlying. But where does delta come from? How is it calculated?

Delta is closely related to option price. If we use an option pricing model to calculate a set of option prices, then the deltas of those options will be produced at the same time. The deltas are a bi-product of the pricing process. Consider the option prices in Table 9.1.

Note that the deltas in Table 9.1 are expressed as percentages. It would be equally valid to express them in decimal form. For example, the 6025 call, priced at 259, has a delta of 33% or 0.33. What does this mean?

Quite simply, it means that, other things being equal, the 6025 call should increase by 33% of an instant rise in the underlying and fall by 33% of an instant decrease in

Table 9.1 LIFFE December 2008 FTSE 100 option prices as at close on 18 June 2008 (LIFFE December 2008 FTSE 100 future = 5825)

Calls	Strike Price	Puts
616	5425	227
547	5525	256
483	5625	288
421	5725	324
362	5825	362
309	5925	405
259	6025	452
213	6125	504
174	6225	561

Now let's add in the option deltas:

Calls (Delta)	Strike Price	Puts (Delta)
616 (75%)	5425	227 (25%)
547 (70%)	5525	256 (30%)
483 (64%)	5625	288 (36%)
421 (58%)	5725	324 (42%)
362 (50%)	5825	362 (50%)
309 (40%)	5925	405 (60%)
259 (33%)	6025	452 (67%)
213 (28%)	6125	504 (72%)
174 (23%)	6225	561 (77%)

the underlying. In this case, the relevant underlying in terms of price is the Dec FTSE future as these are Dec FTSE options. For example, all other things being equal:

- If the FTSE future rises by 3 ticks, the 6025 call should rise by 33% of 3 ticks = 1 tick.
- If the FTSE future rises by 9 ticks, the 6025 call should rise by 33% of 9 ticks = 3 ticks.
- If the FTSE future rises by 15 ticks, the 6025 call should rise by 33% of 15 ticks = 5 ticks.
- If the FTSE future falls by 12 ticks, the 6025 call should fall by 33% of 12 ticks = 4 ticks.
- If the FTSE future falls by 30 ticks, the 6025 call should fall by 33% of 30 ticks = 10 ticks.

By identifying the delta of the option, we can calculate how much the option price *should* change for a given move in the underlying – *all other things being equal*. Remember, we are trying to isolate the effect of the underlying upon an option price. In the real world, all other things are *not* equal. Volatility is not a constant, nor are interest rates and nor is time. Delta focuses purely upon the effect of the underlying upon option prices. At which point, a couple more important points need to be made.

Delta tells us how much an option price should change for an instant move in the underlying; a move in the underlying *right now*. Delta provides a snapshot of the effect of an *instantaneous* move in the underlying. Delta itself changes in response to the underlying moving, time passing, volatility changing, etc. The deltas in Table 9.1 were only applicable at the specific time of their calculation at the close on 18 June, with the underlying FTSE future at 5825, at-the-money volatility at 22.62% (see Table 7.3) and interest rates at the prevailing level. Change any of these assumptions and the deltas also change.

Delta is only really applicable to relatively small moves in the underlying. In the event of the underlying moving significantly, delta itself begins to change. This phenomenon is known as *gamma*, the subject of a subsequent chapter.

Despite the above qualifications, if we want to figure out the extent to which a move in the underlying will affect our options, then we need to use delta. We can predict how much an option price should rise or fall for a given instantaneous move in the underlying. Consider the following exercise.

Exercise 9.1: Using Delta

The Dec FTSE 5925 call has a delta of 0.40 (or 40%). Other things being equal, by how much should the Dec 5925 call change in price if:

1. The Dec FTSE future rises by 10 ticks?
2. The Dec FTSE future rises by 25 ticks?

3. The Dec FTSE future falls by 15 ticks?
4. The Dec FTSE future falls by 40 ticks?

Exercise 9.1: Answers

1. The Dec 5925 call should rise by 4 ticks (i.e. 40% of the 10 tick rise).
2. The Dec 5925 call should rise by 10 ticks (i.e. 40% of the 25 tick rise).
3. The Dec 5925 call should fall by 6 ticks (i.e. 40% of the 15 tick fall).
4. The Dec 5925 call should fall by 16 ticks (i.e. 40% of the 40 tick fall).

Consider a similar exercise focusing upon single stock option prices and deltas.

Exercise 9.2: Using Delta

Given the option prices/deltas in Table 9.2 and all other things being equal:

1. By how much should the 220 call change if ZYX rises by 10?
2. By how much should the 190 put change if ZYX rises by 15?
3. By how much should the 180 call change if ZYX falls by 20?
4. By how much should the 200 put change if ZYX falls by 6?

Exercise 9.2: Answers

1. The 220 call should rise by 3 (i.e. 30% of 10).
2. The 190 put should fall by 6 (i.e. 40% of 15).
3. The 180 call should fall by 14 (i.e. 70% of 20).
4. The 200 put should rise by 3 (i.e. 50% of 6).

Having seen how delta may be used, let's now consider the mathematical properties of delta.

As the underlying rises, call prices also rise, therefore delta is *positive* for calls. There is a positive relationship between call prices and the underlying.

As the underlying rises, put prices fall, therefore delta is *negative* for puts. There is an inverse relationship between put prices and the underlying.

Table 9.2   ZYX 3 month option prices (3 month ZYX future = 200)

Calls (Δ)	Strike Prices	Puts (Δ)
24 (0.70)	180	4 (0.30)
17 (0.60)	190	7 (0.40)
10 (0.50)	200	10 (0.50)
7 (0.40)	210	17 (0.60)
4 (0.30)	220	24 (0.70)

In the real world, in the everyday option markets, market participants don't mention whether a delta is positive or negative unless a complex strategy is under discussion. We are expected to know that a call has a positive delta and that a put has a negative delta; such knowledge is taken as read.

In terms of range, the extremes of delta are zero and one (0% and 100%). That is, the lowest delta that a put or call can have is zero. The highest delta that a call can have is +1.00 (in decimal terms) or +100 (in percentage terms). The highest delta that a put can have is −1.00 (in decimal terms) or −100 (in percentage terms).

In the real world, an option may change in price by more than 100% of the move in the underlying but that is due to other factors such as volatility also changing. The maximum impact of a change in the underlying on an option price is one for one, 100%.

Exercises 9.1 and 9.2 illustrated how delta may be used to predict how much an option price should change for a given move in the underlying. In fact, the textbook definition of delta is "the sensitivity of an option price to a move in the underlying". This simple mathematical relationship is the primary use of delta. However, there is another way of looking at delta, an alternative interpretation of delta that we will now consider.

Intuitively, delta may be interpreted as *the chance of an option being in-the-money by expiry*. By way of illustration, consider the FTSE 100 option prices and deltas in Table 9.3.

The delta of the 6225 call may be viewed as the chance of Dec FTSE exceeding 6225 by Dec expiry. The delta of the 5525 put may be viewed as the chance of Dec FTSE falling below 5525 by Dec expiry.

Remember, option prices are determined by supply and demand from all the various market participants. Option prices reflect the collective view of the market regarding the value of options. And a key determinant in the value of those options is their chance of "success"; their chance of being in-the-money by expiry.

In the two examples above, the delta of the 6225 call (23%) and the delta of the 5525 put (30%) may be viewed as the collective view of the market upon the

Table 9.3 LIFFE December 2008 FTSE 100 option prices as at close on 18 June 2008 (LIFFE December 2008 FTSE 100 future = 5825)

Calls (Delta)	Strike Price	Puts (Delta)
616 (75%)	5425	227 (25%)
547 (70%)	5525	256 (30%)
483 (64%)	5625	288 (36%)
421 (58%)	5725	324 (42%)
362 (50%)	5825	362 (50%)
309 (40%)	5925	405 (60%)
259 (33%)	6025	452 (67%)
213 (28%)	6125	504 (72%)
174 (23%)	6225	561 (77%)

chances of those options being in-the-money by expiry. Specifically, the market believed that the 6225 call had a 23% chance of being in-the-money by expiry and that the 5525 put had a 30% chance of being in-the-money by expiry. The prices of the options reflected these chances, these probabilities. How can we use this information?

As with other pieces of option-related information such as volatilities and skew, deltas may be of use to market participants even if they never intend to trade options. As we have just seen, deltas inform us about the chances that the market is assigning to certain underlying levels being breached. So deltas provide useful information for non-option participants. What about those who *are* interested in trading options, how can they use delta?

Delta may be used to help inform the trading decision. To illustrate this, let's reconsider Table 9.3 which shows FTSE 100 option prices and deltas.

Collectively, the market is assigning a 23% chance of success to the 6225 call. The market believes that there is a 23% chance that the FTSE will exceed 6225 by Dec expiry. Do we agree with this? What chance do we think there is of the FTSE exceeding 6225 by Dec expiry? If we think that the chances of this happening are *greater* than 23%, then we must also believe that the 6225 calls are *underpriced* because (via volatility) the price of the option reflects its chances of succeeding. And if we believe that something is underpriced, what should we do? Buy it!

If, on the other hand, we believe that the chances of the FTSE exceeding 6225 by expiry are *less* than the delta, less than 23%, then it follows that we perceive the 6225 calls to be *overpriced*. We might therefore consider selling these options, with the important rider that selling options naked is dangerous! Nonetheless, this comparison of market delta to our delta is telling us that, in our view, the options are too expensive.

In this way, by intuitively assigning deltas to options and comparing those deltas with the market, we can address the crucial question of whether we consider options to be cheap or expensive. Just like the analysis of implied volatilities and skew, it is another "weapon" in our option armoury.

Now that we have considered this second, intuitive interpretation of delta, we can observe another mathematical property of delta(s).

Ignoring positive and negative signs, *the deltas of corresponding calls and puts sum to 1.00 or 100%.*

For example, from Table 9.3, the delta of the 6225 call (23%) and the delta of the 6225 put (77%) sum to 100%. Intuitively, this must be the case. If there is a 23% chance that the FTSE will be *above* 6225 on Dec expiry, then it follows that there must be a 77% chance that it will be *below* 6225 on Dec expiry.

Similarly, the delta of the 5525 put (30%) and the delta of the 5525 call (70%) must sum to 100%. If there is a 30% chance that the FTSE will be *below* 5525 on Dec expiry, then it follows that there must be a 70% chance of the FTSE being *above* 5525 on Dec expiry.

Consider the following exercise on delta.

Exercise 9.3: Delta

1. What is the delta of an at-the-money call?
2. What is the delta of an at-the-money put?
3. Approximately, what is the delta of a very deep in-the-money call?
4. Approximately, what is the delta of a very far out-of-the-money put?
5. If the delta of a 3 month XYZ 430 call is plus 25%, what is the delta of the 3 month XYZ 430 put?
6. If the delta of the Dec FTSE 5325 put is minus 10%, what is the delta of the Dec FTSE 5325 call?
7. A long at-the-money "straddle" consists of a long at-the-money call and a long at-the-money put. What is the delta of an at-the-money straddle?

Exercise 9.3: Answers

1. Plus (i.e. positive) 50%
2. Minus (i.e. negative) 50%
3. Approaching plus 100%
4. Negative and negligible; approaching minus zero
5. Minus 75%
6. Plus 90%
7. Zero because the delta of the at-the-money call (plus 50%) and the delta of the at-the-money put (minus 50%) cancel each other out

The point of the next exercise is to combine various pieces of option knowledge covered in earlier chapters together with this chapter's consideration of delta.

Exercise 9.4: "Filling in the Gaps" (Put/Call Parity and Delta)

Fill in the missing FTSE option prices and deltas in Table 9.4. Remember that option price equals intrinsic value plus time value and that the deltas of corresponding puts and calls sum to zero (ignoring the plus or minus signs).

Table 9.4 Dec FTSE option prices and deltas
(Dec FTSE 100 future = 5900)

Call Price (Δ)	Strike Prices	Put Prices (Δ)
	5750	100 (33%)
	5800	124 (38%)
	5850	152 (43%)
	5900	180
150 (42%)	**5950**	
120 (36%)	**6000**	
95 (31%)	**6050**	

For the sake of simplicity, ignore the (relatively small) effect of cost-of-carry of the options.

Exercise 9.4: Answers

The completed table should be as follows.

Call Price (Δ)	Strike Prices	Put Prices (Δ)
250 (67%)	**5750**	100 (33%)
224 (62%)	**5800**	124 (38%)
202 (57%)	**5850**	152 (43%)
180 (50%)	**5900**	180 (50%)
150 (42%)	**5950**	200 (58%)
120 (36%)	**6000**	220 (64%)
95 (31%)	**6050**	245 (69%)

Since, as instructed, we have ignored the relatively minor effect of cost-of-carry on the option prices, perfect put/call parity may be observed in the option prices. Further, the deltas of all corresponding calls and puts sum to 100% (ignoring plus or minus signs).

Let's recap what we have learnt about delta thus far and summarise the ways in which delta may be used.

Delta is the first and best known of the four primary Greeks. Delta may be looked at in two ways; in simple mathematical terms and intuitively.

Mathematically, delta explains the relationship between the underlying and option prices. Hence the first and most fundamental use of delta is to predict how much an option price should change for a given move in the underlying.

Intuitively, delta may be interpreted as the chance of an option being in the money by expiry. Hence, a second way that we can use delta is to compare our own deltas to prevailing market deltas to gain some insight into whether options are cheap or expensive.

For what other reasons might we want to consider deltas? How else can we use delta in the real world?

Delta can be used to *equate an option position to a position in the underlying*. We already know that, broadly speaking, buying calls is an alternative to buying the underlying. In the same way, we know that selling calls is a proxy for selling the underlying. We know that buying puts is a proxy for selling the underlying and that selling puts is an alternative to buying the underlying.

Note the use of the words "alternative" and "proxy". Options may be used as an alternative to the underlying; there are key similarities between option positions and underlying positions but they are *not the same*.

First, let's consider the similarities between option positions and positions in the underlying. In what way is an option position a proxy for a position in the underlying?

- Other things being equal, a long call position and a long position in the underlying will both make a profit if the market rises and a loss if the market falls.
- Other things being equal, a short call position and a short position in the underlying will both make a profit if the market falls and a loss if the market rises.
- Other things being equal, a long put position and a short position in the underlying will both make a profit if the market falls and a loss if the market rises.
- Other things being equal, a short put position and a long position in the underlying will both make a profit if the market rises and a loss if the market falls.

These are the ways in which options positions may be likened to positions in the underlying. What about the key differences? Options positions and underlying positions will have different risk/reward profiles. The effect of time is different upon option positions and underlying positions, as is the effect of volatility. So, while we can use options very effectively as an alternative to positions in the underlying, it is important that we understand the different dynamics of options and underlying positions.

We have seen how we can approximate an options position with a position in the underlying. If we want to understand exactly how much underlying an options position approximates to, we need to use delta.

For example, we already know that an at-the-money call has a delta of plus 50%. Other things being equal, for every 1 tick that the underlying increases, the calls will rise by half of a tick (+50% of the 1 tick rise in the underlying). Other things being equal, for every 10 ticks that the underlying falls, the calls will fall in value by 5 ticks (again, +50% of the 10 tick fall in the underlying).

Given the fact that at-the-money calls have a delta of +50%, each at-the-money call that we own is a proxy for owning 50% of the underlying.

For example, one LIFFE BP stock option represents 1000 BP shares; the underlying of one LIFFE BP stock option is 1000 BP shares. If we buy one at-the-money BP call, it is similar to buying 500 BP shares (i.e. 50% of the underlying 1000 shares). If we buy eight at-the-money BP calls, it is a proxy for buying 4000 BP shares (i.e. 50% of 8000 BP shares).

Similarly, if we buy one LIFFE BP put with a delta of 20%, it is similar to selling 200 BP shares (20% of 1000 BP shares). If we buy 30 BP puts with a delta of 20%, it is a proxy for selling 6000 BP shares (20% of 30 000 shares).

In this way, delta may be used to relate options positions to positions in the underlying.

Consider the following exercise.

Exercise 9.5: Using Delta

The underlying of one LIFFE UK equity option is 1000 shares. Equate the following option positions to a position in the underlying stock.

1. Long 5 at-the-money calls
2. Long 12 puts with a delta of 25%

3. Short 20 calls with a delta of 10%
4. Short 10 puts with a delta of 70%

Exercise 9.5: Answers

1. Long 2500 shares (50% of 5000 shares)
2. Short 3000 shares (25% of 12 000 shares)
3. Short 2000 shares (10% of 20 000 shares)
4. Long 7000 shares (70% of 10 000 shares)

By using delta in the above manner, we can instantly equate *any* options position, no matter how complex, to a position in the underlying. Suppose we have executed the following trades in XYZ options over the last few months and that XYZ is currently trading at about £4.00 on the LSE:

Trade Date	Trade	Position Delta
11 Jan	+10 Mar 4.00 calls (Δ 50%)	+5000 shares
18 Jan	−20 Jun 4.50 calls (Δ 20%)	−4000 shares
21 Feb	+10 Sep 3.60 puts (Δ 30%)	−3000 shares
12 Mar	+10 Dec 3.00 puts (Δ 10%)	−1000 shares
Total delta		**−3000 shares**

We can see that the net delta of the above four option trades "equates" to a position in the underlying of short 3000 shares. If we wanted to "flatten off" our book and return the delta to zero, we could simply buy 3000 shares in the market.

Remember, delta is a snapshot of a position. Deltas will change as time passes and the underlying moves around. Nonetheless, delta is useful if we want a snapshot of the extent of our position at a particular price at a particular time.

A later chapter will look at the various ways in which options can be traded against the underlying; the subject of "delta hedging". As its name suggests, delta hedging is only possible if we understand delta. Let's summarise the principal uses of delta:

1. To predict how much option prices should change in response to a move in the underlying; to isolate the effect of a move in the underlying upon option prices.
2. To help inform the option trading decision by comparing market deltas to our deltas.
3. To approximate an options position to a position in the underlying.
4. To "delta hedge" options positions and to trade "gamma" (see later chapters).

We have now covered the nature and principal uses of delta. But in the real world, how and where do we find deltas? How do we find delta in practice?

By far and away the easiest way to find a delta is to ask your broker. Any broker worth their salt will be able to tell you the delta of an option as quickly and easily as they can tell you the price.

Exchange websites such as LIFFE's (www.nyseeuronext.com/liffe) publish deltas as well as prices at the close each night. Other independent websites such as Futuresource (www.futuresource.com) provide free option price and delta information.

Market professionals with access to quote vendors such as Bloomberg and CQG have access to both live and end-of-day deltas.

Finally, anyone with access to a pricing model can calculate deltas as easily as price. As previously stated, deltas are an integral part of the option pricing process; one is a by-product of the other.

Having studied delta in detail, let's now consider the three remaining primary Greeks: theta, vega and rho.

GREEK NUMBER 2: THETA (Θ)

We know that all options erode. All options lose value due to the passage of time. Other things being equal, an option will be worth less tomorrow than it is worth today – but how much less? Theta answers this question. Theta quantifies the effect of time upon option prices. Theta tells how much an option price should change as time passes. Specifically, theta is *the change in the price of an option for a one day decrease in the time to expiry.*

For example, if the Dec FTSE 6025 call is worth 259 today and would, all other things being equal, be worth 257 tomorrow, then it has a theta of 2 ticks (today's value of 259 less tomorrow's value of 257).

For ETOs, options traded on an exchange, theta is expressed in ticks. In the above example, the theta of the Dec 6025 call is 2 (ticks). All other things being equal, the Dec 6025 call should lose 2 ticks of value between today and tomorrow.

This is how we use theta; to predict the effect of time upon our options position. Where does theta come from? How do we discover theta? Just like delta, theta is a by-product of the option pricing process. Consider the LIFFE December FTSE option prices in Table 9.5, the same prices that were used in the previous section on delta.

For the purpose of clear and simple illustration, these thetas are both theoretical and rounded to the nearest half tick. Note that theta is *negative* in all cases since the effect of the passage of time is to *reduce* the value of options.

A pricing model will calculate the theta of any particular option(s). From Table 9.5, we can see that the theta of the 6025 call is −2.0, the theta of the 6125 call is −1.5 and so on. Other things being equal, we can see what the effect of time should be on any particular option. What can we observe about the thetas in Table 9.5?

First, note that options with the same strike have the same theta because of put/call parity. Since calls and puts with the same strike have the same amount of time value, they erode at the same rate.

In terms of moneyness, which options have the greatest theta? The at-the-money options. In the above example, the at-the-moneys are the 5825 calls and puts. The at-the-moneys have a theta of 2.5 ticks, the highest theta of any of the options in

Table 9.5   LIFFE December 2008 FTSE 100 option prices as at close
on 18 June 2008 (LIFFE December 2008 FTSE 100 future = 5825)

Calls	Strike Price	Puts
616	**5425**	227
547	**5525**	256
483	**5625**	288
421	**5725**	324
362	**5825**	362
309	**5925**	405
259	**6025**	452
213	**6125**	504
174	**6225**	561

Now let's add in the option thetas:

Calls (Theta)	Strike Price	Puts (Theta)
616 (−1.5)	**5425**	227 (−1.5)
547 (−1.5)	**5525**	256 (−1.5)
483 (−2.0)	**5625**	288 (−2.0)
421 (−2.0)	**5725**	324 (−2.0)
362 (−2.5)	**5825**	362 (−2.5)
309 (−2.0)	**5925**	405 (−2.0)
259 (−2.0)	**6025**	452 (−2.0)
213 (−1.5)	**6125**	504 (−1.5)
174 (−1.5)	**6225**	561 (−1.5)

the table. Why should this be? Simply, because the at-the-money options have the greatest amount of time value and it is only time value that is affected by the passage of time.

In terms of moneyness, which options have the lowest theta? The furthest out-of-the-money options. We can see that, the further the strike from the money, the lower the theta. So the options with the lowest theta in Table 9.5 are those that are furthest out-of-the-money.

In terms of expiry date, which options have the greatest theta? We know (see Chapter 7) that, other things being equal, shorter-dated options erode at a faster rate than longer-dated options. Therefore, in terms of tenor, shortest-dated options have the greatest theta and longer-dated options have a lower theta. This is logical given that time impacts shorter-dated options more than longer-dated options.

GREEK NUMBER 3: VEGA (KAPPA)

Collectively, the option sensitivities are known as the Greeks. Vega is not a Greek letter, so some market participants (particularly in the USA) use "kappa" as an alternative. We will use vega, the norm in the UK markets.

We already know that volatility is the key variable in pricing options. We also know that as a general rule, as volatility increases, all option prices increase – but by how much? This is the question that vega addresses. Vega quantifies the effect of volatility upon option prices. Specifically, the textbook definition of vega is *the change in the price of an option for a 1% increase in volatility*.

Note that the Greeks are unitary. Theta relates to a 1 day decrease in the time to expiry. Vega relates to a 1% increase in volatility.

For example, if the Dec FTSE 6025 call is worth 259 at the current market volatility and would be worth 265 if volatility rose by 1%, then it has a vega of 6 (the difference between the current option price and the option price if volatility rose by 1%).

For exchange-traded options, as with theta, vega is expressed in ticks. In the above example, the vega of the Dec 6025 call is 6 (ticks). All things being equal, the value of the Dec 6025 call should increase by 6 ticks if volatility increases by 1%.

This is how we use vega; to predict the effect of volatility upon our option position. Where does vega come from? How do we discover vega? Just like delta and theta, vega is a by-product of the option pricing process. Consider the LIFFE December FTSE option prices in Table 9.6, the same prices that were used in the previous sections on delta and theta.

Table 9.6   LIFFE December 2008 FTSE 100 option prices as at close on 18 June 2008 (LIFFE December 2008 FTSE 100 future = 5825)

Calls	Strike Price	Puts
616	**5425**	227
547	**5525**	256
483	**5625**	288
421	**5725**	324
362	**5825**	362
309	**5925**	405
259	**6025**	452
213	**6125**	504
174	**6225**	561

Now let's add in the option vegas:

Calls (Vega)	Strike Price	Puts (Vega)
616 (3)	**5425**	227 (3)
547 (5)	**5525**	256 (5)
483 (6)	**5625**	288 (6)
421 (7)	**5725**	324 (7)
362 (8)	**5825**	362 (8)
309 (7)	**5925**	405 (7)
259 (6)	**6025**	452 (6)
213 (4)	**6125**	504 (4)
174 (2)	**6225**	561 (2)

For the purpose of clear and simple illustration, these vegas are both theoretical and rounded to the nearest tick. Note that vega is *positive* in all cases since a *rise* in volatility will always *increase* the value of options and vice versa.

A pricing model will calculate the vega of any particular option(s). From Table 9.6, we can see that the vega of the 6025 call is 6, the vega of the 6125 call is 4 and so on. Other things being equal, we can see what the effect of volatility changing should be on any particular option. What can we observe about the vegas in Table 9.6?

First, note that options with the same strike have the same vega because of put/call parity. Since calls and puts with the same strike have the same amount of time value, they respond to changes in volatility by the same amount.

In terms of moneyness, which options have the greatest vega? The at-the-money options. In the above example, the at-the-moneys are the 5825 calls and puts. The at-the-moneys have a vega of 8 ticks, the highest vega of any of the options in the table. Why should this be? Simply, because the at-the-money options have the greatest amount of time value and it is only time value that is affected by volatility.

In terms of moneyness, which options have the lowest vega? The furthest out-of-the-money options. We can see that the further the strike from the money, the lower the vega. So the options with the lowest vega in the table are those that are furthest out-of-the-money.

In terms of expiry date, which options have the greatest vega? We know that, other things being equal, longer-dated options have more time value than shorter-dated options. Longer-dated options have more time value to be influenced by volatility than shorter-dated options. Therefore, in terms of tenor, longer-dated options have a greater vega and shorter-dated options have a lower vega.

Rho is the least important of the four main option pricing factors. In the real world, rho is often ignored because of its lack of significance except in extreme circumstances. For what it is worth, rho measures the impact of changes in interest rates upon option prices. Note the last phrase of this sentence. Changes in interest rates may be highly significant to equity markets per se; they are an economic fundamental. But in terms of their impact specifically upon option prices, changes in interest rates tend not to be significant.

The textbook definition of rho is *the change in the price of an option for a 1% rise in interest rates*.

Just like theta and vega, rho is expressed in ticks. Rho will normally be a small number reflecting the lack of significant impact of a 1% change in rates upon option prices. Many traders talk about being "long vega" or "short theta" but in all my years as an options trader, I have never ever heard anyone talk about "trading their rho". De facto, it just doesn't tend to matter in the way that delta, theta and vega are important.

We have now considered each of the four primary Greeks, each of the four main option sensitivities, in some detail. Individually, the Greeks seek to isolate and quantify the effect of a change in one of the four option pricing factors upon option prices.

Table 9.7　LIFFE December 2008 FTSE 100 option prices as at close on 18 June 2008 (LIFFE December 2008 FTSE 100 future = 5825)

Calls	Strike Price	Puts
616	**5425**	227
547	**5525**	256
483	**5625**	288
421	**5725**	324
362	**5825**	362
309	**5925**	405
259	**6025**	452
213	**6125**	504
174	**6225**	561

Now let's add in the option deltas, thetas and vegas:

Calls					Puts			
Price	Delta	Theta	Vega	Strike Price	Price	Delta	Theta	Vega
616	75%	−1.5	3	5425	227	−25%	−1.5	3
547	70%	−1.5	5	5525	256	−30%	−1.5	5
483	64%	−2.0	6	5625	288	−36%	−2.0	6
421	58%	−2.0	7	5725	324	−42%	−2.0	7
362	50%	−2.5	8	5825	362	−50%	−2.5	8
309	40%	−2.0	7	5925	405	−60%	−2.0	7
259	**33%**	**−2.0**	**6**	**6025**	452	−67%	−2.0	6
213	28%	−1.5	4	6125	504	−72%	−1.5	4
174	23%	−1.5	2	6225	561	−77%	−1.5	2

Table 9.7 brings the three key primary Greeks together. As the least important of the primary Greeks, rho is excluded from the following.

Remember, these Greeks are both theoretical and rounded.

Shown together, the Greeks may take on a more intimidating aspect so let's keep things simple. We will focus upon the Dec 6025 call, the option highlighted in the above table. We can see that the price of the option is 259 ticks, each tick being worth £10 giving a value of £2590 per one lot of the Dec 6025 calls.

To assess the extent to which a move in the underlying should affect this value, we need to look at delta. Specifically, all other things being equal and given a delta of 33% (or 0.33), for every tick that the underlying FTSE rises, the 6025 call should rise by 33% of that tick.

To assess the extent to which time should affect this value, we need to look at theta. Specifically, all other things being equal and given a theta of −2.0, the 6025 call should fall in value by 2 ticks between today and tomorrow.

To assess the extent to which a change in volatility should affect this value, we need to look at vega. Specifically, all other things being equal and given a vega of 6, the 6025 call should increase in value by 6 ticks if volatility rises by 1%.

Bringing all three of these measures together, we can begin to analyse various possible scenarios. We can do some "what-ifs?".

For example, what will the 6025 call be worth in 5 days' time if the underlying has risen by 30 and volatility has fallen by 2%? Five days' erosion will reduce the value of the call by 10 ticks (2 ticks theta per day for 5 days). An increase of 30 ticks in the underlying should increase the value of the call by 10 ticks (33% of 30 ticks). Volatility falling by 2% should decrease the value of the calls by 12 ticks (6 ticks vega times 2).

The net effect is that the option should have fallen in value by 12 ticks. Given the scenario detailed above, we would expect the Dec 6025 call to be worth 247 (259 minus 12) in 5 days' time. We can repeat this process for any particular scenario, any given combination of changes in time, underlying and volatility. To reinforce this key use of the Greeks, consider the following exercise based upon options on ZYX shares. Note that the option prices and Greeks have been rounded; in the real world, the numbers would not be so accommodating!

Exercise 9.6: Using the Greeks ("What if?")

1. What should the 200 put be worth in 5 days' time if the underlying (ZYX) has fallen by 10 and volatility has increased by 5%?
2. What should the 190 put be worth tomorrow if the underlying has fallen by 5 and volatility has increased by 1%?
3. What should the 210 call be worth in 2 days' time if the underlying has risen by 5 and volatility has fallen by 1.9%?
4. What should the 220 call be worth in 5 days' time if the underlying has fallen by 10 and volatility has increased by 3%?

Table 9.8 ZYX 3 month option prices (3 month ZYX future = 200)

Calls					Puts			
Price	Delta	Theta	Vega	Strike Price	Price	Delta	Theta	Vega
24	70%	−0.03	0.8	**180**	4	−30%	−0.03	0.8
17	60%	−0.05	1.0	**190**	7	−40%	−0.05	1.0
10	50%	−0.10	1.2	**200**	10	−50%	−0.10	1.2
7	40%	−0.05	1.0	**210**	17	−60%	−0.05	1.0
4	30%	−0.02	0.7	**220**	24	−70%	−0.02	0.7

Exercise 9.6: Answers

1. The 200 put should be worth 20.5. The 200 put should lose 0.5 of a tick due to the passing of 5 days (5 times daily theta of −0.1), gain 5 ticks due to the underlying

falling by 10 (underlying fall of 10 times delta of −50%) and gain 6 ticks due to volatility rising by 5% (rise in volatility of 5% times vega of 1.2).

2. The 190 put should be worth just under 10 (9.95 to be precise). The 190 put should lose 0.05 of a tick due to the passing of 1 day (1 times daily theta of −0.05), gain 2 ticks due to the underlying falling by 5 (fall of 5 times delta of −40%) and gain 1 tick due to volatility rising by 1% (rise in volatility of 1% times vega of 1.0).

3. The 210 call should be worth 7. The 210 call should lose 0.1 of a tick due to the passing of 2 days (2 times daily theta of −0.05), gain 2 ticks due to the underlying rising by 5 (rise of 5 times delta of 40%) and lose 1.9 ticks due to volatility falling by 1.9% (fall in volatility of 1.9% times vega of 1.0).

4. The 220 call should be worth 3. The 220 call should lose 0.1 of a tick due to the passing of 5 days (5 times daily theta of −0.02), lose 3 ticks due to the underlying falling by 10 (fall of 10 times delta of 30%) and gain 2.1 ticks due to volatility rising by 3% (rise in volatility of 3% times vega of 0.7).

Remember, the Greeks are a snapshot, an estimation of the impact of any of the pricing factors upon an option price right now. The Greeks themselves will change over time; we need to reassess the Greeks each time we want to use them to evaluate our position.

We have now seen how the Greeks may be used to estimate the value of any option in any combination of future circumstances. This is of great use; we can estimate how much money we should make if our strategy is right and how much we stand to lose if we are wrong. The above examples and exercises focused upon the values of specific options, now let's consider how the Greeks may be applied to a whole portfolio of options.

Suppose we have been trading FTSE 100 options for the last few months and, in that time, have built up a complex position including FTSE 100 futures and FTSE 100 options with various expiry dates. How can we assess the potential risk and reward attached to our position? The answer; by applying and interpreting the Greeks. Consider the following example.

We have executed the trades in LIFFE's FTSE 100 futures and options over the last few months as shown in Table 9.9. Last night's settlement or closing price is shown in the right-hand column.

Table 9.9 Trades executed in LIFFE FTSE 100 futures and options

Trade Date	Trade	Settlement
12 March	+20 Dec 6025 calls	259
13 April	−20 Sep 6125 calls	88
9 May	−10 Dec 5825 puts	362
10 June	−10 Sep 5725 puts	166
13 June	+10 Dec 5925 puts	405
25 June	−4 Dec futures	5825

Table 9.10   Trades executed (and related Greeks) in LIFFE FTSE 100 futures and options

Trade Date	Trade	Settlement	(Δ) Posn. Δ	(T) Posn. T	(V) Posn. V
12 March	+20 Z 6025C	259	(+0.33) +6.6	(−2.0) −40.0	(6.0) +120.0
13 April	−20 U 6125C	88	(+0.18) −3.6	(−2.5) +50.0	(2.5) −50.0
9 May	−10 Z 5825C	362	(−0.50) +5.0	(−2.5) +25.0	(8.0) −80.0
10 June	+10 U 5725P	166	(−0.28) −2.8	(−3.0) −30.0	(3.5) +35.0
13 June	+10 Z 5925P	405	(−0.60) −6.0	(−2.0) −20.0	(7.0) +70.0
25 June	+2 Z FUTS	5825	(+1.00) +2.0	n/a	n/a
Total	n/a	n/a	**+1.2 Δ**	**−15.0**	**+95.0**

Key: Δ = Delta, T = Theta, V = Vega
Month codes: U = September, Z = December

What is our net position? Are we long or short the FTSE? Are we long or short options? Do we want the market to move around violently or stay exactly where it is? Can we tell? Of course, we could go through each and every trade, working out the individual risk and reward profiles before attempting to combine them. A painstaking and time-consuming process. The only practical way to assess the overall position is to employ the Greeks, as shown in Table 9.10.

Note that, for the purpose of clear and simple illustration, these Greeks are both theoretical and rounded.

For each individual position in Table 9.10, the position delta is simply the product of the individual delta and the quantity traded, the position theta is simply the individual theta times the quantity traded and so on. The total deltas, thetas and vegas are simply the sums of the deltas, thetas and vegas for each respective column. It is these numbers, the numbers highlighted in the bottom row entitled "Total", that are key to the assessment of the overall position. What information can we glean from these Greeks?

The total delta for the whole position including the futures is long 1.2. Right now, the whole position approximates to an underlying position of long 1.2 FTSE futures. For an instantaneous move in the underlying, the whole position will show a profit or loss similar to a position of long 1.2 futures. The value of 1 FTSE futures tick is £10. Therefore, right now and all other things being equal, if the underlying FTSE goes up by 10 ticks, we would expect our overall position to show a profit of about £120 (+1.2 deltas × 10 ticks × £10).

Right now and all other things being equal, if the underlying FTSE goes down by 20 ticks, we would expect our overall position to show a loss of about £240 (+1.2 deltas × −20 ticks × £10).

If we wanted to flatten our position, to reduce this directional risk, then we could simply sell a future. This would leave us long of one fifth (0.2) of a future, a negligible amount. To completely flatten our book and remove even this residual futures position, we could sell 1 call with a 20% delta or buy 2 puts with a 10% delta; any trade that has a delta of short 0.2. This would, of course, also have an impact on theta and vega.

Consider the total theta in Table 9.10. Note that theta is not applicable to the long FTSE futures position; futures don't erode like options (although futures prices are partly a function of time). The total theta for the whole position is −15.0. Taken together and all other things being equal, we would expect our overall position to erode by 15 ticks between now and tomorrow. If we wanted to flatten our book, to reduce or remove the effect of time upon our overall position, we would need to sell some options to reduce our negative theta.

Consider the total vega in Table 9.10. The total vega for the above position is plus 95.0. Taken together and all other things being equal, we would expect our overall position to show a profit of 95 ticks (equivalent to £950) if volatility rose by 1% from its current level. Taken together and all other things being equal, we would expect our overall position to show a loss of 190 ticks (equivalent to £1900) if volatility fell by 2% from its current level. If we wanted to flatten our book, to reduce or remove the effect of volatility upon our overall position, we would need to sell some options to reduce our long vega.

Consider the following exercise which uses the same FTSE options position as a basis.

Exercise 9.7: What if?

Trade Date	Trade	Settlement	(Δ) Posn. Δ	(T) Posn. T	(V) Posn. V
12 March	+20 Z 6025C	259	(+0.33) +6.6	(−2.0) −40.0	(6.0) +120.0
13 April	−20 U 6125C	88	(+0.18) −3.6	(−2.5) +50.0	(2.5) −50.0
9 May	−10 Z 5825P	362	(−0.50) +5.0	(−2.5) +25.0	(8.0) −80.0
10 June	+10 U 5725P	166	(−0.28) −2.8	(−3.0) −30.0	(3.5) +35.0
13 June	+10 Z 5925P	405	(−0.60) −6.0	(−2.0) −20.0	(7.0) +70.0
25 June	+2 Z FUTS	5825	(+1.00) +2.0	n/a	n/a
Total	n/a	n/a	**+1.2 Δ**	**−15.0**	**+95.0**

How much should the above position make or lose if:

1. The FTSE rises by 100 over the next 5 days and volatility rises by 1%?
2. The FTSE rises by 40 over the next 2 days and volatility falls by 2%?
3. The FTSE falls by 150 over the next 10 days and volatility rises by 4%?

Exercise 9.7: Answers

1. The position should make a profit of 140 ticks which equates to £1400. Breakdown:
   Profit from 100 rise in underlying times net long 1.2 deltas = +120 ticks = +£1200
   Loss from passing of 5 days times −15 daily theta = −75 ticks = −£750
   Profit from 1% increase in volatility times +95 vega = +95 ticks = +£950
   Net profit = +£1200 − £750 + £950 = +£1400

2. The position should make a loss of 172 ticks which equates to £1720. Breakdown:
   Profit from 40 rise in underlying times +1.2 deltas = +48 ticks = +£480
   Loss from passing of 2 days times −15 daily theta = −30 ticks = −£300
   Loss from 2% decrease in volatility times +95 vega = −190 ticks = −£1900
   Net loss = +£480 − £300 − £1900 = −£1720
3. The position should make a profit of 50 ticks which equates to £500. Breakdown:
   Loss from 150 fall in underlying times +1.2 deltas = −180 ticks = −£1800
   Loss from passing of 10 days times −15 daily theta = −150 ticks = −£1500
   Profit from 4% increase in volatility times +95 vega = +380 ticks = +£3800
   Net profit = −£1800 − £1500 + £3800 = +£500

We have now covered the nature and uses of the four primary Greeks: delta, theta, vega and rho. Each of these primary Greeks isolates and quantifies the relationship between each of the four main option pricing factors (underlying, time, volatility and interest rates) and option prices. Note the use of the word "isolates".

The primary Greeks quantify the effect of each of the four main option pricing factors on option prices, *all other things being equal*. Specifically:

- Delta quantifies the effect of a change in the underlying upon option prices, all other things being equal.
- Theta quantifies the effect of the passage of time upon option prices, all other things being equal.
- Vega quantifies the effect of a change in volatility upon option prices, all other things being equal.
- Rho quantifies the effect of a change in interest rates upon option prices, all other things being equal.

In the real world, however, "other things" are not very often equal. The underlying is likely to be moving around, time is certainly passing and volatility is likely to be changing. In fact, changes in the underlying are likely to lead to changes in volatility. In short, the Greeks are inter-related. The primary Greeks (delta, vega, theta and rho) focus upon the impact of various variables upon option prices. If we want to quantify the inter-relationships of the various primary Greeks, then we need to consider the secondary and even tertiary Greeks. The most important of the secondary Greeks is *gamma*. Gamma relates to the fact that option deltas change as the underlying moves around. To understand this, consider the following extreme example.

Shares in ABC are trading at a price of £5.00. Consider the 1 month ABC £5.00 call. It has a delta of 50% because it is exactly at-the-money. If the share price of ABC doubles today to £10.00, then the £5.00 call will no longer be *at*-the-money but rather deep *in*-the-money. As such, the delta of the call will be significantly higher than 50%, perhaps 90%. The delta of the option has changed in response to the underlying changing. This is gamma.

If the share price of ABC now plummets to £1.00, then the £5.00 call will no longer be deep *in*-the-money but rather far *out*-of-the-money. As such, the delta of the call will be significantly lower than 50%, perhaps 10%. Again, the delta of the option has changed in response to the underlying changing. This is gamma.

We can see that as the underlying changes, option deltas change. As the underlying changes, option deltas change – but by how much? This is what gamma tells us.

Gamma quantifies how much option deltas should change for a given move in the underlying, all other things (e.g. time, volatility, etc.) being equal. Specifically, gamma is *the change in the delta of an option for a 1 tick move in the underlying*.

For example, (cet.par.) if the delta of the Sep FTSE 5825 call is 0.500 (or 50.0%) at the current underlying price of 5825 and would be 0.501 (or 50.1%) if the underlying FTSE rose by 1 tick to 5826, then the gamma of the Sep 5825 call is 0.001 (or 0.1%).

As we can see, gamma is of a relatively small magnitude for a 1 tick move in the underlying. In the real world, traders tend to consider changes in option deltas over rather larger movements in the underlying. Notwithstanding this, the standard expression of gamma is for a 1 tick move in the underlying.

We can use gamma to predict how much an option delta should change for a given move in the underlying. Why would we want to do this? Sophisticated option users "trade their gamma". That is, they trade the underlying stock or future against their long option positions to benefit from the changes in delta caused by movement in the underlying. "Gamma trading" and its counterpart, "being whipped", are considered in depth at a later stage when we consider the trading of options in conjunction with the underlying.

Which options have the greatest gamma? Let's consider this question from two perspectives: moneyness and tenor.

In terms of moneyness, it is *at*-the-money options that have the greatest gamma since they have the greatest amount of time value. Intuitively, this makes sense. The options that have the greatest theta also have the greatest gamma. Those options that lose the most due to the passage of time also provide the greatest profit potential in terms of gamma trading.

In terms of tenor, other things being equal, shorter-dated options have greater gamma than longer-dated options. This again makes intuitive sense. Other things being equal, shorter-dated options erode at a faster rate than longer-dated options. Again, those options that lose the most due to the passage of time also provide the greatest profit potential in terms of gamma trading. The following example illustrates this point.

Consider two exactly at-the-money stock options, an option with 1 year to expiry and an option with 1 minute to expiry. Both options have a delta of 50%. The underlying stock now rises by a small amount. As a result, the delta of the 1 year call also rises by a small amount. But the delta of the 1 minute option rises to nearly 100% since it is almost certain to be in-the-money when it expires in 1 minute's time. The gamma of the longer-dated option is minimal, the delta of the shorter-dated option much greater. This rather extreme example illustrates the wider point that, other things being equal, shorter-dated options have greater gamma than longer-dated options.

We could continue studying the secondary, tertiary and further Greeks ad infinitum, quantifying the impact of various factors upon the various Greeks themselves until we knew to within a thousandth of a tick how much an option price should change in any given circumstances. But in practical terms, this would be pointless. Very few real world users of options need to drill down to such levels of detail, nor do most real world users have the time or resources to do so. And so, at this point, we will draw a line under the Greeks for the time being. The practical importance of gamma will become evident when we consider option strategy, specifically trading options in conjunction with their underlying. Before turning to option strategy, let's briefly summarise the Greeks.

SUMMARY OF CHAPTER 9

There are four primary Greeks, one for each of the four main pricing factors:

1. **Delta** – the relationship between the *underlying* and option prices
2. **Theta** – the relationship between *time* and option prices
3. **Rho** – the relationship between *interest rates* and option prices
4. **Vega** – the relationship between *volatility* and option prices

In practical terms, rho is the least important of the primary Greeks.

The most important secondary Greeks is *gamma* which explains the relationship between the underlying and option deltas. Broadly speaking, the following relationships hold true:

- Long options = negative theta (losing due to time passing), long vega and long gamma
- Short options = positive theta (making due to time passing), short vega and short gamma

Long options positions give us profit potential if the underlying moves but lose due to the passage of time. Short options positions expose us to movement in the underlying but benefit from the passing of time. This is the essential dynamic of options positions, a dynamic that we will now consider in greater detail as we embark upon option strategy.

10
Basic Option Strategy

We have already seen that options may be traded as an alternative to trading an underlying share. For example, if we want to profit from a share rising in price, then we have the following three basic choices:

1. Buy the share itself (either the physical shares or stock futures, CFDs, etc.)
2. Buy some calls
3. Sell some puts

Other things being equal, all three of the above choices will deliver a profit if the share price rises and a loss if it falls. All three are "bullish" choices. So are they the same? No! Indeed, the *only* thing that unites the three choices is their "bullish" nature. Consider the profit and loss profiles of the three choices:

1. Buying the actual share, whether physically or via a CFD, potential profit to the upside is unlimited and is (depending upon the specific share price) matched by commensurately big losses to the downside (limited only by zero). Buying the actual share is, to all intents and purposes, a 50/50 "shot". Big potential profits matched by big potential losses.
2. Buy some calls. Our potential profits to the upside are unlimited and, if we are wrong and the share price falls, we can only lose the premium paid for the call. Even if the company goes bust and the share price falls to zero, we can only lose the price paid for the options. Unlimited potential profit against limited risk.
3. Sell some puts. Our potential losses to the downside are large, limited only by zero and our profits to the upside are limited to the premium received for the puts. Even if the company discovers the secret of eternal youth or free energy, our profits to the upside are limited to the premium received for the options. Limited potential profit against big potential losses (limited only by zero).

Which of the above is the best choice? It is tempting to say choice number 2, buying some calls, because of the attractive risk/reward profile. But that would be too simplistic. In the above example, there is a critical piece of information that is missing. Before reading on, try to think what it might be. Consider how, in a broader context, we decide whether we want to buy or sell anything.

The missing piece of information is *price*; specifically the prices of the calls and puts under consideration. Extreme examples best illustrate this point. Let's say we are looking to exploit our view that share XYZ will rise in price in the coming weeks. XYZ is currently trading at £5.00. If the 1 month £5.00 calls and puts are both trading at £0.01, then our choice of trade is simple. Buy the £5.00 calls at 1p! We can only ever lose 1p and our potential profit is unlimited. At the other extreme, if the 1 month £5.00 calls and puts are both trading at £4.90, then our choice of trade is equally simple. Sell the £5.00 puts at £4.90! We can only ever lose £0.10 (if the share price falls to zero in the next month) and our potential profit is £4.90. Of course, in the real world we would be extremely suspicious if the puts were trading at such an extraordinarily high price; it would mean that an awful lot of people believed with near certainty that XYZ was about to go bust.

Furthermore, in the real world, options are unlikely to be trading at such extreme prices. 1p would be an amazingly low price for a 1 month at-the-money call. £4.90 would be an equally amazingly high price for a 1 month £5.00 put. In the real world, the options are likely to be trading at a more realistic price; perhaps 20 or 30 or 40 pence. In that case, our choice of option trade would be less clear cut. It would essentially depend on *how far* and *how quickly* we expected the share price to rise. Before considering a more detailed example, a key question needs to be answered. What will determine whether the at-the-money options are worth 1p or 30p or indeed £4.90? Pause to consider this for a moment before reading on.

Remember, the value of any option is a function of four variables; underlying value (in relation to the option strike price), time to expiry, interest rates and volatility. The first three variables are, at any particular moment, known. Underlying share price, time to expiry and prevailing interest rates are all a matter of fact at any particular moment in time. It is *volatility* that is the key variable. Volatility will determine whether a 1 month at-the-money option is worth 1p (implying an extremely low volatility) or £4.90 (implying an extremely high volatility) or 25p (implying a "middling" volatility). Remember, it is by considering the implied volatility of an option price that we can accurately assess whether it is relatively cheap or expensive. We could simply consider the price of the option but, in so doing, we run the very real risk of either buying relatively expensive options or selling relatively cheap options. Why ignore volatility? Why ignore such good information when it is so freely available? Why, for the sake of such a small task, risk the chance of making less profit or sustaining a greater loss?

All of which brings us to an important point. No matter how simple or how complex our option trading, our choice of option trade will be determined by two considerations:

1. Our view on the underlying
2. Our view on volatility – because it is volatility that determines whether options are relatively cheap or expensive

Table 10.1 Closing prices of December BP options on 22 October 2007 (BP share price (LSE) = 605 (i.e. £6.05))

Calls	Strike Prices	Puts
53	**560**	8
38	**580**	13
26	**600**	21
16	**620**	31
9	**640**	44

Initially, most investors will find it easier to form a view on the underlying than on volatility but, as option traders gain experience, they will find themselves focusing ever more closely upon volatility rather than market direction. The vast majority of my trades are now volatility led. That is not to say that I ignore direction but rather that I tend to consider volatility first and market direction second.

For now, given that the readers of this book are aiming to learn about options, we will continue to consider direction first and volatility second. However, as we progress, we will attach increasing emphasis to the price of the options, to volatility.

Consider the real world example taken from the LIFFE market in Table 10.1.

Given the above prices, what are our choices of trade if we believe that the BP share price will rise in the next month?

1. We could buy the physical shares on the LSE at a price of £6.05. Our potential profits are unlimited and our potential losses are £6.05, the full value of the share. The trade has, to all intents and purposes, a 50/50 chance of success.
2. We could buy some calls. For example, we could buy the 640 calls at the prevailing price of 9 ticks per contract. Our potential profit to the upside is unlimited. Our potential losses to the downside are limited to 9 ticks (with a monetary value of £90) per contract bought. We can only lose the premium paid. Our risk/reward is –£90/+infinity.
3. We could sell some puts. For example, we could sell the 560 puts at 8 ticks per contract. Our potential profit to the upside is limited to 8 ticks (with a monetary value of £80) per contract sold. Our potential losses to the downside are limited only by zero. In the event that BP shares become worthless, the 560 puts will be worth 560. We sold them for 8 so, in the event that the BP share price falls to zero, our net loss will be 552 (with a monetary value of £5520) per contract sold. Our risk reward is –£5520/+£80.

Which is the best choice? Intuitively, it is tempting to say that choice number 2, buying the 640 calls, is best. It is certainly true that this offers the best risk/reward. But what is working against us if we buy the calls? In a broader sense, what "hurts" option buyers? What is continually working against option buyers?

The answer is *time*. Consider how the passage of time will impact the three strategy choices listed above.

1. Buying the physical shares at £6.05. The only way that time affects this trade is in terms of the "cost-of-carry", the amount of interest foregone on the money paid out for the shares. Aside from this cost-of-carry, there is no "erosion" on the trade; the value of the physical shares is not eroded by the passage of time.
2. Buying the 640 calls at 9. If the BP share price remains unchanged until expiry, the value of the options will erode and our options will expire worthless; we will lose 9 ticks per contract.
3. Selling the 560 puts at 8. If the BP share price remains unchanged until expiry, the value of the options will erode and the options we have sold will expire worthless; we will make a profit of 8 ticks per contract.

In summary, time works for us if we choose to sell the puts, against us if we choose to buy calls, and is insignificant if we trade the share itself. This brings us to an important general observation:

•   When we buy options, our risk/reward is "good" but time works against us.
•   When we sell options, our risk/reward is "bad" but time works in our favour.

Before moving on to an exercise that helps clarify these principles, let's consider the way that option trades are represented graphically. Specifically, let's compare and contrast the expiry payoff charts (Figures 10.1 and 10.2) for choices 2 and 3 above; buying the 640 calls at 9 and selling the 560 puts at 8.

In Figure 10.1, note that profit and loss is shown on the vertical axis with the BP share price shown on the horizontal. The line depicts the payoff of the strategy *on expiry*. If we wanted to look at the payoff between now and expiry, we would need to construct a highly complex 3D surface that would be intimidatingly difficult to understand. It is for this reason that payoff charts focus upon the payoff on expiry, a much simpler proposition.

In Figure 10.2, again, note that profit and loss is shown on the vertical axis with the BP share price shown on the horizontal. The line depicts the payoff of the strategy *on expiry*.

The charts are representative of the way that option payoffs are shown graphically by just about everyone; they are industry standard. Many people find that these charts help; they find it easier to analyse option trades graphically than by simply looking at the raw numbers. We will consider some more complicated examples of such charts when we look at option spreads in later chapters.

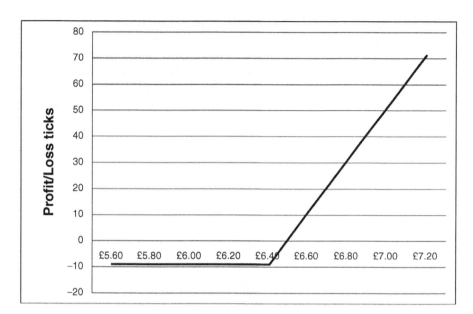

Figure 10.1 Long Sep 640 call at 9; expiry payoff

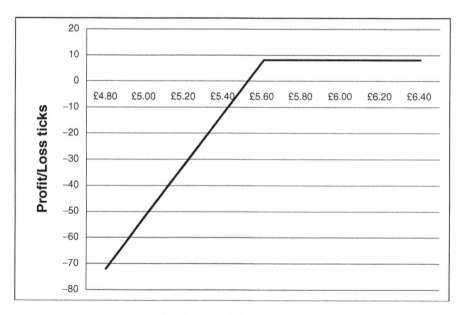

Figure 10.2 Short Sep 560 put at 8; expiry payoff

The above examples all focus upon possible choices of trade if our view on the underlying share is "bullish"; if we believe that the share price will rise. The following exercise assumes a "bearish" view, a view that the share price will fall. Exactly the same principles apply. Our choice of trade is dictated by our views on the underlying and volatility; are the options "cheap" or "expensive"? Buying options results in a favourable risk/reward and vice versa. The passage of time works for us when we sell options and against us when we buy them. Bear these principles in mind when considering the following exercise.

Exercise 10.1: Option Strategy

We wish to exploit our view that the price of XYZ will fall over the coming month. We cannot go short of physical XYZ shares; that is, we cannot sell shares that we do not own. We can, however, sell XYZ futures or CFDs. Prevailing XYZ futures and option prices are as follows:

XYZ 1 month future = £5.00 (500 pence)		
1 Month Calls	Strike Price	1 Month Puts
20	500	20

1. If we go short of XYZ futures at £5.00, what is our risk/reward?
2. Is the trade significantly affected by the passage of time?
3. Which two option trades could be used as alternatives to "shorting" XYZ futures?
4. How should we decide which of the two option trades to employ?
5. What are the risk/reward profiles of the two option trades?
6. Draw the expiry payoff charts for the two trades
7. How are these trades affected by time?

Exercise 10.1: Answers

1. Risk/reward is unlimited loss (if the share goes up towards infinity!) against a maximum profit of £5.00 (if the share price falls to zero). In practical terms, a 50/50 trade.
2. No, trading the futures is *not* significantly affected by the passage of time.
3. The two option alternatives to shorting the future are buying puts or selling calls. Both are proxies for shorting the underlying. Other things being equal, both option alternatives will be profitable if we are correct and the share price falls. Both option alternatives will result in a loss if we are wrong and the share price rises.
4. Both of the above option trades are "bearish" choices; they will both be profitable if the share price falls and vice versa. How do we choose which of the two alternatives

to employ? By looking at the price of the two options under consideration. Here, both options are priced at 20 ticks (with a monetary value of £200) per contract. If we consider 20 ticks to be a relatively low price for these options (because current market volatility is relatively low), then we should buy the 500 puts at 20. If we consider 20 ticks to be a relatively high price for these options (because current market volatility is relatively high), then we should sell the 500 calls at 20, with the important rider that selling calls "naked" is dangerous. (See subsequent chapters for further detail).

5. With regard to the risk reward profiles of the two option trades, if we buy the 500 puts at 20, then we can lose 20 (the premium paid) and make 480 (the maximum possible value of the put minus the price paid for them) in the event that the share price falls to zero. If we sell the 500 calls at 20, then we have unlimited potential losses to the upside (in the event that the share price tends towards infinity) and our potential profit is limited to 20 (the premium received).

6. The expiry payoff charts for the two option trades are as shown in Figures 10.3 and 10.4

In Figure 10.3, note that profit and loss is shown on the vertical axis with the BP share price shown on the horizontal. The line depicts the payoff of the strategy *on expiry*.

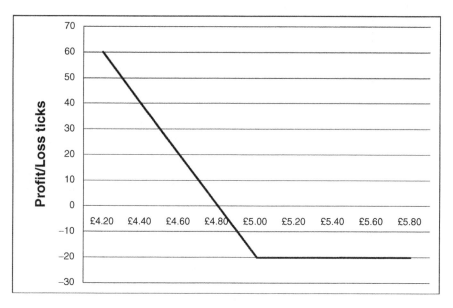

Figure 10.3   Long 500 put at 20; expiry payoff

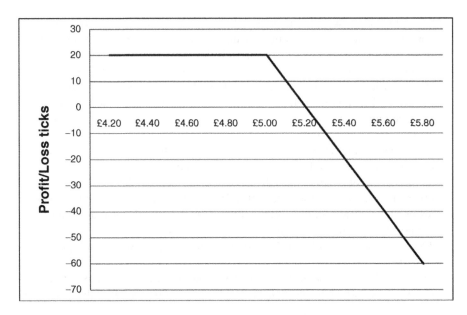

Figure 10.4 Short 500 call at 20; expiry payoff

In Figure 10.4, note that profit and loss is shown on the vertical axis with the BP share price shown on the horizontal. The line depicts the payoff of the strategy *on expiry.*

7. With regard to the impact of the passage of time upon the two option trades, if we buy the puts, then time will work against us; the options will erode. If we sell the calls, then time will work in our favour as the options erode in value.

To summarise the above, if we believe that the price of XYZ will fall, we could sell XYZ futures. Remember, it is not normally possible to short the physical shares. Selling XYZ futures is, effectively, a 50/50 "bet" in that we can both make and lose lots of money. Time is not a significant factor.

Instead of selling XYZ futures, we could buy some XYZ puts. Our loss is limited to the premium paid and we can make large profits to the downside but time is working against us; the options will erode in value.

Instead of selling XYZ futures or buying XYZ puts, we could sell XYZ calls. Our potential losses are unlimited and our profit is limited to the premium received but time is working in our favour.

The essential dynamic; an attractive or ugly risk/reward against positive or negative time decay. Our choice of option trade will depend upon our perception of price. If we consider the options to be cheap, then we should do what we do with anything that we think is cheap – we should buy them. If we perceive the options to be expensive, then we should do what we do with anything that is expensive – we should sell them, with the vitally important rider that this exposes us to significant risk.

Let's return to the question of *how* we decide whether options are cheap or expensive. We already know that options are relatively cheap when volatility is relatively low and that options are relatively expensive when volatility is relatively high. As option traders, we need to build up an idea of what constitutes "high" and "low" volatility in our particular areas of interest. The point has already been made that different assets will have different "normal" ranges of volatility. For example, having traded FTSE 100 Index options for many years, I know that 8 or 9% is about as low as market volatility ever gets in FTSE options. When "vol" in the FTSE gets down towards these levels, I know from experience that FTSE options are about as cheap as they ever get. In such circumstances, depending upon my view on the underlying market, I am likely to be looking to be long of FTSE options rather than short. Whether or not I decide to go ahead and buy some FTSE options will depend upon my view on the FTSE over the forthcoming period. It might be that I think the FTSE is going to remain within a narrow range over the coming weeks, in which case the low market volatility is justified and I may do nothing. On the other hand, if I believe that the FTSE is about to rally, I might buy some "cheap" calls or, if I think the FTSE is likely to fall, buy some "cheap" puts. This is logical, common sense, the practical application of the theory previously outlined.

I mentioned earlier that the majority of my option trades are volatility led. Indeed, it may well be that I do not have a directional view on the underlying, just a view on volatility.

Following on from the above FTSE examples, if I find that FTSE volatility is approaching its lows, I may well consider that the market is about to move but not be sure in which direction. In short, I may have a view on volatility but not direction. I know that I want to be long of options but cannot simply buy calls (because I am not bullish) and I cannot simply buy puts (because I am not bearish). So what should I do? Consider this for a moment.

The answer is that I should buy both calls *and* puts. I should buy a strategy called a "straddle" (calls and puts with the same strike) or a "strangle" (out-of-the-money calls and out-of-the-money puts). Straddles and strangles are examples of "volatility spreads" because they focus upon volatility rather than direction. These strategies will be considered in greater detail in a later chapter.

SUMMARY OF CHAPTER 10

The two key considerations when deciding upon option strategy are:

1. Our view on the underlying; is it going up, down or sideways?
2. Our view on volatility; are the options relatively cheap or expensive?

If we perceive the options to be cheap because volatility is low, then we should buy calls if we are bullish, we should buy puts if we are bearish, and we should buy both calls *and* puts if we have no directional view.

To my mind, when we believe options are cheap, our decision is simple; buy some options! But what about when options are not cheap? What should we do when volatility is high? Simplistically, the answer is to sell some options. But there is a problem. Selling options in isolation (known in the market as selling options "naked") exposes us to significant, perhaps infinite, risk. Subjectively, in my opinion, that is unacceptable. Unlimited risk is a non-starter. Does that mean that we cannot sell options? Does that mean that we can only trade options when they are cheap? No. Of course we can sell options. When volatility is high and options are therefore expensive, selling options is the right thing to do. But there are good ways and bad ways of doing this. There are intelligent ways and unintelligent ways of doing this. To my mind, subjectively, there are two compelling reasons why it is wrong to sell options naked. First, naked short options equate to significant risk and that is unacceptable, particularly when it is not matched by a correspondingly large profit. But the truly compelling argument against selling options naked is the second reason. Why is it wrong to sell options naked? Because there are better alternatives. We don't need to expose ourselves to unlimited risk, so why would we do so? All of which moves us neatly onto the subject of option spreads.

11
Option Spreads

Calls and puts can be combined in a wide variety of ways. Some of these combinations have become familiar enough to be recognised as option strategies. The following list, while no means exhaustive, contains some of the most widely used of these recognized option strategies. Any genuine option practitioner, whether broker, trader or analyst would recognise these strategies although the exact names of these strategies may vary from market to market:

Collars (aka fences, combos, min/max, etc.)
Call spreads and put spreads
Straddles and strangles
Butterflies and condors
Calendars and diagonals

The majority of these spreads are used primarily to speculate, the exception being the collar or fence. Of the strategies listed above, only the collar is a truly defensive strategy, a strategy used primarily to hedge an existing position in the underlying.

There are many more recognised option strategies than those listed above, often with ever more exotic names such as jelly-rolls and seagulls and Christmas trees, but we will focus upon the strategies listed above.

All of these option strategies have evolved for one of two reasons:

- To reduce the *cost* of owning options and/or
- To reduce the *risk* of selling options

Remember that the two main reasons for using options are protection (hedging an existing underlying position or holding) and speculation (risking money in order to make more money). As previously stated, of the strategies listed above, the only truly protective strategy is the collar, the detail of which we will now consider.

GLOSSARY

Natural long: A person or business that always owns a particular asset, such as a wheat farmer who is "naturally" long of wheat or a copper mining company that is "naturally" long of copper.

Natural short: A person or business that always needs to buy a particular asset, such as a bread baker who is "naturally" short of wheat or an airline that is "naturally" short of jet fuel. They cannot conduct their business without buying the requisite raw materials.

12
The Collar (Fence)

Option strategies often have a variety of names depending upon the specific market in which they are traded. "Collar" is prevalent in interest rate and forex markets, "fence" is typically used in commodities markets, "min/max" is often used in metals and LIFFE's official name for this strategy is a "combo". Despite this, "collar" is the term that I am used to hearing in LIFFE's equity and index markets but all of the above terms may be used to describe this strategy. So what is a collar? A collar is an option strategy designed to protect an existing position in the underlying. Collars could be used in isolation but to do so would be highly risky. In order to understand how and why collars are used, it is worth revisiting the more basic ways in which derivatives in general may be used to protect underlying positions.

Consider a fund manager who invests in UK equities. Our fund manager is a "natural long" of UK shares. What does our fund manager, our natural long of equities, hope that the UK stock market will do? And what is his fear?

Clearly, our fund manager hopes that UK equities will rise in value and is fearful of a falling stock market. How could he hedge his long equity position? How could he protect his portfolio against a falling UK stock market? Given that our manager's exposure relates to the UK stock market, FTSE 100 Index derivatives might seem a sensible choice to hedge his basket of UK equities.

Derivatives, in this case FTSE 100 Index futures and options, offer a variety of hedging choices. The simplest thing that our fund manager could do is sell some FTSE futures. He is protecting himself against the market falling but is simultaneously removing any possibility of profit should the market rise. By selling futures against his long equity portfolio, he has locked himself in. Therein lies the problem. If our fund manager hedges his long equity portfolio by selling index futures and the market falls, then he has made a good choice. However, if the market rises, he has a potential problem. By locking in with futures, he is no longer making a profit to the upside. If all of his competitors are in the same position, then things are not too bad, although investors will tend to expect positive returns when the market rises. However, if our fund manager's competitors haven't locked themselves in by selling futures, then they will make money to the upside, putting our fund manager at a competitive disadvantage, a potentially disastrous situation in such a competitive industry.

Instead of selling futures to hedge, our fund manager could buy some FTSE 100 Index puts, options that allow him to sell the FTSE if he needs to, if he wants to. The key word is "if". If our fund manager hedges his long equity portfolio by buying some FTSE puts, then he will only exercise those puts, only exercise his right to sell the FTSE, in the event that the FTSE falls. This is *not what he wants to happen* nor what he expects to happen. What he wants is for the UK stock market to rally and for his FTSE puts to expire worthless. He expects the market to rally and his FTSE puts are simply insurance in case he is wrong and the market falls. Yet again we see the way in which options can be directly related to insurance against adverse price movement.

Buying puts to protect a long position allows our fund manager to "have his cake and eat it". He is protected against adverse price movement but still gets to participate in any favourable price movement. So where is the catch? What is the problem with buying puts? What is the problem with simply buying anything?

The answer, of course, is the cost. Options cost money and businesses tend not to like cost. I remember the finance director of a well-known company telling me that "we don't mind buying options . . . so long as they cost us nothing". There is no getting around the fact that options, just like insurance, cost money. People tend to understand the need for insurance; it is something that we have come to accept as part of the cost of everyday life. The problem is that options are not perceived in the same way. Price insurance is somehow seen as different to insurance on a car or home contents. The strategy known as the "fence" or "collar" has evolved as a direct result of this reluctance to spend money on options, on price insurance. So how does it work?

Let's return to our fund manager with his portfolio of UK equities and consider his position in more detail. He finds himself faced with the following LIFFE FTSE 100 Index derivatives prices. These option prices, while theoretical, are closely based on FTSE option prices during June 2008.

Our fund manager has considered and then discarded the idea of hedging by selling FTSE futures at 5825 because it locks him in and stops him benefiting from a rally in the FTSE. He has considered hedging by buying, for example, the 5525 puts but has balked at the cost of 257 ticks (equivalent to £2570) per put purchased. How can our fund manager achieve protection without incurring such substantial costs? The answer is by giving away some of his upside. In practical terms, this means selling upside calls against the downside puts that he is buying for protection. Consider the following example from the FTSE option prices shown in Table 12.1.

Remember that our fund manager has an existing long equity portfolio which he wishes to protect. This is achieved by buying, for example, the appropriate number of 5525 puts. The cost of buying these protective puts is offset by the sale of the same number of 6025 calls. The puts are bought for 257 while the calls are sold for the same price, making the combined trade cost free. Together, these two trades constitute a

Table 12.1   LIFFE 6 month FTSE 100 option prices (LIFFE 6 month 2008 FTSE 100 future = 5825)

Calls	Strike Price	Puts
616	**5425**	227
547	**5525**	257
483	**5625**	288
421	**5725**	324
362	**5825**	362
309	**5925**	405
257	**6025**	452
213	**6125**	504
174	**6225**	561

collar, in this case the long 5525/6025 collar; "long" because it is protecting a long underlying position. What are the possible outcomes for the combined underlying and collar position between now and expiry?

If the market expires below 5525, then the fund manager will benefit from being short the FTSE (via his long puts) at 5525. Hence, his worst case scenario between now and expiry is 5525. No matter how low the underlying stock market falls between now and expiry, he has the right to be short the FTSE at 5525. What if the market rallies between now and expiry?

If the market rises above 6025, then the fund manager will lose on his short calls. Whoever owns the calls will exercise their right to go long the FTSE at 6025, forcing our fund manager to be short the FTSE at that price. However, 6025 is a significantly better selling price than 5825, the price of the FTSE future when the trade was first established.

We can see that the fund manager's worst case scenario is 5525 and his best 6025. Should the FTSE be between these parameters upon option expiry, then both options will expire worthless since neither will have any value.

A collar places parameters upon potential profit and loss. Both the best and worst case scenarios are known. In fact, the basic dynamic of the collar is that protection is bought at the expense of profit above a certain level. In the above example, protective downside puts are bought at the expense of "blue sky" profit. The alternative would have been to pay for the protective puts with cold, hard cash but the fundamental premise of trading the collar is that simply buying options is considered too expensive.

The above example focused upon a long collar, a collar used to protect a long underlying position. Before considering the short collar, we need to consider a couple of important supplementary issues.

First, it is worth considering the motivation behind trading a collar. Broadly speaking, the motivation for trading a collar rather than outright options is to reduce the cost of protection. But what about the specific circumstances in which a collar is or is not appropriate? Remember that the two key considerations when deciding upon options strategy in general are:

- Our view upon the underlying
- Our view upon volatility (are the options "cheap" or "expensive"?)

How do these two considerations impact our choice of hedging strategy? In answering this question, the first point to make is that the boundaries between hedging and speculation begin to blur as we become more sophisticated in our use of derivatives as hedging tools. Let's reconsider in greater detail the previous example of a fund manager looking to protect a long equity portfolio.

The fund manager's job is to invest in UK equities and, as a result, he is always long of UK equities. Consequently, a rising UK stock market is good for the fund manager, a falling market is bad. His risk is to the downside. Our fund manager could choose to ignore this risk, to do nothing. However, given that stock markets tend to correct downwards on a reasonably regular basis, our fund manager would be well advised to consider protecting his long portfolio. Let's assume he decides to hedge his equity portfolio as a matter of good practice. Furthermore, he decides that LIFFE FTSE 100 Index derivatives are the most appropriate instruments for this hedging. The prevailing prices of these futures and options shown in Table 12.1 are repeated in Table 12.2.

Table 12.2 LIFFE 6 month FTSE 100 option prices (LIFFE 6 month 2008 FTSE 100 future = 5825)

Calls	Strike Price	Puts
616	**5425**	227
547	**5525**	257
483	**5625**	288
421	**5725**	324
362	**5825**	362
309	**5925**	405
257	**6025**	452
213	**6125**	504
174	**6225**	561

Given the above prices, how could our fund manager protect his long equity portfolio? As before, he has the following choices:

1. Sell futures at 5825. Downside protection is achieved but only at the expense of any upside profit potential. Bearing in mind the two key considerations when choosing option strategy, under what circumstances might this hedging choice be appropriate? The answer is when the fund manager is convinced that the market is going down. In such circumstances, why "waste" money on options? Why

not simply accept today's price? If the fund manager is sure that the market will fall, then selling futures to hedge his long equity portfolio makes sense. He is not worried about being locked in at today's price because he perceives today's price to be the best price over the forthcoming period. Of course, our fund manager may be wrong about the market falling. In such circumstances he may still be conceding competitive edge but being wrong is always likely to have a cost.

2. Buy 5525 puts at 257. Downside protection is achieved and upside potential is retained. Bearing in mind the two key considerations when choosing option strategy, under what circumstances might this hedging choice be appropriate? The answer is when the fund manager believes that the market will go up. He needs to be protected to the downside but wants to retain upside potential; buying puts is the solution. As long as they are cheap enough! If the puts are relatively cheap because market volatility is relatively low, then the decision is easy; the puts may be bought. So, in terms of the decision-making process, puts may be bought to protect a long underlying position when we believe the market is going up and that options are relatively cheap. More specifically, with reference to the above example, our fund manager can buy protective 5525 puts at a cost of 257 when he believes that the underlying will rise by at least 257, the cost of the puts, between now and expiry. Remember, our fund manager has bought protective puts rather than sell futures because he believes that the underlying will rise. He is not looking to profit from the puts themselves; they are simply price insurance. And he can only pay the price of that insurance if he believes that he will get this cost back from a commensurate rise in the underlying.

3. Trade a long collar. Specifically, buy the 5525 puts and sell the 6025 calls. Downside protection is achieved at the expense of upside potential. Again, bearing in mind the two key considerations when choosing option strategy, under what circumstances might this hedging choice be appropriate? The answer is when the fund manager believes that the market will go up but considers options to be too expensive to buy outright. Given his bullish market view, the fund manager would like to have simply bought puts, but has balked at their cost. The puts are too expensive to buy outright. Instead, our fund manager finances his purchase of protective puts by selling upside calls.

Let's summarise this decision-making process. Remember that we are considering the hedging choices available to a fund manager looking to protect a long equity portfolio. Our assumption is that the fund must be protected; to do nothing is unacceptable. We know that the key determinants of our choice of hedging trade are our view on the underlying and our view on volatility; are the options cheap or expensive?

If the fund manager is convinced that the market is going to fall, sell futures to hedge. If our fund manager believes that the market will rise and that options are relatively cheap, buy puts to hedge.

Table 12.3   LIFFE 6 month FTSE 100 option prices (LIFFE 6
month 2008 FTSE 100 future = 5825)

Calls	Strike Price	Puts
616	**5425**	227
547	**5525**	257
483	**5625**	288
421	**5725**	324
362	**5825**	362
309	**5925**	405
257	**6025**	452
213	**6125**	504
174	**6225**	561

If the fund manager believes that the market will rise and that options are not cheap
enough to buy outright, trade the collar; finance the protective put purchase by selling
upside calls.

By deciding upon our view on the underlying and volatility, we can identify the
appropriate hedging choice. Let's drill down a little deeper. How do we choose which
expiry month to trade? How do we choose our option strikes? Let's expand upon the
above example to address these questions. As ever, our fund manager has a portfolio
of UK equities. He believes that the UK stock market will rise but needs protection.
He considers FTSE options to be too expensive to buy outright and has therefore
decided to employ a collar. The FTSE derivatives prices shown in Table 12.1 are
repeated in Table 12.3.

Our fund manager has decided to trade a long FTSE collar to protect his portfolio.
But which strikes should he choose and for which expiry?

The starting point of any hedging strategy should always be commercial. At what
level must our fund manager have protection? Over what period is that protection
required?

In terms of timing, he needs to choose options which expire roughly in line with
his underlying exposure, options which cover him for the duration of his underlying
risk. Physical equities do not expire; the underlying exposure is ongoing, so how can
he decide which expiry month to choose? He could trade 1 month collars, "rolling"
them forward as we approach each expiry. This allows him to reassess his needs
and views on a monthly basis. In the real world, however, this may mean significant
costs in terms of brokerage fees, bid/offer spreads and so on. If such costs render
monthly collars impractical, then the fund manager could employ 3 month collars,
"rolling" them forward each quarter. Less flexibility than successive 1 month collars
but less costly as well. Alternatively, our fund manager could employ 1 year collars,
only needing to re-hedge once a year. Even less flexibility than the shorter-dated
alternatives but incurring relatively low trading costs and requiring relatively little
time and attention. So which choice is best? The reality is that there is no simple
answer to the question of tenor. Broadly speaking, the options chosen should cover

the period for which protection is required. Whether that should be one long-dated collar or a series of shorter-dated collars is impossible to answer without addressing detailed views and circumstances. In reality, experience teaches us which strategy to employ. Regardless, it is surely better to be protected to some degree than not to be protected at all. Broadly speaking, for those in close contact with the market, trading regularly and interested in short-term moves, a shorter-dated option solution is likely to suit. My company runs a hedge fund with a core long equity position which we tend to protect with short-dated collars. This strategy suits us because we are in close contact with the market on a minute-to-minute basis. We look at 60 minute charts as well as daily, weekly and monthly studies. Others who have less inclination or insufficient resources to follow the market so closely may find that longer-dated options better suit their specific needs.

In terms of the strikes chosen for the puts and calls comprising a collar, we need to establish the exact level at which we want or need to be protected. Logically, this should be the strike of the protective leg of our collar. This is common sense; a response to our commercial requirements. In the specific case of our fund manager, he needs to establish the level at which he wants or needs to be protected. If this is 5525, then buy the 5525 puts. If it is 5650, then buy the 5650 puts, and so on.

Having addressed our need for protection, we can then bring our market view to bear. The basic dynamic of the collar is the exchange of potential "blue sky" profit for protection.

Having established the level at which we need protection, we now need to consider how much of our upside we want to give away to finance our protection. In the real world, many collars are structured to be zero cost. That is, the cost of the protective option is cancelled out by the income from the sale of the "blue sky" option. In the specific case of our fund manager, given that he needs protection at 5525, he should buy the 5525 puts at a cost of 257. So far so good. He now looks at the prevailing call prices and decides to sell the 6025 call at 257 because it covers the cost of the puts exactly. Is this correct? Subjectively, no. This is the point at which our fund manager should be bringing his market view into play. This is the point at which hedging and speculation start to merge.

Remember that our fund manager is trading a protective collar because he believes that the market has a chance of rising and he wishes to participate in this favourable movement. How far does he think the underlying can rise by the expiry of the options? If he believes that the likely extent of any upside move is 6025, then why not sell the 6025 calls at 257? If he is correct and the market rallies to 6025 on expiry, then this is the optimal choice. His underlying equity portfolio has benefited from the full extent of the upward move and yet the options he has sold have still expired worthless. A "win/win". Had he sold a lower strike call, then he would have received a larger premium but foregone a larger potential profit on the underlying. Had he sold a higher strike call, then he would have received a smaller premium without making a larger profit on the underlying.

It is worth repeating that this is not how collar strikes tend to be chosen in the real world. In reality, market participants tend to choose collar strikes to ensure zero cost;

so much so that many market participants talk about "zero cost collars". Zero cost is seen, incorrectly, as the main reason for trading collars.

Let's summarise the exact decision-making process relating to long collars; collars used to protect a long underlying position.

1. At what point on the downside is protection required? This is the put that should be purchased.
2. Realistically, how much potential is there to the upside by expiry? This is the call that should be sold.

Of course, if the cost of the protective put hugely exceeds the income from the financing call, then the strategy may not be viable and we may need to adopt a different strategy, perhaps sell a lower strike call in the knowledge that we may be missing out on potential upside. Nonetheless, the decision-making process detailed above is both logical and optimal. Option strategy is matched to commercial needs and market view.

We can see that the collar combines both commercial considerations and market view. Many companies seek to use derivatives purely for hedging purposes. They quite deliberately avoid speculative trading. But we can see that whenever derivatives are used to hedge, both commercial requirements *and* market view come into play. And like it or not, market view means speculation. There is no such thing as pure hedging. We live and work in a competitive world. Hedging with futures locks us into a price. Fine in absolute terms but what about our competitors? What about the rest of the market? Locking ourselves in at today's price implies a belief that today's price is better than tomorrow's expected price. We are back to speculation. Our aim may well be purely to hedge, but we cannot avoid the reality that market view will enter the hedging process to some degree. This should not deter us from hedging with derivatives. It is, after all, what derivatives were invented for.

Thus far, we have focused upon protection of a long underlying position such as the long equity portfolio of a fund manager. Derivatives can, of course, be used equally effectively to manage a short underlying position. The best examples of natural shorts are to be found in the commodities world, companies such as airlines (natural shorts of jet fuel), bakers (natural shorts of wheat), chocolate manufacturers (natural shorts of cocoa) and so on. Increasing commodity prices and increasing volatility in commodity markets have driven such companies towards the commodity derivatives markets in unprecedented numbers. The following exercise uses a simplistic example of such a company to illustrate the ways in which derivatives may be used to protect a natural short. Exactly the same principles and processes apply as with natural longs; bear these in mind as you address the exercise.

Exercise 12.1: Hedging with Derivatives

We are in charge of hedging at a large chocolate company. Our exposure is to the price of cocoa because we cannot make chocolate without it. Specifically, we are

Table 12.4   LIFFE cocoa 3 month derivatives prices

3 Month Future = 1500		
3 Month Calls	Strike Prices	3 Month Puts
112	**1400**	12
76	**1450**	26
47	**1500**	47
28	**1550**	78
15	**1600**	115

exposed to the price of cocoa rising which will increase our costs. The price of cocoa falling is good for our company since it will reduce our costs. We have decided that we must be hedged at all times. To do nothing, to ignore price risk is not acceptable. We have decided to use LIFFE cocoa derivatives to hedge our company's price risk. Since we negotiate physical cocoa prices with our suppliers on a quarterly basis, we decide to use 3 month LIFFE cocoa derivatives to hedge our exposure. Prevailing LIFFE cocoa 3 month derivatives prices are shown in Table 12.4.

LIFFE cocoa is quoted in pounds sterling per tonne. Hence the 3 month futures price quoted above equates to £1500 per tonne.

One LIFFE cocoa future corresponds to 100 tonnes of physical cocoa. One LIFFE cocoa option corresponds to one LIFFE cocoa future. Our company needs to buy 500 tonnes of cocoa every quarter. Therefore, given that our company wants to be fully hedged, we need to trade 5 contracts (equivalent to 500 tonnes of physical cocoa) each quarter. From a commercial perspective, our company cannot afford to pay more than £1600 per tonne for cocoa.

What is the correct derivatives trade if:

1. We are sure that the cocoa price is about to rise
2. We believe that the price of cocoa will fall to £1000 per tonne in the next 3 months and we believe that cocoa options are currently cheap (because "vol" is low)
3. We believe that the price of cocoa will fall to £1400 per tonne in the next 3 months and we believe that cocoa options are currently expensive (because "vol" is high)
4. We believe that the price of cocoa will fall to £1450 per tonne in the next 3 months and we believe that cocoa options are currently expensive (because "vol" is high)

Exercise 12.1: Answers

1. Buy cocoa futures at £1500. Why "waste" money on options if we are convinced that today's price is as low as it will be for the coming 3 months?
2. Buy calls. This is logical since we perceive the calls to be cheap (because market "vol" is low) and believe that the market will fall. We could buy the 1500, 1550 or 1600 calls to hedge. Any of these would provide the necessary upside protection.

However, given that we only need protection at a price of £1600 per tonne and that we believe that the market will fall, buying the 1600 calls at 15 would seem the best choice. In the event that our market view is wrong and the market rallies, we are protected at 1600 (the strike of the call) plus 15 (the cost of the call) which equals 1615. The cost of the option needs to be factored into the hedging equation. Of course, what we want to happen is for the market to fall, as we expect, allowing us to buy the company's physical cocoa at a lower price. The calls are simply an insurance policy; we want and expect them to expire worthless.

3. Trade a short collar. Specifically, buy the 1600 calls (to protect our upside exposure) and sell the 1400 puts (to finance the call purchase). We cannot logically buy calls outright since we perceive them to be expensive (because market "vol" is high). However, we need to buy the 1600 call since this is the price level at which we require protection. Which put should be sold to finance this call purchase? Given our market view that the market will not fall below 1400, it seems logical to sell the 1400 put. The net cost of the collar is just 3 ticks (15 ticks paid for the long 1600 call less 12 ticks received for the short 1400 put) against 15 ticks for the outright calls. Cost is reduced by a hefty 80%. Our best case scenario between now and expiry is cocoa falling to 1400. Below this level, the 1400 puts that we have sold will be exercised and we will be obliged to buy cocoa futures at a price of 1400. This, however, is a significantly better buying price than the current futures price of 1500. Our worst case scenario between now and expiry is cocoa rising to 1600. Above this level, we will exercise our 1600 calls (claim on our "insurance") and buy cocoa futures at a price of 1600. No matter how high the price of cocoa rises over the next 3 months, we have the right to buy cocoa futures at 1600.

4. Again, trade a short collar but this time with different strikes. Specifically, buy the 1600. calls and sell the 1450 puts. We cannot logically buy calls outright since we perceive them to be expensive. However, we need to buy the 1600 call since this is the price level at which we require protection. Which put should be sold to finance this call purchase? Given our view that the market will not fall below 1450, it seems logical to sell the 1450 put. The net price of the collar is a credit to us of 11 ticks (15 ticks paid for the long 1600 call less 26 ticks received for the short 1450 put). We have not only reduced the cost of protection but brought income in! In doing so, we have limited our best buying price between now and expiry to 1450. Below this level, the 1450 puts that we have sold will be exercised and we will be obliged to buy cocoa futures at 1450. This is still a better buying price than the current price of 1500. Our worst case scenario between now and expiry is the price of cocoa rising to 1600. Above this level, we will exercise your 1600 calls (claim on our "insurance") and buy cocoa futures at 1600. As before, no matter how high the price of cocoa rises in the next 3 months, we have the right to buy futures at 1600.

We can see that the basic dynamic of the collar is the exchange of protection for profit potential. And that exchange needs to be attractive. Regardless, as previously stated, all option strategies including the collar have evolved to either limit the risk of selling options or the cost of owning options. The collar has evolved quite specifically to address the problem of protective options costing money. When options are cheap, when hedgers are happy to spend money on what they perceive to be cheap protection, the solution is simple; buy options outright. But when cost is an issue, when buying options outright is considered too expensive, the collar comes into its own.

As previously stated, the collar is essentially defensive or protective in nature. The collar is all about protecting an existing underlying position. Let's now turn our attention to the long list of option strategies that have evolved for the purpose of speculation. Let's remind ourselves of that list:

Call spreads and put spreads
Straddles and strangles
Butterflies and condors
Calendars and diagonals

As previously stated, there are far more option strategies than those listed above. These, however, are the most popular and widely used of the speculative option strategies.

Examples of these strategies will come from the set of LIFFE BP option prices shown in Table 12.5, the settlement (closing) prices for 21 July 2008. All prices have been rounded to the nearest whole tick (i.e. 1p).

Remember, option strategies have evolved for two reasons. The first is to reduce the *cost* of owning options. The second is to reduce the *risk* of selling options. Some option strategies combine these two features; limited cost often equates to limited potential and vice versa.

Table 12.5 LIFFE September BP option prices (BP share price (LSE) = 522 (i.e. £5.22), LIFFE BP September future = 519 (i.e. £5.19))

Calls	Strike Prices	Puts
86	440	6
69	460	10
53	480	14
39	500	20
28	520	29
19	540	40
12	560	54
7	580	70
4	600	87
3	620	106
1	640	125

Remember also the two-part decision-making process when choosing option strategies. Our choice of option strategy will be determined by two things. The first is our view on the underlying (bullish, bearish, neutral, etc.). The second is our view on volatility; are options relatively cheap or expensive?

With these two key considerations in mind, let's turn our attention to the first of the speculative option strategies, call spreads. We will first consider long call spreads then long put spreads, before considering both call and put spreads from a short perspective.

13
Long Call Spreads
(Bull Call Spreads)

GLOSSARY

Vertical spread: an option strategy comprising options with the same expiry dates
  but different strike prices
Leg: a constituent part of an option spread
Bull spread: an option spread designed to exploit a bullish (i.e. upward) view on the
  underlying

What is a call spread? A call spread consists of two "legs", a long call "leg" and
a short call "leg". A long call spread, sometimes called a *bull* call spread (because it
is bullish in nature) consists of a long call with a lower strike and a short call with a
higher strike.

For example, from the matrix of Sep BP option prices (Table 12.5), buying the
540/560 call spread consists of two legs, buying the 540 call at 19 and simultaneously
selling the 560 call at 12. The cost of the call spread is 7 ticks (equivalent to £70) per
call spread, the difference between the 19 ticks paid for the 540 call and the 12 ticks
received from the sale of the 560 call. These 7 ticks represent the maximum loss on
buying the call spread. If BP is at or below 540 (i.e. £5.40) on Sep expiry, then both
the 540 and 560 calls will expire worthless. The maximum possible value of the call
spread is 20, the difference between the two strike prices of 540 and 560. If BP is at
or above 560 (i.e. £5.60) on Sep expiry, then the 540 call will be worth exactly 20
more than the 560 call.

For example, if BP is priced at exactly 560 (i.e. £5.60) on Sep expiry, then the
540 call will be worth exactly 20 and the 560 call will be worthless. The difference
between the value of the two calls is 20. If BP is priced at exactly 600 (i.e. £6.00) on
Sep expiry, then the 540 call will be worth exactly 60 and the 560 call will be worth
40. Again, the difference between the values of the two calls is 20.

Given that the maximum possible value of the call spread is 20 and that the price of the call spread is 7, the maximum possible profit is 13, the difference between the maximum value and the price.

So, the risk/reward for buying the 540/560 call spread at 7 is –7/+13. If we buy this spread, we can make 13 and lose 7, odds of roughly 2 to 1. Why would we do this? In practice, the starting point for long vertical spreads (same month, different strikes) such as the 540/560 call spread is a directional view – specifically, a bullish view, a belief that the underlying is going up. In the case of the 540/560 call spread, BP needs to be above 540 (i.e. £5.40) on expiry for the spread to have any value. The second part of the equation is volatility, the prices of the options.

If we believe that BP is going up and that BP options are relatively cheap (because volatility is relatively low), what should we do? Buy BP calls! To take an extreme example, if in the matrix of prices (Table 12.5), at-the-money BP calls are trading at just 1 tick (equivalent to £10) per contract and we believe that BP is going to rally, we can simply buy these very cheap at-the-money calls for 1 tick. We can only ever lose 1 tick (i.e. £10) per contract and our upside profit potential is unlimited. So why buy a call spread, why limit our upside? Because, in this case, we do *not* perceive BP calls to be cheap. We either perceive BP calls to be expensive or we are not sure. Broadly speaking, trading call spreads rather than outright calls reduces the significance of volatility, a point that will become clearer when we consider the vega of call spreads.

To return to the two-part decision-making process, we buy a call spread when we believe that the underlying will rise and that options are not cheap enough to purchase outright. In the case of the Sep 540/560 call spread, we could simply buy the 540 calls for 19. Our maximum loss would be 19 and our upside unlimited. But we may perceive 19 to be too much to pay for these calls. We may wish to reduce the cost of owning these options. So we sell a higher call, in this case the 560 call, against the 540 call in order to significantly reduce the cost involved. Specifically, by selling the 560 call at 12, we are reducing the cost of owning the 540 calls by that amount. Buying the 540 calls outright would cost 19. Buying the 540/560 call spread costs 7, a cost reduction of about two thirds. But in reducing the cost of the trade, we have also reduced our upside potential. Buying the 540 calls outright gives unlimited upside potential. Buying the 540/560 call spread reduces upside potential profit to 13. Clearly, if we believed that the BP share price was about to double, then we would not want to limit our upside in this way. We would be more than happy to pay 19 for the outright calls *because we would perceive that price to be cheap* in relation to our views on the underlying (very bullish) and volatility (about to explode!).

To use the vernacular, "you pays your money and you takes your choice". We can accept greater cost and have greater upside or limit our cost and limit our upside. Consider the expiry payoff chart (Figure 13.1) for being long the Sep 540/560 call spread at 7.

Note that profit and loss is shown on the vertical axis with the BP share price shown on the horizontal. The line depicts the pay-off of the strategy *on expiry*.

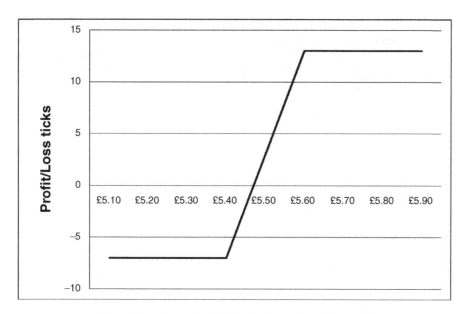

Figure 13.1   Long Sep 540/560 call spread; expiry payoff

We can see that loss is limited to 7 if BP is at or below 540 on expiry. Profit is limited to 13 if BP is at or above 560 on expiry. The breakeven price of BP on expiry is 547. That is, if BP is at exactly 547 on expiry, then the call spread will be worth 7 (the 540 call worth 7 and the 560 call worthless), the price that we originally paid for it.

The risk/reward for the trade is –7 versus +13, odds in our favour of roughly 2 to 1. Intuitively, do these odds seem like good or bad value for BP being above 560 by Sep expiry? This is a useful "quick and dirty" way of assessing the trade. Note the use of the word "roughly" and the phrase "quick and dirty". Considering the odds attached to the spread is perfectly valid but it is also rough and ready.

Thus far we have considered the payoff of the call spread upon expiry. But option spreads don't have to be held until expiry. Just like shares, futures or outright options, option spreads are transferable; they may be traded in and out of at will. What about the value of the call spread between the trade date and expiry?

Remember that the three main factors affecting the value of options are the underlying, time and volatility. How will these factors impact the value of a call spread?

We may assess the impact of the underlying, the BP share price in this case, on both an intuitive and mathematical level. Broadly speaking, as the underlying rises, the value of the call spread also rises. Intuitively, this is hardly surprising given the bullish nature of the long call spread. We would expect it to gain value as the market rises and lose as the market falls. This is fine in broad terms but if we want to be more precise, if we wish to quantify the likely effect of a rise in the BP share price upon our call spread, then we need to consider the delta of the call spread.

The delta of the Sep 540 call is +40% and the delta of the Sep 560 call is +29%. Given that buying the Sep 540/560 call spread involves buying the 540 call and selling the 560 call, the net delta of the spread is +11% (long a 40% delta call and short a 29% delta call).

If we buy the Sep 540/560 call spread for 7 and the market instantly rises from its current level of 522 to 532, then the value of the spread should rise, probably by around 1 tick, equivalent to about 11% (the net delta of the spread) of the 10p rise in the underlying BP share price.

If the underlying BP share price falls by 20p, then we would expect the value of the call spread to fall by about 2p, equivalent to about 11% (the net delta of the spread) of the 20p fall in the underlying.

Remember that the starting point for buying the call spread is a bullish view on the underlying. If we are right in our view and the BP share price rises, we can sell our spread and bank the profit or hold the position in the hope of further rises. If we are wrong about BP and the market falls, we can either trade out of the call spread or hold in the hope of a change in fortune. Regardless, the parameters of profit and loss at the extremes are known. We can only ever lose 7 and we can only ever make 13.

As previously stated, the net delta of the 540/560 call spread is +11%. For every 10p that the BP share price rises or falls, the value of the call spread should only change by about 1 tick. This is a fairly small change and brings us to an important point. Broadly speaking, call spreads are fairly conservative strategies. Risk and reward are both known and, depending upon the width of the spread (i.e. the difference between the two call strikes), will tend to change in value quite slowly. If we want to have a similar size of potential profit as with outright calls, then we need to trade call spreads in bigger sizes than we would the outright calls. In the specific example of the Sep 540/560 call spread, the cost of buying the spread for 7 is about one third of the cost of buying the 540 calls outright for 19. If we want our incremental profits to be of a similar magnitude to those generated by the outright calls, then we need to buy two to three times as many of them. This idea will be expanded upon when we consider the selection of specific strikes for a call spread.

So much for the effect of the underlying upon a call spread. What about the impact of time and volatility? As with the underlying, the effect of these factors may be considered upon an intuitive or mathematical level.

Remember that the starting point for buying a call spread is a bullish view upon the underlying. Volatility is a secondary consideration and it is therefore no surprise that volatility is not generally of great significance for call spreads unless the strikes are far apart. In the case of the Sep 540/560 call spread, volatility is of little significance since the strikes are adjacent. However, if we do want to quantify the effect of volatility upon the spread, we can look at the net vega of the spread (the vega of the long call leg less the vega of the short call leg). What about the effect of time upon our call spread?

In practice, since call spreads are usually bought to exploit a bullish underlying view, they are normally out-of-the-money. That is to say, both long and short legs are usually out-of-the-money. Of course, this is not a rule, call spreads don't have to be out-of-the-money, just as outright calls don't have to be out-of-the-money, they just usually are. After all, we are far more likely to want to speculate on something that has not yet happened (out-of-the-money) than something that has already happened (in-the-money). How will the passage of time impact out-of-the-money call spreads? Consider our example, the Sep 540/560 call spread. Given that the underlying BP share price is 522, this is an example of an out-of-the-money call spread. Both legs, the long 540 call and the short 560 call are currently out-of-the-money. Time will impact both of the legs of the spread in the same way but to different degrees.

Specifically, time will erode our long 540 call more than it erodes our short 560 call. This is logical, since the 540 call currently has more time value (19 ticks) than the 560 call (12 ticks). The net effect of time upon our call spread is to reduce its value. If we want to quantify this effect, we need to consider the net theta of the call spread. If, for example, the theta of the 540 call is –0.5 and the theta of the 560 call is –0.3, then the net theta of the 540/560 call spread is –0.2, the difference between the two individual thetas. In lay terms this means that, other things being equal, our 540/560 call spread should lose about 0.2 of a tick (equivalent to £2 per spread) per day. Over a 5 day period, other things being equal, the spread should lose about 1 tick (equivalent to £10 per spread).

In general, then, out-of-the-money call spreads will erode due to the passing of time. But what if our directional view is right? What if BP rises as expected and our 540/560 call spread becomes in-the-money? Remember that time decay or erosion only affects the time value of options. Time decay has no impact upon intrinsic value. In relation to our long Sep 540/560 call spread, whichever option has the greatest amount of time value will erode the fastest. Broadly speaking, this means that whichever option is closest to the prevailing underlying will erode the fastest. So, as the price of BP rises towards our long call strike of 540, time will be working against us. As the price of BP moves towards 550, the mid-point of the two call strikes, the net theta of the spread will move closer and closer to zero, and as the price of BP rises further towards and then through 560, time decay will start to work in our favour. Once the price of BP has breached our short call leg of 560, time is working in our favour. Other things being equal, as time passes, the value of our now in-the-money call spread will move closer towards its maximum possible value of 20. And if our Sep 540/560 call spread is still in-the-money upon Sep expiry (because BP is at or above 560), then the spread will be worth 20.

Let's summarise what we have learnt of call spreads thus far. A long call spread comprises a long call and a short call, the short call having a strike price above that of the long call. The value of the call spread is the difference between the two option premiums. If we buy the call spread for this price, then this is our maximum loss. If, on expiry, the underlying is at or below our long call strike, we will lose this amount.

If we buy the spread, then our maximum possible profit is the maximum value of the spread (the difference between the two strikes) less the price paid. The extremes of both risk and reward are known.

We may consider buying call spreads if we are bullish on the underlying but are not prepared to buy outright calls because we do not perceive them to be cheap enough. Broadly speaking, buying call spreads is a directional trade rather than a volatility driven trade.

Other things being equal:

- A rise in the underlying will increase the value of our long call spread and vice versa (long delta).
- Volatility will not be significant unless the strike prices are far apart (vega neutral).
- The passage of time will erode the value of *out*-of-the-money call spreads (negative theta).
- The passage of time will increase the value of *in*-the-money call spreads (positive theta).

How should we choose the tenor and exact strikes of a long call spread? Remember, a long call spread is a directional trade, specifically a bullish trade, so it makes sense that the exact nature of our view on the underlying is key.

There are two basic ways of viewing a long call spread. It may be viewed as an expiry play, a trade designed to optimize the return on a given view within a given time frame. Alternatively, a long call spread may be viewed as a simple directional play, a proxy for owning the underlying where cost and risk are limited at the expense of also limiting profit potential. Regardless of how we view the long call spread, common sense dictates that we should choose options with an expiry date that lines up with our view on the timing of the anticipated upward move in the underlying. For example, if we are anticipating that BP will rally over the next three months, then it makes sense to use 3 month options. If our view is longer term, then it seems sensible to use longer-dated options, and so on. What about choosing the exact strikes that make up our long call spread? How should they be chosen?

When buying vertical spreads such as call spreads and put spreads, the choice of short strike is simple; sell your target! That is, the short strike of the call spread should be the level to which we think the underlying will rise in the appropriate period. For example, if our view is that BP will rise to around 560 by Sep expiry, then we should sell the Sep 560 call, sell our target. We should then buy a more expensive, lower strike call such as the Sep 540 call to make up our call spread. How we choose that lower strike call should depend upon how much we wish to spend on the spread and how likely we believe that the underlying rise will happen. In terms of optimising returns on our view, it is usually better to buy a large number of narrow call spreads rather than a smaller number of wider call spreads. This will, however, depend upon the specific option prices in question. Consider the example shown in Table 13.1 using the Sep BP option prices from Table 12.5.

Table 13.1 LIFFE September BP option prices (BP share price (LSE) = 522 (i.e. £5.22), LIFFE BP September future = 519 (i.e. £5.19))

Calls	Strike Prices	Puts
86	**440**	6
69	**460**	10
53	**480**	14
39	**500**	20
28	**520**	29
19	**540**	40
12	**560**	54
7	**580**	70
4	**600**	87
3	**620**	106
1	**640**	125

We wish to trade the appropriate option strategy given that we believe that BP will rally to about 560 by Sep expiry and that the options are not cheap enough to buy outright.

Given that our view relates to the next 2 months or so, it makes sense to use 2 month (in this case September) options. Further, given that our upside target for this period is around 560 (i.e. £5.60), it makes sense to choose the Sep 560 call as the short leg of our call spread. But which calls should be bought for the long leg? We could buy either the Sep 520 call or the Sep 540 call against the sale of the Sep 560 call. Which is the best choice? Obviously the 520 call will cost more (28 ticks) than the 540 call (19 ticks) because it conveys the right to buy BP at a lower price (520) than the 540 call (540). As a result, the Sep 520/560 call spread costs 16 (i.e. 28 minus 12) whereas the Sep 540/560 call spread costs 7 (i.e. 19 minus 12). How do the two alternatives compare?

The Sep 520/560 call spread costs 16 and has a maximum value of 40 (the difference between the two strikes). The risk/reward on buying this spread is therefore −16 against +24, "odds" of 3 to 2 on our investment (usually expressed as 6 to 4 in the racing world). The Sep 540/560 call spread costs 7 and has a maximum value of 20 (the difference between the two strikes). The risk/reward on buying this spread is therefore −7 against +13, "odds" of about 2 to 1 on our investment.

Purely in odds terms, the 540/560 call spread offers a superior return to the 520/560 call spread but the 520/560 call spread starts to acquire intrinsic value at a lower underlying level (520) than the 540/560 call spread (540). The wider call spread starts "working" at a lower level, at an earlier stage.

How can we choose between the two alternatives? Well, we may approach the decision intuitively and weigh up the value of the odds on offer. Or we may be a little bit more scientific. We can calculate the exact payoff for a given investment if we are right in our views on the timing and extent of the anticipated upward move.

If we have 100 ticks (equivalent to £1000) to invest, we can buy 6 lots of the wider Sep 520/560 call spread at a price of 16 or we can buy 14 lots of the narrower Sep 540/560 call spread at a price of 7. Remember, we are doing this because we believe that BP will rally to about 560 by Sep expiry. How do the payoffs of the two alternatives compare if we are right in our view and BP is at exactly 560 on Sep expiry?

The wider 520/560 call spread will yield a profit of 24 ticks (£240) per call spread. We can afford 6 of the spreads with our trading capital of 100 ticks (£1000) so our profit will be 6 times 24 ticks which equals 144 ticks (£1440).

The narrower 540/560 call spread will yield a profit of 13 ticks (£130) per call spread. We can afford 14 of the spreads with our 100 ticks (£1000) so our profit will be 14 times 13 ticks which equals 182 ticks (£1820).

Given that we are right (a rather big "if" in the market!), we are better off trading the *540/*560 call spread than the *520/*560 call spread. If we are looking to optimise returns on our specific view, we will generally be better off trading a large number of narrow spreads than a smaller number of wider spreads. This may seem counterintuitive to some but is generally correct. It does, however, depend upon the exact option prices under consideration.

Long call spreads are widely used in option markets. They are one of the basic building blocks of option strategy. Call spreads are easy to understand and easy to manage since the extremes of both risk and reward are known. They also largely take the thorny question of volatility out of the equation since they involve buying one option and selling another. Long call spreads may be used highly effectively as a directional (specifically bullish) "punt". It should not surprise us to discover that the subject of the next section, long put spreads, may be just as effectively used to exploit a bearish (i.e. downward) directional view.

14
Long Put Spreads
(Bear Put Spreads)

What is a put spread? A put spread consists of two legs, a long put and a short put. A long put spread, sometimes called a bear put spread (because it is bearish in nature) consists of a long put with a higher strike and a short put with a lower strike.

For example, from the matrix of Sep BP option prices (Table 14.1, repeated from Table 12.5), buying the 500/460 put spread consists of two legs, buying the 500 put at 20 and simultaneously selling the 460 put at 10. The cost of the put spread is 10 ticks (equivalent to £100 per spread), the difference between the 20 ticks paid for the 500 put and the 10 ticks received from the sale of the 460 put. These 10 ticks represent the maximum loss on buying the put spread. If BP is at or above 500 (i.e. £5.00)

Table 14.1 LIFFE September BP option prices (BP share price (LSE) = 522 (i.e. £5.22), LIFFE BP September future = 519 (i.e. £5.19))

Calls	Strike Prices	Puts
86	440	6
69	460	10
53	480	14
39	500	20
28	520	29
19	540	40
12	560	54
7	580	70
4	600	87
3	620	106
1	640	125

on Sep expiry, then both the 500 and 460 puts will expire worthless. The maximum possible value of the put spread is 40, the difference between the two strike prices of 500 and 460. If BP is at or below 460 (i.e. £4.60) on Sep expiry, then the 500 put will be worth exactly 40 more than the 460 put.

For example, if BP is priced at exactly 460 (i.e. £4.60) on Sep expiry, then the 500 put will be worth exactly 40 and the 460 put will be worthless. The difference between the value of the two puts is 40. If BP is priced at exactly 400 (i.e. £4.00) on Sep expiry, then the 500 put will be worth exactly 100 and the 460 put will be worth 60. Again, the difference between the values of the two puts is exactly 40.

Given that the maximum possible value of the put spread is 40 and that the price of the put spread is 10, the maximum possible profit is 30, the difference between the maximum value and the price.

So, the risk/reward for buying the 500/460 put spread at 10 is −10/+30. If we buy this spread, we can make 30 and lose 10, "odds" of 3 to 1. Why would we do this?

As with long call spreads, the starting point for vertical spreads (same month, different strikes) such as the 500/460 put spread is a directional view. Specifically, a bearish view, a belief that the underlying is going down. In the case of the 500/460 put spread, BP needs to be below 500 (i.e. £5.00) on expiry for the spread to have any value. The second part of the equation is volatility and its impact upon the prices of the options.

If we believe that BP is going down and that BP options are relatively cheap (because market volatility is relatively low), what should we do? Buy BP puts! To take an extreme example, if in the Table 14.1 at-the-money BP puts are trading at just 1 tick (equivalent to £10) per contract and we believe that BP is going to fall, we can simply buy these very cheap at-the-money puts for 1. We can only ever lose 1 tick (i.e. £10) per contract and our profit to the downside is limited only by zero. So why buy a put spread? Why limit our profit potential? Because, in this case, we do *not* perceive BP puts to be cheap. We either perceive BP puts to be expensive or we are not sure. Broadly speaking, trading put spreads rather than outright puts allows us to take volatility out of the equation.

To return to the two-part decision-making process, we buy a put spread when we believe that the underlying will fall and that options are not cheap enough to purchase outright. In the case of the Sep 500/460 put spread, we could simply buy the 500 puts for 20. Our maximum loss would be 20 and our upside 480 (the maximum value of the 500 put less the price paid for it). But we may perceive 20 to be too much to pay for these puts outright. We may wish to *reduce the cost* of owning these options. So we sell a lower put, in this case the 460 put, against the 500 put in order to significantly reduce the cost involved. Specifically, by selling the 460 put at 10, we are reducing the cost of owning the 500 puts by that amount. Buying the 500 puts outright would cost 20. Buying the 500/460 put spread costs 10, a cost reduction of 50%. But in reducing the cost of the trade, we have also reduced our upside potential. Buying the 500 puts outright gives downside profit potential of 480 (in the event that BP falls to zero). Buying the 500/460 put spread reduces downside profit potential to

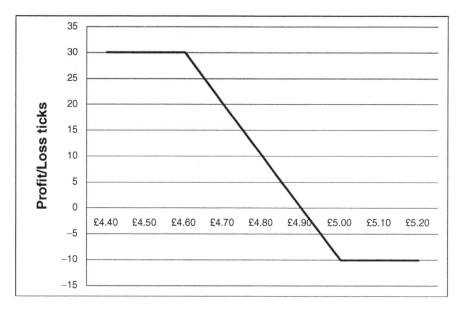

Figure 14.1 Long Sep 500/460 put spread; expiry payoff

30. Clearly, if we believe that the BP share price is about to plunge, we don't want to limit our downside profit potential in this way. We would be more than happy to pay 20 for the outright puts *because we would perceive that price to be cheap* in relation to our views on the underlying (very bearish) and volatility (about to explode!).

As with call spreads and outright calls, "you pays your money and you takes your choice". Greater cost and greater profit potential or less cost and less profit potential. Consider the expiry payoff chart in Figure 14.1 for being long the Sep 500/460 put spread at 10.

Note that profit and loss is shown on the vertical axis with the BP share price shown on the horizontal. As before, the line depicts the payoff of the strategy on expiry.

We can see that loss is limited to 10 if BP is at or above 500 (i.e. £5.00) on expiry. Profit is limited to 30 if BP is at or below 460 (i.e. £4.60) on expiry. The breakeven price of BP on expiry is 490 (i.e. £4.90). If BP is at 490 on expiry, then the put spread will be worth 10 (500 put worth 10 and the 460 put worthless) which is what we originally paid for it.

The risk/reward for the trade is −10 versus +30, "odds" of roughly 3 to 1. Intuitively, do these odds seem like good or bad value for BP being below 460 by Sep expiry? This is a useful "quick and dirty" way of assessing the trade. Note the use of the word "roughly" and the phrase "quick and dirty". Considering the odds attached to the spread is perfectly valid but it is also rough and ready.

Thus far we have considered the payoff of the put spread upon expiry. But we don't have to hold put spreads until expiry. Just like shares, futures or outright options, option spreads are transferable; they may be traded in and out of at will. What about the value of the put spread between the trade date and expiry?

Remember that the three main factors affecting the prices of options are the underlying, time and volatility. How will these factors impact the value of a put spread?

As with call spreads, we may assess the impact of the underlying, the BP share price in this case, on both an intuitive and mathematical level. Broadly speaking, as the underlying falls, the value of put spreads rises. Intuitively, this is hardly surprising given the bearish nature of long put spreads. We would expect a put spread to gain value as the market falls and lose as the market rises. This is fine in broad terms but if we want to be more precise, if we wish to quantify the likely effect of a change in the BP share price upon our put spread, then we need to consider the delta of the spread.

The delta of the Sep 500 put is −36% and the delta of the Sep 460 put is −21%. Given that buying the Sep 500/460 put spread involves buying the 500 put and selling the 460 put, the net delta of the spread is −15% (long a −36% delta put and short a −21% delta put).

If we buy the Sep 500/460 put spread for 10 and the market instantly falls from its current level of 522 to 502, then the value of the spread should rise, probably by around 3 ticks, equivalent to about 15% (the net delta of the spread) of the 20p fall in the underlying BP share price.

If the underlying BP share price rises by 10p, then we would expect the value of the put spread to fall by about 1.5p, equivalent to about 15% (the net delta of the spread) of the 10p rise in the underlying.

Remember that the starting point for buying the put spread was a bearish view on the underlying. If we are right in our view and the BP share price falls, we can sell our spread and bank the profit or hold the position in the hope of further falls. If we are wrong about BP and the market rises, then we can either trade out of the put spread at a loss or hold in the hope of a change in fortune. Regardless, as with call spreads, the parameters of profit and loss at the extremes are known. We can only ever lose 10 and we can only ever make 30.

As previously stated, the net delta of the 500/460 put spread is −15%. For every 10p that the BP share price rises or falls, the value of the put spread should only change by about 1.5 ticks. This is a fairly small change and brings us again to the important point that put spreads are relatively conservative strategies (unless the strikes are far apart). Risk and reward are both known and, depending upon the width of the spread (i.e. the difference between the two put strikes), will tend to change in value quite slowly. If we want to have a similar size of potential profit as with outright puts, then we need to trade put spreads in bigger sizes than we would trade the outright puts. In the specific example of the Sep 500/460 put spread, the cost of buying the spread (10) is half of the cost of buying the outright 500 puts (20). If we want our incremental profits to be of a similar magnitude to the outright puts, then we need to buy roughly twice as many of them. This idea will be expanded upon when we consider the selection of specific strikes for a put spread.

So much for the effect of the underlying upon a put spread. What about the impact of time and volatility? As with the underlying, the effect of these factors may be considered upon an intuitive or mathematical level.

Remember that the starting point for buying a put spread was a bearish view upon the underlying. Volatility was a secondary consideration and it is therefore no surprise that volatility is not generally of great significance for put spreads unless the strikes are far apart. In the case of the Sep 500/460 put spread, volatility is of little significance since the strikes are relatively close to one another. However, if we do want to quantify the effect of volatility upon the spread, we can look at the net vega of the spread (the vega of the long put leg less the vega of the short put leg). What about the effect of time upon our put spread?

In practice, since put spreads are usually bought to exploit a bearish underlying view, they are usually out-of-the-money. That is to say, both the long and the short leg are usually out-of-the-money. Of course, this is not a rule; put spreads don't *have* to be out-of-the-money, just as outright puts don't *have* to be out-of-the-money, they just usually are. This is logical since we are far more likely to want to speculate on something that has not yet happened (out-of-the-money) than something that has already happened (in-the-money). How will the passage of time impact out-of-the-money put spreads? Consider our example, the Sep 500/460 put spread. Given that the underlying BP share price is 522, this is an example of an out-of-the-money put spread. Both legs, the long 500 put and the short 460 put are currently out-of-the-money. Time will impact both of the legs of the spread in the same way but to different degrees.

Specifically, time will erode our long 500 put more than it erodes our short 460 put. This is logical, since the 500 put currently has more time value (20 ticks) than the 460 put (10 ticks). The net effect of time upon our put spread is to reduce its value. If we want to quantify this effect, we need to consider the net theta of the put spread. If, for example, the theta of the 500 put is -0.40 and the theta of the 460 put is -0.15, then the net theta of the 500/460 put spread is -0.25, the difference between the two individual thetas. In lay terms this means that, other things being equal, our 500/460 put spread should lose about a quarter of a tick (equivalent to £2.50 per spread) per day. Over a 4 day period, other things being equal, the spread should lose about 1 tick (equivalent to £10 per spread).

In general, then, out-of-the-money put spreads will erode due to the passing of time. But what if our directional view is right? What if BP falls as expected and our 500/460 put spread becomes in-the-money? Remember that time decay or erosion only affects the time value of options. Time decay has no impact upon intrinsic value. In relation to our long Sep 500/460 put spread, whichever option has the greatest amount of time value will erode the fastest. Broadly speaking, this means that whichever option is closest to the prevailing underlying will erode the fastest. So, as the price of BP falls towards our long put strike of 500, time will be working against us. As the price of

BP moves towards 480, the mid-point between the two put strikes, the net theta of the spread will move closer and closer to zero, and as the price of BP falls further towards and then through 460, time decay will start to work in our favour. Once the price of BP has breached our short put leg of 460, time is working in our favour. Other things being equal, as time passes, the value of our now in-the-money put spread will move closer towards its maximum possible value of 40. And if our Sep 500/460 put spread is still in-the-money upon Sep expiry (because BP is at or below 460), then the spread will be worth 40.

Let's summarise the Greeks in relation to long put spreads. Other things being equal:

- A fall in the underlying will increase the value of our long put spread and vice versa (short delta).
- Volatility will not be significant unless the strike prices are far apart (vega neutral).
- The passage of time will erode the value of out-of-the-money put spreads (negative theta).
- The passage of time will increase the value of in-the-money put spreads (positive theta).

How should we choose the tenor and constituent strikes of a long put spread? Remember, a long put spread is a directional trade, specifically a bearish trade, so it makes sense that the exact nature of our view on the underlying is key.

There are two basic ways of viewing a long put spread. It may be viewed as an expiry play, a trade designed to optimise the return on a given view within a given timeframe. Alternatively, a long put spread may be viewed as a simple directional play, a proxy for shorting the underlying where cost and risk are limited at the expense of limiting profit potential. Regardless of how we view the long put spread, common sense dictates that we should choose options with an expiry date that lines up with our view on the timing of the anticipated downward move in the underlying. For example, if we are anticipating that BP will fall in price over the next 3 months, then it makes sense to use 3 month options. If our view is that BP will fall between now and year-end, then it seems sensible to use December options. What about choosing the exact strikes that make up our long put spread? How should they be chosen?

Remember how we choose our short strike for vertical spreads such as call and put spreads? Sell our target! That is, the short strike of the put spread should be the level to which we think the underlying will fall in the appropriate period. For example, if our view is that BP will fall to around 460 (i.e. £4.60) by Sep expiry, then we should sell the Sep 460 put, sell our target. We should then buy a more expensive, higher strike put such as the Sep 500 put to make up our put spread. How we choose that higher strike put should depend upon how much we wish to spend on the spread and how likely we believe that the fall in the underlying will happen. In terms of optimising returns on our view, it is usually better to buy a large number of narrow put spreads than a smaller number of wider put spreads. This will, however, depend

Table 14.2 LIFFE September BP option prices (BP share price (LSE) = 522 (i.e. £5.22), LIFFE BP September future = 519 (i.e. £5.19))

Calls	Strike Prices	Puts
86	**440**	6
69	**460**	10
53	**480**	14
39	**500**	20
28	**520**	29
19	**540**	40
12	**560**	54
7	**580**	70
4	**600**	87
3	**620**	106
1	**640**	125

upon the specific option prices in question. Consider the example in Table 14.2 of using the Sep BP option prices, repeated from Table 12.5.

We wish to trade the appropriate option strategy given that we believe that BP will fall to about 460 (i.e. £4.60) by Sep expiry and that the options aren't cheap enough to buy outright.

Given that our view relates to the next 2 months or so, it makes sense to use 2 month (in this case September) options. Given that our downside target for this period is around 460 (i.e. £4.60), it further makes sense to choose the Sep 460 put as the short leg of our put spread. But which puts should be bought for the long leg? We could buy either the Sep 500 put or the Sep 480 put against the sale of the Sep 460 put. Which is the best choice? Obviously, the 500 put will cost more (20 ticks) than the 480 put (14 ticks) because it conveys the right to sell BP at a higher price. As a result, the Sep 500/460 put spread costs 10 (i.e. 20 minus 10) whereas the Sep 480/460 put spread costs 4 (i.e. 14 minus 10). How do the two alternatives compare?

The Sep 500/460 put spread costs 10 and has a maximum value of 40 (the difference between the two strikes). The risk/reward on buying this spread is therefore −10 against +30, "odds" of 3 to 1 in our favour.

The Sep 480/460 call spread costs 4 and has a maximum value of 20 (the difference between the two strikes). The risk/reward on buying this spread is therefore −4 against +16, "odds" of 4 to 1 in our favour.

Purely in odds terms, the 480/460 put spread offers a superior return to the 500/460 put spread but the 500/460 put spread starts to acquire intrinsic value at a higher underlying level (500) than the 480/460 put spread (480). The wider put spread starts "working" at a higher level, at an earlier stage.

How can we choose between the two alternatives? Well, we may approach the decision intuitively and weigh up the value of the odds on offer. Or we may be a little bit more scientific. We can calculate the exact payoff for a given investment if we are right in our views on the timing and extent of the anticipated downward move.

If we have 20 ticks (equivalent to £200) to invest, we can buy 2 lots of the wider Sep 500/460 put spread at a price of 10 or we can buy 5 lots of the narrower Sep 480/460 put spread at a price of 4. The investment (£200) is the same in both cases. Remember, we are doing this because we believe that BP will fall to about 460 by Sep expiry. How do the payoffs of the two alternatives compare if we are right in our view and BP is at exactly 460 on Sep expiry?

The wider 500/460 put spread will yield a profit of 30 ticks (£300) per put spread. We can afford 2 of the spreads with our 20 ticks (£200) so our profit will be 2 times 30 ticks which equals 60 ticks (£600).

The narrower 480/460 put spread will yield a profit of 16 ticks (£160) per put spread. We can afford 5 of the spreads with our 20 ticks (£200) so our profit will be 5 times 16 ticks which equals 80 ticks (£800).

Given that we are precisely correct in our view in terms of direction, extent and timing of underlying move (a rather big "if" in the market!) we are better off trading the 480/460 put spread. If we are looking to optimise returns on our specific view, we will generally be better off trading a large number of narrow spreads than a smaller number of wider spreads. This may seem counterintuitive to some but is generally correct. This does, however, depend upon the exact option prices under consideration.

Both long put spreads and long call spreads are widely used in option markets. They are basic building blocks of option strategy. Let's summarise the attraction of such long vertical spreads:

- Easy to understand and easy to manage since the extremes of both risk and reward are known
- Questions of volatility are largely taken out of the equation since one option is bought and another option sold against it
- They may be used highly effectively as directional (either bullish or bearish) "punts". The following exercise focuses upon this use of vertical spreads

Exercise 14.1: Call and Put Spreads

We are speculators in Capita stock options as traded on the LIFFE market. We are not prepared to buy Capita options outright because we do not perceive them to be cheap enough. Instead, we have decided to buy call or put spreads to exploit our directional view. We have up to 100 ticks (equivalent to £1000) to invest. September Capita option prices are given in Table 14.3.

Identify the appropriate call or put spreads to buy with our 100 ticks (£1000) given the following views:

1. We believe that the Capita share price will rally towards 720 (i.e. £7.20) by Sep expiry.

Table 14.3 LIFFE September Capita option prices as at the close on 22 July 2008 (Capita share price = 665 (i.e. £6.65))

Calls (Δ)	Strike Price	Puts (Δ)
75 (0.84)	**600**	7 (0.16)
59 (0.77)	**620**	11 (0.23)
44 (0.67)	**640**	17 (0.33)
32 (0.55)	**660**	26 (0.45)
23 (0.45)	**680**	36 (0.55)
15 (0.33)	**700**	49 (0.67)
10 (0.24)	**720**	64 (0.76)

Key: Δ = Delta

2. We believe that the Capita share price will fall towards 600 (i.e. £6.00) by Sep expiry.

Identify the associated expiry payoff and net delta in each case.

Exercise 14.1: "Answers"

Note the inverted commas around "answers". Choosing option strategy is a subjective process. While we can identify the optimal option trade for a particular outcome, that outcome is clearly not yet known when the trade is being considered. All that this exercise seeks to demonstrate is how to identify the optimal trade for a specific outcome.

1. Buy 20 lots of the Sep 700/720 call spread at 5 (equivalent to £50 per spread). Our total investment is 100 ticks (equivalent to £1000) and this is our maximum loss. The maximum value of the 700/720 call spread is 20 (the difference between the two strikes). Our maximum profit is therefore 15 ticks per spread (maximium value of 20 less the cost of the spread). Hence the maximum profit on 20 spreads is 300 ticks (equivalent to £3000). Our risk/reward is −£1000 against +£3000, a 3 to 1 "shot".

   We could also have bought a smaller amount of a wider call spread; the 680/720 call spread, for example. Specifically, we could have bought 7 of these spreads with our 100 ticks of trading capital. Each of the 680/720 call spreads costs 13 (i.e. 23 for the 680 call less 10 for the 720 call) so buying 7 of these spreads would cost 91 ticks (i.e. £910). The maximum value of the 680/720 call spread is 40 (the difference between the two strikes). The maximum profit is therefore 27 ticks per spread (maximum value of 40 less the cost of the spread). Hence, the maximum profit on 7 spreads is 189 ticks (equivalent to £1890). Our risk/reward is −£910 against +£1890, "odds" of roughly 2 to 1.

The "odds" for the wider 680/720 call spread are clearly inferior to those of the narrower 700/720 call spread. However, the 680/720 call spread will start to "work", will start to gain intrinsic value at a lower underlying share price than the 700/720 call spread. All of this should be borne in mind when selecting the appropriate spread.

In terms of the effect of an underlying move upon the two call spreads right now, the 680/720 call spread has a net delta of +21% (long a 45% delta call and short a 24% delta call) which means that, other things being equal, for every 10p that the underlying rises, the call spread should rise by about 2p (21% of the underlying rise of 10p). If we own 7 of the 680/720 call spreads, we can therefore expect to make about 14 ticks (equivalent to £140) for every 10p that the underlying stock rises.

The narrower 700/720 call spread has a smaller net delta of +9% (long a 33% delta call and short a 24% delta call) which means that, other things being equal, for every 10p that the underlying rises, the call spread should rise by about 1p (9% of the underlying rise of 10p). If we own 20 of the 700/720 call spreads, we can therefore expect to make about 20 ticks (equivalent to £200) for every 10p that the underlying stock rises.

Comparing the two call spreads, we can again see that buying a greater number of the narrower spread results in a better incremental payoff than buying a smaller number of the wider spread.

2. Buy 25 lots of the Sep 620/600 put spread at 4 (equivalent to £40 per spread). Our total investment is 100 ticks (equivalent to £1000) and this is our maximum loss. The maximum value of the 620/600 put spread is 20 (the difference between the two strikes). Our maximum profit is therefore 16 ticks per spread (maximum value of 20 less the cost of the spread). The maximum profit on 25 spreads is therefore 400 ticks (equivalent to £4000). Our risk/reward is −£1000 against +£4000, "odds" of 4 to 1 in our favour.

We could also have bought a smaller amount of a wider put spread; the 640/600 put spread, for example. Specifically, we could have bought 10 of these spreads with our 100 ticks of trading capital. Each of the 640/600 put spreads costs 10 (i.e. 17 for the 640 put less 7 for the 600 put) so buying 10 of these spreads would cost 100 ticks (i.e. £1000). The maximum value of the 640/600 put spread is 40 (the difference between the two strikes). Hence the maximum profit is 30 ticks per spread (maximum value of 40 less the cost of the spread). The maximum profit on 10 spreads is therefore 300 ticks (equivalent to £3000). Our risk/reward is −£1000 against +£3000, "odds" of 3 to 1 in our favour.

We could also have bought an even smaller amount of an even wider put spread; the 660/600 put spread, for example. Specifically, we could have bought 5 of these spreads with our 100 ticks of trading capital. Each of the 660/600 put spreads costs 19 (i.e. 26 for the 660 put less 7 for the 600 put) so buying 5 of these spreads would cost 95 ticks (i.e. £950). The maximum value of the 660/600 put spread is 60 (the difference between the two strikes). Hence, the maximum profit is

41 ticks per spread (maximum value of 60 less the cost of the spread). The maximum profit on 5 spreads is therefore 205 ticks (equivalent to £2050). Our risk/reward is −£950 against +£2050, "odds" of roughly 2 to 1 in our favour.

The "odds" for the widest 660/600 put spread are clearly inferior to those of the narrower 640/600 put spread which in turn are inferior to those of the narrowest 620/600 put spread. However, the 660/600 put spread will start to "work", will start to gain intrinsic value at a higher underlying share price than the 640/600 put spread which in turn will start to "work" 20p earlier than the 620/600 put spread. As ever in trading, "you pays your money, you takes your choice". How confident are you that your target of 600 will be reached by expiry? Is 600 a very precise target, perhaps a big support level or key retracement, or is it simply the lower end of a wide target range? All of these factors should be borne in mind when choosing the appropriate spread.

In terms of the effect of an instantaneous underlying move upon the various put spreads, the 660/600 put spread has a net delta of −29% (long a −45% delta put and short a −16% delta put) which means that, other things being equal, for every 10p that the underlying falls, the put spread should rise by about 3p (29% of the underlying fall of 10p). If we own 5 of the 660/600 put spreads, we can therefore expect to make about 15 ticks (equivalent to £150) for every 10p that the underlying stock falls.

The 640/600 put spread has a net delta of −17% (long a −33% delta put and short a −16% delta put) which means that, other things being equal, for every 10p that the underlying falls, the put spread should rise by a little over 1.5p (17% of the underlying fall of 10p). If we own 10 of the 640/600 put spreads, we can therefore expect to make little more than 15 ticks (equivalent to £150) for every 10p that the underlying stock falls.

The 620/600 put spread has a net delta of −7% (long a −23% delta put and short a −16% delta put) which means that, other things being equal, for every 10p that the underlying falls, the put spread should rise by between 0.5p and 1p (7% of the underlying fall of 10p). If we own 25 of the 620/600 put spreads, we can therefore expect to make between 12.5 and 25 ticks (equivalent to between £125 and £250) for every 10p that the underlying stock falls.

Comparing the three put spreads, we can see that while the net payoffs are broadly similar, buying the greatest number of the narrowest spread results in the best incremental payoff.

Having looked at vertical spreads from a long perspective, we now need to consider such call and put spreads from a short perspective. While many of the features of short vertical spreads (simplicity, vega neutrality, etc.) are the same as for long vertical spreads, the motivation for shorting such spreads is very different. Let's start by considering short call spreads.

15
Short Call Spreads
(Bear Call Spreads)

Remember, a call spread consists of two legs, a long call and a short call. We have already seen that a long call spread, sometimes called a bull call spread (because it is bullish in nature), consists of a long call with a lower strike and a short call with a higher strike. A short call spread, sometimes called a bear call spread (because it is bearish in nature), consists of a short call with a lower strike and a long call with a higher strike.

For example, from the matrix of Sep BP option prices in Table 15.1, selling the 540/560 call spread consists of two legs, selling the 540 call at 19 and simultaneously buying the 560 call at 12. The price of the call spread is 7 ticks (equivalent to £70 per spread), the difference between the 19 received from the sale of the 540 call and the 12 paid out for the 560 call. These 7 ticks represent the maximum profit on selling the call spread. If BP is at or below 540 (i.e. £5.40) on Sep expiry, then both the 540 and 560 calls will expire worthless. The maximum possible value of the call spread is 20, the difference between the two strike prices of 540 and 560. If BP is at or above 560 (i.e. £5.60) on Sep expiry, then the 540 call will be worth exactly 20 more than the 560 call.

Given that the maximum possible value of the call spread is 20 and that the price received for the call spread is 7, the maximum possible loss is 13, the difference between the maximum value of the spread and its price.

So, the risk/reward for selling the 540/560 call spread at 7 is +7/−13. If we sell this spread, we can make 7 and lose 13, "odds" of roughly 1 to 2 against. Why would we do this?

Remember that, in practice, the starting point for long vertical spreads (same month, different strikes) such as long call spreads and long put spreads is a directional view. Specifically, a bullish view in the case of long calls spreads and a bearish view in the case of long put spreads. Volatility and its effect upon the price of options are likely

Table 15.1   LIFFE September BP option prices (BP share price
(LSE) = 522 (i.e. £5.22), LIFFE BP September future = 519
(i.e. £5.19))

Calls	Strike Prices	Puts
86	**440**	6
69	**460**	10
53	**480**	14
39	**500**	20
28	**520**	29
19	**540**	40
12	**560**	54
7	**580**	70
4	**600**	87
3	**620**	106
1	**640**	125

to be secondary considerations; specifically, deterring us from buying outright calls
or outright puts.

In the case of short vertical spreads in practice (i.e. short call spreads and short
put spreads), it is likely that the primary driver behind the trade will be the option
prices themselves. Specifically, our starting point is likely to be the view that options
are too expensive because we believe that market volatility is currently unjustifiably
high. As a result, we know that we want to be short of options. The exact choice of
which options to short will depend upon our view of the underlying market. Consider
the following decision-making process.

We are speculators in BP options. We believe that all BP options are currently
overpriced. This view may be intuitive, a result of familiarity with BP option prices
or the result of a more technical approach involving the study of implied volatilities.
Either way, our starting point is a view that BP options are currently too expensive.
As speculators, what do we do with things that we perceive to be expensive? We sell
them. So we want to sell BP options but which ones? This is the point at which our
underlying view comes into play.

Simply, if we are bearish (or at the very least not bullish), we could sell calls. If
we are right in our bearish views on both the underlying and volatility, then we will
profit from both a fall in the underlying and a fall in volatility. Both dimensions of
our view will work for us. If we are bullish (or at the very least not bearish), we
could sell puts. If we are right in our bullish view on the underlying and bearish
view on volatility, then we will profit from both a rise in the underlying and a fall
in volatility. Both dimensions of our view will again work for us. In simple terms,
we can match our choice of trade to our views on underlying direction and volatility.
But there is a problem. Selling options outright equates to unlimited risk (literally,
unlimited to the upside in the case of short calls, limited only by zero to the downside

Table 15.2 LIFFE September BP option prices (BP share price (LSE) = 522 (i.e. £5.22), LIFFE BP September future = 519 (i.e. £5.19))

Calls	Strike Prices	Puts
86	**440**	6
69	**460**	10
53	**480**	14
39	**500**	20
28	**520**	29
19	**540**	40
12	**560**	54
7	**580**	70
4	**600**	87
3	**620**	106
1	**640**	125

in the case of short puts). Selling options outright is sometimes known as selling options "naked". In this context, selling options "naked" specifically means selling options in isolation, selling options with nothing against them, either other options or underlying. As the name suggests, selling options naked is dangerous. Subjectively, selling options naked is unacceptable because of the unlimited risk that it conveys. This is my point of view, a point of view that has stood me in good stead through stock market crashes, terrorist incidents and, latterly, a credit crisis. Others may disagree; they may feel that it is necessary to take risk to make reward. I can only agree to disagree with such views. Selling options naked is unacceptable not just because of the unlimited risk that it conveys but also because *there are better choices available*. In a nutshell, there are "good" ways and "bad" ways of selling options. To be precise, if we believe that options are too expensive, sell spreads rather than outrights. Consider the example in Table 15.2 using the BP option prices shown in Table 15.1.

As before, we are speculators in BP options. We currently have no positions in BP. Our view is that Sep BP options are currently too expensive because Sep market volatility is currently too high. We therefore want to be short of Sep BP options. Our view on the underlying is that the share price of BP is likely to fall (or at the very least not rise) between now and Sep expiry. As a result of these views, we have two basic choices of strategy. We can sell Sep BP Calls outright or we can sell Sep BP call spreads. Let's compare and contrast the two trades.

First, we can sell BP calls outright. For example, we can sell the Sep 560 calls at 12. Our potential profit is limited to the 12 ticks (equivalent to £120) that we receive per call sold. We will realise this maximum profit if BP stays below 560 (i.e. £5.60) between now and Sep expiry. Our maximum loss is unlimited. As the share price of BP rises towards infinity, our potential losses also rise towards infinity. To summarise, if we sell the Sep 560 calls naked at 12, we can make 12 against losing an infinite amount. Not, in my humble opinion, an attractive risk/reward profile.

Let's compare this with the second alternative, selling call spreads. For example, we can sell the Sep 560/600 call spread at 8 (short the 560 call at 12 and long the 600 call at 4). Our potential profit is limited to the 8 ticks (equivalent to £80) that we receive per spread sold. As with the outright call sale, we will realise this maximum profit if BP stays below 560 (i.e. £5.60) between now and Sep expiry. The maximum possible value of the 560/600 call spread is 40, the difference between the two strikes. The spread will be worth this maximum value if BP is at or above 600 (i.e. £6.00) upon expiry. Our maximum loss on selling the spread at a price of 8 is therefore 32 (the maximum possible value of the spread less the price received for it). No matter how high the share price of BP rises, we can only ever lose 32 (equivalent to £320) per spread sold. To summarise, if we sell the Sep 560/600 call spread at 8, we can make 8 against losing 32.

Remember, both of the above choices of trade are driven by exactly the same views upon the underlying (bearish/not bullish) and volatility (bearish/options currently overpriced). Now compare and contrast the risk/reward profiles of the two trades.

Selling the Sep 560 calls outright at 12 gives us unlimited exposure and profit potential of 12 ticks (£120) per contract. In rough terms, we are giving away "odds" of infinity to 1. Selling the Sep 560/600 call spread at 8 gives us exposure of 32 ticks (£320) and profit potential of 8 ticks (£80) per spread sold. In rough terms, we are giving away "odds" of 4 to 1.

Which is the "better" trade? Remember, these are real prices from the LIFFE market. They are not made up to suit my view. Let's consider this question in both relative and absolute terms.

In relative terms, selling the call spread is surely preferable to selling naked calls since the call spread exposes us to odds of four to one while selling the naked calls exposes us (in theory at least!) to odds of infinity to one. Can the share price of BP go to infinity? No, not in practice but it can rise very far and very fast under the right circumstances (such as discovering the secret of cheap, clean, renewable energy). Potential risk is de facto unlimited. So, in relative terms, selling the call spread "beats" selling naked calls. What about in absolute terms?

In absolute terms, selling the naked calls can make us 12 ticks per contract sold while selling the call spread can make us 8 ticks. But if we sell 50% more spreads than we sell outrights, then we can make the same amount (12 ticks) and our exposure is simultaneously increased by 50% to 48 ticks (i.e. $32 \times 150\%$).

For example, if we sell 2 Sep 560 calls at 12, we can make 24 and lose an unlimited amount. If we sell 3 Sep 560/600 call spreads, we can make exactly the same amount (24) and lose 96 (i.e. 3×32).

Now, which is better; reward of 24 versus unlimited risk or reward of 24 versus risk of 92? Selling the call spreads is surely the better choice. We can see that if we want to make the same absolute amount from selling call spreads as from selling outright calls, then we need to trade in bigger size; we should sell more call spreads than we would outright calls. How much bigger depends upon the premiums being taken in. In the above example, it makes intuitive sense to trade one and a half times more spreads than outrights to get the same absolute potential return.

In terms of risk/reward on expiry, we can see that selling call spreads is a better choice than selling outright calls. But what about between the trade date and expiry? Remember, option spreads do not have to be held until expiry. Just like other option spreads, we may trade in and out of short call spreads at will.

We know that the three main factors affecting the value of any option strategy are the underlying, time and volatility. How will changes in these factors impact the value of a short call spread?

First, let's consider the impact of changes in the underlying upon a short call spread. On an intuitive level, it is clear that a short call spread is a bearish trade, hence its alternative name of bear call spread. Other things being equal, it will perform well to the downside and poorly to the upside. Broadly speaking, if we sell a call spread, we are likely to profit if the underlying falls and lose if the underlying rises.

If we want to quantify the extent of these potential profits and losses, then we need to consider the net delta of the spread. Let's return to our example of a bear call spread, selling the Sep BP 560/600 call spread at 8.

The delta of the Sep 560 call is 29% and the delta of the Sep 600 call is 13%. Given that selling the Sep 560/600 call spread involves selling the 560 call and buying the 600 call, the net delta of the spread is −16% (short a 29% delta call and long a −13% delta call).

Other things being equal, if we sell the Sep 560/600 call spread for 8 and the market instantly falls from its current level of 522 to 502, then the value of the call spread that we have sold should fall by around 3 ticks (making a profit of about £30 per spread), equivalent to about 16% (the net delta of the spread) of the 20p fall in the underlying BP share price.

If the underlying BP share price rises by 10p, then we would expect the value of the call spread we have sold to rise by about 1.5p (making a loss of about £15 per spread), again equivalent to about 16% (the net delta of the spread) of the 10p rise in the underlying. By using the net delta of the spread in this way, we can estimate the likely effect of an instantaneous move in the underlying upon the value of the spread. If the instant underlying move is particularly large, then we need to bear the effects of gamma in mind. Regardless, as with all vertical spreads, the parameters of profit and loss at the extremes are known. We can only ever make 8 and we can only ever lose 32.

Before addressing the effects of time and volatility upon the value of bear call spreads, we need to consider the nature of bear call spreads in practice. In reality, the majority of bear call spreads that trade are out-of-the-money. That is to say, both short and long legs are usually out-of-the-money. Of course, this is not a rule, bear call spreads don't have to be out-of-the-money, just as short outright calls don't have to be out-of-the-money, they just usually are.

How will the passage of time impact out-of-the-money call spreads? Consider our example, the Sep BP 560/600 call spread. Given that the underlying BP share price is 522, this is an example of an out-of-the-money call spread. That is to say, both legs of the trade, the short 560 call and the long 600 call, are currently out-of-the-money. The passage of time will erode both legs of the spread in the same way but to different degrees.

Specifically, time will erode our short 560 call more quickly than it erodes our long 600 call. This is logical, since the 560 call is closer to the money than the 560 call and therefore has more time value to erode. The net effect of the passage of time upon our short call spread is to reduce its value.

If we want to quantify this effect, then we need to consider the net theta of the call spread. If, for example, the theta of the 560 call is -0.30 and the theta of the 600 call is -0.15, then the net theta of the 560/600 call spread is -0.15, the difference between the two individual thetas. In lay terms this means that, other things being equal, our short 560/600 call spread should lose about 0.15 of a tick (equivalent to £1.50) per spread sold per day. Over a 5 day period, other things being equal, the spread should lose about 0.75 of a tick (equivalent to £7.50) per spread sold.

In general then, out-of-the-money call spreads will erode due to the passing of time. As long as we are correct in our underlying view, correct in our view that the underlying will not rise, then our short call spread will remain out-of-the-money. But what if our directional view is wrong? What if BP rises and our short 560/600 call spread becomes in-the-money?

Time decay only affects the time value of options. Time decay does not affect intrinsic value. In relation to our short Sep 560/600 call spread, whichever option has the greatest amount of time value will erode the fastest. Broadly speaking, this means that whichever option is closest to the prevailing underlying will erode the fastest. As long as the price of BP remains below our short call strike of 560, time will be working in our favour. As the price of BP moves towards 580, the mid-point of the two call strikes, the net theta of the spread will move closer and closer to zero, and as the price of BP rises further towards and then through 600, time decay will start to work against us.

Once the price of BP has breached our long call leg of 600, time is working against us. Other things being equal, as time passes, the value of the now in-the-money call spread that we have sold will move closer and closer towards its maximum possible value of 40. And if the Sep 560/600 call spread is still in-the-money upon Sep expiry (because BP is at or above 600), then the spread will be worth 40 and we will realise our maximum loss of 32 ticks (equivalent to £320) per spread sold.

How will changes in volatility impact the value of bear call spreads? This is an important question, given that the starting point for selling call spreads is often a bearish view upon volatility, a belief that options are currently overpriced. This belief, combined with a view that the underlying is unlikely to rise, is the driver behind selling a call spread. Given a bearish view on both volatility and the underlying, the ideal trade would be to sell calls outright. Selling calls naked would benefit from both falling volatility and a fall in the underlying. The trade fits the views. The problem is that such a trade also exposes us to unlimited loss. If (as in my view) this is deemed unacceptable, then a compromise has to be made. A higher, protective call has to be bought to turn the short naked calls into a short call spread. The problem of unlimited loss is addressed but, simultaneously, our ability to benefit from falling volatility is compromised as well.

As previously stated, speculators in the real world tend to sell out-of-the-money call spreads; call spreads where both legs are out-of-the-money. Selling an out-of-the-money call spread involves selling a call that is out-of-the-money (the short leg) and buying a call that is further out-of-the-money (the long leg). The short leg has more time value than the long leg because it is closer to the money. The short leg will therefore lose more value due to volatility falling than the long leg. The short leg has a higher vega than the long leg.

As ever, if we want to quantify the effects of volatility upon the value of a bear call spread, then we need to consider the net vega of the spread.

Consider our previous example of a short call spread, selling the Sep 560/600 call spread at 8. In terms of the effect of volatility upon our spread, if the Sep 560 call has a vega of 2.2 and the Sep 600 call has a vega of 1.2, then the net vega of the spread is -1.0 (short a 2.2 vega call and long a 1.2 vega call). Other things being equal, this means that the Sep 560/600 call spread should decrease in value by 1 tick (equivalent to £10) for a 1% fall in volatility.

We can see that the net vega and net theta of the Sep 560/600 call spread are not particularly large. If we sell this spread with the express intention of profiting from volatility falling and time passing, then we may not consider these Greeks particularly attractive. If we wanted to benefit more from volatility falling and time passing, we could sell a wider call spread, such as selling the 560/640 call spread and/or a spread closer to the money, such as selling the 520/600 call spread. Both of these alternatives will have a larger net vega and larger net theta than the 560/600 call spread, therefore both will benefit more from volatility falling and time passing but both alternatives expose us to significantly more risk than the 560/600 call spread. As ever, potential risk must be weighed against potential reward; "you pays your money and you takes your choice".

Let's summarise the Greeks in relation to short (bear) call spreads. Other things being equal:

- A fall in the underlying is beneficial since it will decrease the value of a short call spread and vice versa (short delta).
- A fall in volatility will decrease the value of short out-of-the-money call spreads (negative vega) and is therefore beneficial.
- A fall in volatility will increase the value of short in-the-money call spreads (positive vega) and is therefore detrimental.
- The passage of time will erode the value of short out-of-the-money call spreads (negative theta) and is therefore beneficial.

- The passage of time will increase the value of short in-the-money call spreads (positive theta) and is therefore detrimental.

Broadly speaking, short call spreads are a less risky alternative to selling naked calls. Both trades are chosen due to a belief that the underlying and/or volatility will fall. Selling naked calls conveys unlimited risk whereas the parameters of both risk and reward are known when selling call spreads.

Bear call spreads may be as wide or as narrow as desired. Broadly speaking, the wider the spread, the greater the potential for both risk and reward. Broadly speaking, the wider the spread, the greater the Greeks, the greater the effect of changes in the underlying, time and volatility.

How should we choose the tenor and constituent strikes of a bear call spread? Common sense dictates that the exact nature of our views on volatility and the underlying are key. If we are selling a call spread because of a bearish view on the underlying, then common sense dictates that we should choose options with an expiry date that lines up with our view on the timing of the anticipated downward move in the underlying. For example, if we are anticipating that BP will fall in price over the next 3 months, then it makes sense to use 3 month options. If our view is that BP will fall between now and year-end, then it seems sensible to use December options. What about choosing the exact strikes that make up our short call spread? How should they be chosen?

If we are selling a call spread as an expiry play, it would seem to make sense to choose the short leg of our bear call spread on the basis of whatever level we feel the underlying will *not* breach by expiry. If, for example, there is huge resistance at the 550 (£5.50) level, then it would seem to make sense to choose to sell the 550 (£5.50) call. If, on the other hand, the first level of significant resistance is at 575 (£5.75), then it might make more sense to choose the 580 (£5.80) call as the short leg of the spread. As with most trading-related matters, this is largely subjective, largely dependent upon our market view.

If we are selling a call spread as a "safe" way of shorting calls, then it would seem to make sense to choose a spread with a significant short net vega, a spread that will profit significantly from a fall in volatility. This is very much a balance of risk against reward. We know that, broadly speaking, wider bear call spreads and closer to the money bear call spreads will have the greatest vega. However, they also convey the greatest risk. As ever, the exact choice of spread sold will depend on the trader's views, desire for reward and appetite for risk.

16
Short Put Spreads
(Bull Put Spreads)

A put spread consists of two legs: a short put and a long put. We have already seen that a long put spread, sometimes called a bear put spread (because it is bearish in nature) consists of a long put with a higher strike and a short put with a lower strike. A short put spread, sometimes called a bull put spread (because it is bullish in nature), consists of a short put with a higher strike and a long put with a lower strike.

Exercise 16.1: Bull Put Spreads

Given the option prices in Table 16.1, consider the following questions about selling the Sep 500/460 put spread. Note that, for the purpose of clear and simple illustration, these Greeks are both theoretical and rounded.

1. What are the two legs of the spread?
2. What is the risk/reward on the spread?
3. What is the net delta of the spread? Other things being equal, what should the spread be worth if the BP share price rises by 10p?
4. What is the net theta of the spread? Other things being equal, what should the spread be worth in 4 days' time?
5. What is the net vega of the spread? Other things being equal, what should the spread be worth if market volatility falls by 3%?
6. For what reasons might this put spread be sold?

Exercise 16.1: Answers

1. Selling the 500/460 put spread consists of two legs, selling the 500 put at 20 (the short leg) and simultaneously buying the 460 put at 10 (the long leg).

Table 16.1 LIFFE September BP option prices and Greeks as at the close on 21 July 2008 (BP share price (LSE) = 522 (i.e. £5.22))

Calls					Puts			
Vega	Theta	Delta	Price	Strike Price	Price	Delta	Theta	Vega
1.30	−0.10	0.88	86	**440**	6	0.12	−0.10	1.30
1.70	−0.15	0.79	69	**460**	10	0.21	−0.15	1.70
2.25	−0.25	0.73	53	**480**	14	0.27	−0.25	2.25
2.80	−0.40	0.64	39	**500**	20	0.36	−0.40	2.80
3.30	−0.55	0.52	28	**520**	29	0.48	−0.55	3.30
2.75	−0.50	0.40	19	**540**	40	0.60	−0.50	2.75
2.20	−0.30	0.29	12	**560**	54	0.71	−0.30	2.20
1.65	−0.20	0.20	7	**580**	70	0.80	−0.20	1.65
1.20	−0.15	0.13	4	**600**	87	0.87	−0.15	1.20
0.85	−0.15	0.08	3	**620**	106	0.92	−0.15	0.85
0.55	−0.10	0.04	1	**640**	125	0.96	−0.10	0.55

2. The sale price of the put spread is 10 ticks (equivalent to £100) per spread, the difference between the 20 received for the sale of the 500 put and the 10 paid out for the 460 put. These 10 ticks represent the maximum profit on selling the put spread. If BP is at or above 500 (i.e. £5.00) on Sep expiry, then both the 500 and 460 puts will expire worthless. The maximum possible value of the put spread is 40, the difference between the two strike prices of 500 and 460. If BP is at or below 460 (i.e. £4.60) on Sep expiry, then the 500 put will be worth exactly 40 more than the 460 put. Given that the maximum possible value of the spread is 40 and that the price received for the spread is 10, the maximum possible loss is 30, the difference between the maximum value and the price. So, the risk/reward for selling the 500/460 put spread is +10/−30, "odds" of roughly 1 to 3 against.

3. The net delta of the spread is +15% (short a −36% put and long a −21% put). Other things being equal, if the BP share price rises by 10p, the put spread should fall in value by about 15% (the net delta) of 10p (the fall in the underlying), a fall in value of 1.5p (equivalent to £1.50) per spread sold.

4. The net theta of the spread is −0.25 (short a −0.40 theta put and long a −0.15 theta put). Other things being equal, the spread should decay by about 0.25 of a tick (equivalent to £2.50 profit per spread sold) between today and tomorrow. Other things being equal, the spread should be worth about 9 (the spread's current value of 10 less 4 days' erosion at a rate of 0.25 per day) in 4 days' time.

5. The net vega of the spread is −1.10 (short a 2.80 vega put and long a 1.70 vega put). Other things being equal, for every 1% that volatility falls, the spread should lose about 1.1 ticks in value (equivalent to £11 profit per spread sold). In the event that market volatility falls by 3%, the put spread should fall in value by between 3 and 3.5 ticks, other things being equal, giving it a value of between 6.5 and 7 ticks.

6. The rationale for selling the Sep 500/460 put spread is either a view that the Sep puts are overpriced (because market volatility is currently too high) and/or a view that the underlying BP share price will not fall between now and expiry. Given these views, selling outright puts seems an appropriate trade, a trade that benefits from both falling volatility and a rising underlying. However, selling puts naked conveys significant risk to the downside. This downside risk may be limited by purchasing a lower, protective put, turning the short outright puts into a short put spread. See the next chapter for a detailed comparison.

17
Selling Naked Puts versus Selling Put Spreads

Following on from the answer to part (6) in Exercise 16.1, let's now compare selling naked puts to selling put spreads. Specifically, let's compare selling Sep 500 puts naked to selling Sep 500/460 put spreads. The rationale for the two trades is the same, a view that the Sep puts are overpriced (because market volatility is currently too high) and/or a view that the underlying BP share price will not fall between now and expiry. Remember that, in practice, the starting point for long vertical spreads such as long call spreads and long put spreads is usually a directional view. Volatility and its effect upon the price of the options are likely to be secondary considerations. Specifically, relatively high volatility is deterring us from buying outright calls or outright puts.

In the case of short vertical spreads such as short call spreads and short put spreads, it is likely that the primary driver behind the trade will be option prices. Specifically, our starting point is likely to be the view that options are too expensive because we believe that market volatility is currently unjustifiably high. As a result, we know that we want to be short of options. The exact choice of which options to short will depend upon our view on the underlying market. Consider the following decision-making process.

We are speculators in BP options. We believe that all BP options are currently overpriced. We know that we want to sell BP options. Which options should we sell? This is the point at which our underlying view comes into play.

If we are bullish (or at the very least not bearish), then we could sell puts. If we are right in our bullish view on the underlying and bearish view on volatility, then we will profit from both a rise in the underlying and a fall in volatility. Both dimensions of our view will work for us.

In simple terms, we can match our choice of trade to our views on underlying direction and volatility. But there is a problem. Selling puts naked equates to significant risk to the downside. Remember, selling puts naked specifically means selling puts without anything against them, either other options or underlying. Subjectively, this is unacceptable because of the significant risk that it conveys. I must re-emphasise that this is *my* point of view, a point of view that has evolved over 25 years of trading options, a quarter century that has included a number of stock market crashes, company collapses and sundry financial crises. Personally, I have absolutely no interest in exposing myself to unlimited downside in equity markets. Others may disagree; they may feel that it is necessary to take such risk to make worthwhile reward. As ever, I can only agree to disagree with such views.

But selling puts naked is unacceptable not just because of the significant risk that it conveys but also because *there are better choices available*. Remember, there are "good" ways and "bad" ways of selling options. To be precise, if we believe that puts are too expensive, sell put spreads rather than outright puts. Consider the following exercise.

Exercise 17.1: Selling Puts vs Selling Put Spreads

We are speculators in BP options. We currently have no positions in BP. Our view is that Sep BP options are currently too expensive because Sep market volatility is currently too high. We therefore want to be short of Sep BP options. Our view on the underlying is that the share price of BP is likely to rise (or at least not fall) between now and Sep expiry. As a result of these views, we have two basic choices of strategy. We can sell Sep BP Puts outright or we can sell Sep BP put spreads. Specifically, we have to choose between:

1. Selling the Sep 500 puts at 20 and
2. Selling the Sep 500/460 put spread at 10

Compare the expiry payoffs of the two alternative trades. Which is "better"?

Exercise 17.1: Answers

1. Selling the Sep 500 puts at 20. Our potential profit is limited to the 20 ticks (equivalent to £200) that we receive per put sold. We will realise this maximum profit if BP stays above 500 (i.e. £5.00) between now and Sep expiry. In the event that the price of BP falls to zero, the 500 puts will be worth 500. Our maximum loss is therefore 480 (the maximum possible value of the puts less the price received for them). To summarise, if we sell the Sep 500 puts "naked" at 20, we can make 20 against losing 480, "odds" of 1 to 24 against us.
2. Selling the Sep 500/460 put spread at 10. Our potential profit is limited to the 10 ticks (equivalent to £100) that we receive per spread sold. We will realise this maximum profit if BP stays above 500 (i.e. £5.00) between now and Sep expiry.

The maximum possible value of the 500/460 put spread is 40, the difference between the two strikes. The spread will be worth this maximum value if BP is at or below 460 (i.e. £4.60) upon expiry. Our maximum loss on selling the spread at a price of 10 is therefore 30 (the maximum possible value of the spread less the price received for it). No matter how low the share price of BP falls, we can only ever lose 30 (equivalent to £300) per spread sold. To summarise, if we sell the Sep 500/460 put spread at 10, we can make 10 against losing 30, "odds" of 1 to 3 against us.

Which is the "better" trade? Remember, both trades are driven by exactly the same views upon the underlying (bullish/not bearish) and volatility (bearish/options currently overpriced). Now compare and contrast the risk/reward profiles of the two trades.

Selling the Sep 500 puts outright at 20 gives us exposure of 480 ticks (£480) and profit potential of 20 ticks (£120) per put sold. Roughly speaking, we are conceding "odds" of 24 to 1. Selling the Sep 500/460 put spread at 10 gives us exposure of 30 ticks (£300) and profit potential of 10 ticks (£100) per spread sold. In rough terms, we are conceding "odds" of 3 to 1.

Which is the "better" trade? Remember, these are real prices from the LIFFE market. The prices haven't been chosen to suit my view. Consider the question in both relative and absolute terms.

In relative terms, selling the put spread is surely preferable to selling naked puts since the put spread exposes us to odds of 3 to 1 while selling the naked puts exposes us (in theory at least!) to odds of 24 to 1. Can the share price of BP go to zero? Highly unlikely in practice but impossible? A list of companies that "could not possibly" go bust includes Enron, Worldcom, Railtrack, Marconi, Northern Rock, Bear Sterns, Lehman and so on. In relative terms, selling the put spread "beats" selling the naked puts. What about in absolute terms?

In absolute terms, selling the naked puts can make us 20 ticks per contract while selling the put spread can make us 10 ticks. But if we sell twice as many spreads as outrights, then we can make the same amount (20 ticks) and our exposure is simultaneously doubled to 60 ticks (i.e. 30 × 2) per spread sold.

For example, if we sell 1 Sep 500 put at 20, we can make 20 and lose 480. If we sell 2 Sep 500/460 put spreads at 10, we can make exactly the same amount (20) and lose 60 (i.e. 2 × 30).

Now, which is better; reward of 20 versus risk of 480 or reward of 20 versus risk of 60? Selling the put spreads is surely the better choice. We can see that if we want to make the same absolute amount from selling put spreads as from selling outright puts, then we need to trade in bigger sizes; we should sell more put spreads than we would outright puts. How much bigger depends upon the premiums being taken in. In the above example, it made intuitive sense to trade twice as many spreads as outrights in order to achieve the same absolute potential return.

In terms of risk/reward on expiry, we can see that selling put spreads is a better choice than selling outright puts. But what about between the trade date and expiry? Remember, all option spreads are transferable; we don't have to hold them until expiry. Just like other option spreads, short put spreads may be traded in and out of at will.

We know that the three main factors affecting the value of any option strategy are the underlying, time and volatility. How will changes in these factors impact the value of a short (bull) put spread?

Other things being equal:

- A rise in the underlying is beneficial since it will decrease the value of a short put spread and vice versa (long delta).
- A fall in volatility will decrease the value of short out-of-the-money put spreads (negative vega) and is therefore beneficial.
- A fall in volatility will increase the value of short in-the-money put spreads (positive vega) and is therefore detrimental.
- The passage of time will erode the value of short out-of-the-money put spreads (negative theta) and is therefore beneficial.
- The passage of time will increase the value of short in-the-money put spreads (positive theta) and is therefore detrimental.

Consider our previous example of a short put spread, selling the Sep 500/460 put spread at 10. In terms of the effect of volatility upon our spread, if the Sep 500 put has a vega of 2.80 and the Sep 460 put has a vega of 1.70, then the net vega of the spread is -1.10 (short a 2.80 vega put and long a 1.70 vega put). Other things being equal, this means that the Sep 500/460 put spread should decrease in value by 1.1 ticks (equivalent to £11 per spread) per 1% fall in volatility. In terms of the effect of the passage of time upon our spread, if the Sep 500 put has a theta of -0.40 and the Sep 460 put has a theta of -0.15, then the net theta of the spread is -0.25 (short a -0.40 theta put and long a -0.15 theta put). Other things being equal, this means that the Sep 500/460 put spread should decrease in value by 0.25 of a tick (equivalent to £2.50 per spread) per day.

We can see that the net vega and net theta of the Sep 500/460 put spread are not particularly large. If we have sold this spread with the express intention of profiting from volatility falling and time passing, then we may not consider these Greeks particularly attractive. If we wanted to benefit more from volatility falling and time passing, we could sell a wider put spread, such as selling the 500/400 put spread and/or a spread closer to the money, such as selling the 520/460 put spread. Both of these alternatives will have a larger net vega and net theta than the 500/460 put spread; both will benefit more from volatility falling and time passing but both alternatives expose us to significantly more risk than the 500/460 put spread. As ever, potential risk must be weighed against potential reward; as always in trading, "you pays your money and you takes your choice".

Broadly speaking, short put spreads are a less risky alternative to selling naked puts. Both trades are chosen due to a belief that volatility will fall and/or the underlying will not fall. Selling naked puts conveys significant risk to the downside whereas the parameters of both risk and reward are known when selling put spreads.

Bull put spreads may be as wide or as narrow as desired. Broadly speaking, the wider the spread, the greater the potential for both risk and reward. Broadly speaking, the wider the spread, the greater the Greeks, the greater the effect of changes in the underlying, time and volatility.

How should we choose the tenor and constituent strikes of a bull put spread? As ever, common sense dictates that the exact nature of our views on volatility and the underlying are key.

If we are selling a put spread because of a bullish view on the underlying, then common sense dictates that we should choose options with an expiry date that lines up with our view of the timing of the anticipated upward move in the underlying. For example, if we are anticipating that BP will rise in price over the next 3 months, then it makes sense to use 3 month options. If our view is that BP will rise between now and year-end, then it seems sensible to use December options. What about choosing the exact strikes that make up our short put spread? How should they be chosen?

If we are selling a put spread as an expiry play, it would seem to make sense to choose the short leg of our bull put spread on the basis of whatever level we feel the underlying will not fall below by expiry. If, for example, there is significant support at the 500 (£5.00) level, then it would seem to make sense to choose to sell the 500 (£5.00) put. If, on the other hand, the first level of significant support is around 485 (£4.85), it might make more sense to choose the 480 (£4.80) put as the short leg of the spread. As with most trading-related matters, this is largely subjective, largely dependent upon our view.

If we are selling a put spread as a "safe" way of shorting puts, then it would seem to make sense to choose a spread with a significant short net vega, a spread that will profit significantly from a fall in volatility. This is very much a balance of risk against reward. We know that, broadly speaking, wider bull put spreads and closer to the money bull put spreads will have the greatest vega. However, they also convey the greatest risk. As ever, the exact choice of spread sold will depend on the trader's views, desire for reward and appetite for risk.

18
Long Verticals versus Short Verticals

We have already seen the way in which call and put spreads may be used to exploit a directional view on the underlying. For example, buying call spreads may be used to exploit a bullish view on the underlying. An alternative trade would be to sell put spreads, a trade that also exploits a bullish (or at least not bearish) view on the underlying. So which should we choose? If we are bullish on the underlying, should we buy call spreads or sell put spreads?

Broadly speaking, the answer depends upon our exact view on the underlying. Specifically, if we are *positively bullish*, then buying call spreads seems logical. If, rather than being positively bullish, we are simply *not bearish*, then selling put spreads seems logical. So far so good. But our choice of trade will also depend upon whether we want the "odds" (risk/reward) in our favour or the "odds" against us. Remember, vertical spreads may be viewed as fixed odds "bets", directional trades where the extremes of both risk and reward are known. Do we want the odds of the "bet" in our favour or the odds of the "bet" against us? Instinctively, the majority of traders would prefer the former, to have the odds in their favour but, as ever in the markets, there is a price to pay for this. That price is time decay. In practice, most call and put spreads that are traded are out-of-the-money. Out-of-the-money call and put spreads have negative theta, they erode due to the passing of time. So, if we buy out-of-the-money call spreads to exploit a bullish view, then the odds are likely to be in our favour but time against us. If nothing happens, if the underlying stays around its current level, then our long call spread is likely to lose value as time passes, costing us money, day by day. If, on the other hand, we sell out-of-the-money put spreads to exploit a bullish view, then the odds are likely to be against us but time is working in our favour. If nothing happens, if the underlying stays around its current level, then our short put spread is likely to lose value as time passes, making us money, day by day.

Exactly the same applies to the choice between long put spreads and short call spreads. Both may be used to exploit a bearish view on the underlying. So which is the better choice? Consider the following exercise.

Exercise 18.1: Long Vertical Spreads versus Short Vertical Spreads

We are speculators in BP options. We currently have no position in BP. We believe that the BP share price will fall between now and Sep expiry. We cannot buy outright BP puts because we do not perceive them to be cheap enough. Nor can we sell BP calls "naked" because we are unwilling to accept unlimited risk. We have therefore narrowed our choice of strategies to two alternatives:

(a) Buy the Sep 480/460 put spread at 4
(b) Sell the Sep 560/580 call spread at 5

Which is the appropriate choice if:

1. We believe that the price of BP will fall towards 450 (£4.50) by Sep expiry?
2. We have no specific view on the price of BP but believe that it will *not* rise between now and Sep expiry?

Identify the expiry payoffs of the trades (a) and (b). How will the passage of time and changes in market volatility affect the two trades?

Table 18.1   LIFFE Sep BP option prices and Greeks at close on 21 July 2008 (BP share price (LSE) = 522 (i.e. £5.22)) – repeated from Table 16.1

Calls					Puts			
Vega	Theta	Delta	Price	Strike Price	Price	Delta	Theta	Vega
1.30	−0.10	0.88	86	**440**	6	0.12	−0.10	1.30
1.70	−0.15	0.79	69	**460**	10	0.21	−0.15	1.70
2.25	−0.25	0.73	53	**480**	14	0.27	−0.25	2.25
2.80	−0.40	0.64	39	**500**	20	0.36	−0.40	2.80
3.30	−0.55	0.52	28	**520**	29	0.48	−0.55	3.30
2.75	−0.50	0.40	19	**540**	40	0.60	−0.50	2.75
2.20	−0.30	0.29	12	**560**	54	0.71	−0.30	2.20
1.65	−0.20	0.20	7	**580**	70	0.80	−0.20	1.65
1.20	−0.15	0.13	4	**600**	87	0.87	−0.15	1.20
0.85	−0.15	0.08	3	**620**	106	0.92	−0.15	0.85
0.55	−0.10	0.04	1	**640**	125	0.96	−0.10	0.55

Note that, for the purpose of clear and simple illustration, these Greeks are both theoretical and rounded.

Exercise 18.1: Answers

1. If we believe that the price of BP will fall towards 450 (£4.50) by Sep expiry, then trade (a) is the more appropriate choice since it will deliver the better payoff if we are correct in our view. Specifically, buying the 480/460 put spread at 4 exposes us to a potential loss of 4 ticks (equivalent to £40) and a potential profit of 16 ticks (equivalent to £160) per spread purchased. The risk reward is −4 against +16, "odds" of 4 to 1 in our favour.

   Trade (b), selling the 560/580 call spread at 5, exposes us to a potential loss of 15 ticks (equivalent to £150) and a potential profit of 5 ticks (equivalent to £50) per spread sold. The risk reward is −15 against +5, "odds" of 3 to 1 against us.

   Clearly, if we are correct in our view, trade (a) delivers a significantly better payoff upon expiry than trade (b). The flip side of this is that, if nothing happens and BP stays around its current price of 522 (£5.22) until Sep expiry, both spreads will erode and expire worthless, giving us a profit of 5 ticks per spread on trade (b) and a loss of 4 ticks per spread on trade (a).

2. If we have no specific view on BP but simply believe that it will *not* rally between now and Sep expiry, then trade (b) may be the appropriate choice, depending upon our attitude to risk. For example, if our perception is that BP will remain range-bound between now and Sep expiry, if we believe that BP will drift sideways or down a little over the period, then selling the call spread rather than buying the put spread makes sense, as long as we are comfortable with the "odds" being against us (see above).

Changes in volatility are likely to have little effect on the value of either of the spreads since both spreads have relatively small net vegas.

HEALTH WARNING!
As ever in trading, our exact choice of trade is largely subjective. All that the above exercise seeks to illustrate is a structured approach to the choice of option trade.

SUMMARY OF CHAPTERS 13 TO 18

Collectively, call and put spreads are known as vertical spreads. They involve the simultaneous purchase and sale of two options of the same type (call or put) and same series (underlying and month) but with different strikes.

Long vertical spreads involve buying the more expensive option (the lower strike call or the higher strike put) and selling the cheaper option (the higher strike call or the lower strike put). The difference between the premium paid out for the more expensive option and the premium received for the cheaper option is the cost of the spread. This is the maximum loss. The difference between the two strike prices is the maximum possible value of the spread. This maximum value less the cost of the spread is the maximum possible profit.

Potential risk and potential reward are both known. The cost of owning options is reduced but so is potential profit.

Long vertical spreads may be viewed as a conservative way of trading a directional view. Specifically, long call spreads may be used to exploit a bullish view on the underlying and long put spreads may be used to exploit a bearish view on the underlying.

Short vertical spreads involve selling the more expensive option (the lower strike call or the higher strike put) and buying the cheaper option (the higher strike call or the lower strike put). The difference between the premium received for the more expensive option and the premium paid out for the cheaper option is the price received for the spread. This is the maximum profit. The difference between the two strike prices is the maximum possible value of the spread. This maximum value less the price received for the spread is the maximum possible loss.

As with long verticals, potential risk and potential reward are both known. The risk associated with selling options is reduced but so is potential profit.

Short vertical spreads may be viewed as a "safer" way of selling premium than selling "naked" options. Specifically, selling call spreads is a "safer" way of selling calls and selling put spreads is a "safer" way of selling puts.

Vertical spreads may be as wide or as narrow as desired. Broadly speaking, the narrower the spread, the more conservative the trade and vice versa.

Vertical spreads should be entered as a spread (i.e. both legs executed simultaneously) and closed as a spread. Don't be tempted to "leg out" of vertical spreads (trade out of one leg and leave the other leg open) unless you are closing the short leg first and are aware that you then have a long outright position.

All true option market participants are familiar with call and put spreads. If your broker doesn't understand such spreads, then they are not an option broker.

Vertical spreads are relatively simple and user-friendly. As such, call and put spreads are a good starting point for anyone new to option spread trading.

Over the following six chapters we will consider straddles and strangles. These are sometimes collectively referred to as "volatility strategies" since the driver behind these trades is often a view on volatility rather than a directional view on the underlying. As with vertical spreads, we will first consider long straddles and strangles before considering both straddles and strangles from a short perspective. We will then consider refinements of short straddles and strangles, the wonderfully named "iron butterfly" and "iron condor".

19
Long Straddles

What is a long straddle? A long straddle consists of two legs, a long call and a long put with the same strike and from the same series. Buying a straddle involves buying both options simultaneously.

For example, from the matrix of Sep BP option prices (Table 19.1, repeated from Table 16.1), buying the 520 straddle consists of two legs, buying the 520 call at 28 and simultaneously buying the 520 put at 29. The cost of the straddle is 57 ticks (equivalent to £570) per straddle, the sum of the 28 paid for the 520 call and the 29 paid for the 520 put. These 57 ticks represent the maximum loss on buying the straddle. This loss will occur if BP is at exactly 520 (i.e. £5.20) on Sep expiry, since both the 520 calls and 520 puts will expire worthless. The maximum possible value of the straddle is unlimited to the upside and limited only by zero to the downside.

Table 19.1 LIFFE Sep BP option prices and Greeks at close on 21 July 2008 (BP share price (LSE) = 522 (i.e. £5.22))

Calls					Puts			
Vega	Theta	Delta	Price	Strike Price	Price	Delta	Theta	Vega
1.30	−0.10	0.88	86	**440**	6	0.12	−0.10	1.30
1.70	−0.15	0.79	69	**460**	10	0.21	−0.15	1.70
2.25	−0.25	0.73	53	**480**	14	0.27	−0.25	2.25
2.80	−0.40	0.64	39	**500**	20	0.36	−0.40	2.80
3.30	−0.55	0.52	28	**520**	29	0.48	−0.55	3.30
2.75	−0.50	0.40	19	**540**	40	0.60	−0.50	2.75
2.20	−0.30	0.29	12	**560**	54	0.71	−0.30	2.20
1.65	−0.20	0.20	7	**580**	70	0.80	−0.20	1.65
1.20	−0.15	0.13	4	**600**	87	0.87	−0.15	1.20
0.85	−0.15	0.08	3	**620**	106	0.92	−0.15	0.85
0.55	−0.10	0.04	1	**640**	125	0.96	−0.10	0.55

The risk/reward for buying the 520 straddle at 57 is a potential loss of 57 ticks (equivalent to £570) per straddle against unlimited potential profit, favourable "odds" of infinity to 1. Why would we buy this straddle?

Remember the two key factors when deciding upon option strategy are our view on the underlying and our view on volatility (are the options cheap or expensive?). If we are buying a straddle, then we are simultaneously buying both a call and a put. So do we have a view on the underlying? Are we bullish or bearish? No! If we were bullish, we would be buying calls, not puts. And if we were bearish, we would be buying puts and not calls. If we don't have a view on the underlying, it follows that we *must* have a view on volatility. We must have a view on whether the options are cheap or expensive.

The driver behind a long straddle is a view on volatility. Specifically, a view that market volatility is currently too low, that the options are currently underpriced. We know that we want to be long options, that is our starting point. Because we are neither bullish nor bearish, we need to buy both calls and puts. Our view is not that the market will rise or that it will fall but that it is likely to do either. We believe that the market will be volatile, that the market will move; we just don't know which way. Hence, we "cover all the bases"; we buy both calls and puts, we buy a straddle.

Let's reconsider our example of a long straddle in more detail. Buying the Sep 520 straddle involves two legs, buying the 520 call at 28 and buying the 520 put at 29. The cost of the straddle is therefore 57 ticks (equivalent to £570) per straddle, the sum of the two premiums. This is our maximum loss, a loss that we will realise if the underlying BP share price is at exactly 520 (£5.20) on Sep expiry because both the 520 call and the 520 put will expire worthless. Remember that the rationale for buying the straddle is a belief that the options are too cheap because market volatility is currently too low. We expect the underlying to become more volatile, we expect BP to move away from its current price of 522 (£5.22), but we aren't sure in which direction.

If the price of BP starts to rise, then the 520 call that we own will start to gain value. The 520 put will simultaneously start to lose value but can only fall in value to zero. If the price of BP rises towards infinity, the value of the 520 call will also rise towards infinity, giving us an infinite profit! Theoretically correct but not very real world. To use a less extreme example, if the share price of BP rises to 950 (£9.50) by Sep expiry, then the value of the 520 call that we own will rise to at least 430, the intrinsic value of the option under such circumstances. This will give us a profit of at least 373 ticks (equivalent to £3730) per straddle, the difference between the value of the straddle and the price originally paid for it.

If the price of BP starts to fall, then the 520 put that we own will start to gain value. The 520 call will simultaneously start to lose value but can only fall in value to zero. If the price of BP falls to zero, then the value of the 520 put will be 520, giving us a profit of 463 (equivalent to £4630) per straddle. Again, mathematically correct but not very real world. To use a less extreme example, if the share price of BP falls to

400 (£4.00) by Sep expiry, then the value of the 520 put that we own will rise to at least 120, the intrinsic value of the option under such circumstances. This will give us a profit of at least 63 ticks (equivalent to £630) per straddle, the difference between the value of the straddle and the price originally paid for it.

The expiry breakeven points for the straddle are 57 *above* 520 (577 or £5.77) and 57 *below* 520 (463 or £4.63). If the BP share price is at exactly £5.77 on Sep expiry, then the Sep 520 call will be worth exactly 57 and the 520 put will expire worthless. The 520 straddle will be worth 57 which is the price that we originally paid for it.

If the BP share price is at exactly £4.63 on Sep expiry, then the Sep 520 put will be worth exactly 57 and the 520 call will expire worthless. The 520 straddle will again be worth 57 which is the price that we originally paid for it.

The above information is depicted in the expiry payoff chart shown in Figure 19.1.

Note that profit and loss is shown on the vertical axis with the BP share price shown on the horizontal. As before, the line depicts the payoff of the strategy on expiry.

Thus far we have considered the payoff of the long straddle upon expiry. But what about the value of the straddle between the trade date and expiry?

Remember that the three main factors affecting the value of options are the underlying, time and volatility. How will these factors impact the value of a long straddle?

Remember also that the driver behind trading a long straddle is a view upon volatility, a view that the options are cheap, rather than a directional view upon the underlying. We are unsure about underlying direction; that is why we are buying both a call and a put. Given the above, it is not surprising that the delta of a straddle such

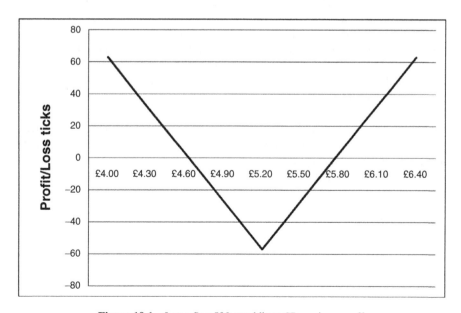

Figure 19.1 Long Sep 520 straddle at 57; expiry payoff

as that in the above BP example is not particularly significant. In practice, it is at-the-money straddles that tend to be bought rather than those away from the money. This doesn't have to be the case, it just usually is. The delta of an exactly at-the-money straddle is zero. The long call leg has a delta of +50% which is precisely cancelled out by the −50% delta of the long put leg. Even when the straddle is not precisely at-the-money, the delta of one leg works in the opposite direction to the delta of the other leg. In the case of our long Sep BP 520 straddle, the delta of the long call leg is +52% and the delta of the long put leg is −48%. The net delta of the long straddle is therefore just +4%. Other things being equal, for every 10p that the underlying rises, the straddle will increase in value by about 0.5 of a tick (equivalent to £5). For every 20p that the underlying falls, the straddle will decrease in value by about 1 tick (equivalent to £10). Not particularly significant swings in profit or loss but remember that if the underlying moves significantly, gamma will begin to "kick in" and the delta of the straddle will start to grow (see Chapter 33). The long gamma of a long straddle is significant; hardly surprising since it comprise two long at-the-money options. The counterpart of this significant long gamma is equally significant time decay, which takes us neatly on to theta.

We know that, in terms of moneyness, it is *at*-the-money options that erode at the fastest rate. Given that a straddle will normally (though not necessarily) consist of two at-the-moneys, it is hardly surprising that it will be significantly affected by the passage of time. To quantify this impact, we need to consider the net theta of the straddle. In the case of our long Sep BP 520 straddle, the theta of both the long call leg and the long put leg is −0.55. The net theta of the long straddle is therefore −1.10, the sum of the two individual thetas. Other things being equal, the straddle will lose 1.1 ticks of value (equivalent to £11) per straddle for every day that passes. If the market remains unchanged over the forthcoming period, then this net theta will grow as expiry approaches. In practice, it will become harder and harder to hold the long straddle position if nothing happens. If nothing happens, the long straddle will "bleed" value as time passes.

Of course, we would only buy a straddle in the anticipation of increased volatility, another way of saying that we expect the underlying to move away from its current level. If this happens, then the net theta of the straddle will start to fall as the options move away from the money. If we are correct in our view and the underlying moves significantly away from its current level, then our concern over time erosion will be negated by the beneficial impact of delta and, possibly, increasing vega. All of which moves us neatly on to the impact of volatility upon a long straddle.

Remember that the driver behind trading a long straddle is a view upon volatility, a view that the options are cheap, rather than a directional view upon the underlying. Remember also that, in practice, long straddles tend to be close-to-the-money. As such, buying a long straddle will involve buying two options, often at- or close-to-the-money options. Such options have the highest vega since they have the most time value. We can therefore expect a long straddle to change significantly in price as market volatility changes. If we want to quantify these changes in value, then we need to consider the net vega of the long straddle. In the case of our long Sep BP 520 straddle, the vega of both the long call leg and the long put leg is 3.30. The net vega of the long straddle is therefore 6.60, the sum of the two individual vegas. Other things being equal, the straddle will gain 6.6 ticks of value (equivalent to £66) per straddle for every 1% that market volatility increases. We should not underestimate the potential impact of such changes. Under the right circumstances, the market volatility of equity and index options can increase by a huge amount, particularly intra-day. To give just one example of this (and there are many), on the first day of the stock market crash of 1987, the FTSE 100 Index fell by about 10%. Despite this 10% fall in the underlying, out-of-the-money FTSE calls were worth more at the end of the day than they had been worth at the beginning! The impact of volatility, specifically a huge rise in FTSE market volatility, was enormous.

Let's summarise the Greeks for a long straddle. Other things being equal:

- In practice, most long straddles are either at- or close-to-the-money. Such long straddles are close to delta neutral; a change in the underlying will have little impact upon the value of a long straddle.
- A rise in volatility will increase the value of a long straddle (long vega).
- The passage of time will erode the value of a long straddle (negative theta).

How should we choose the tenor and exact strikes of a long straddle? Remember, a long straddle is a volatility-driven trade, which is why long straddles tend to be close-to-the-money, to maximise the profitable impact of increasing volatility. That said, it is rare for speculators to buy straddles in practice because they tend to be expensive (buying two at-the-money options) and they tend to erode quickly (long two high theta at-the-money options). That is certainly not to say that speculators *never* buy straddles, just that they tend to be used only when market volatility is particularly low. In such circumstances, the risk of buying at-the-money options is reduced since less investment is being made than when volatility is at a higher level.

If straddles are not often bought in practice, which strategy *do* speculators tend to use when they want to be long options but do not have a directional view on the underlying? The answer is the long strangle, a less costly variation of the long straddle that we have just considered.

20
Long Strangles

What is a long strangle? Just like a long straddle, a long strangle consists of two legs, a long call and a long put. The difference is that whereas a long straddle consists of a put and a call with the same strike, a strangle consists of an out-of-the-money put and an out-of-the-money call. As with a long straddle, the options come from the same series and buying a strangle involves buying both of the options simultaneously.

For example, from the matrix of Sep BP option prices (Table 20.1, repeated from Table 16.1), buying the 460/580 strangle consists of two legs, buying the 460 put at 10 and simultaneously buying the 580 call at 7. The cost of the strangle is 17 ticks (equivalent to £170) per strangle, the sum of the 10 paid for the 460 put and the 7 paid for the 580 call. These 17 ticks represent the maximum loss on buying the strangle. If BP is between 460 (i.e. £4.60) and 580 (i.e. £5.80) on Sep expiry, then both the 580

Table 20.1 LIFFE Sep BP option prices and Greeks at close on 21 July 2008 (BP share price (LSE) = 522 (i.e. £5.22))

Calls					Puts			
Vega	Theta	Delta	Price	Strike Price	Price	Delta	Theta	Vega
1.30	−0.10	0.88	86	**440**	6	0.12	−0.10	1.30
1.70	−0.15	0.79	69	**460**	10	0.21	−0.15	1.70
2.25	−0.25	0.73	53	**480**	14	0.27	−0.25	2.25
2.80	−0.40	0.64	39	**500**	20	0.36	−0.40	2.80
3.30	−0.55	0.52	28	**520**	29	0.48	−0.55	3.30
2.75	−0.50	0.40	19	**540**	40	0.60	−0.50	2.75
2.20	−0.30	0.29	12	**560**	54	0.71	−0.30	2.20
1.65	−0.20	0.20	7	**580**	70	0.80	−0.20	1.65
1.20	−0.15	0.13	4	**600**	87	0.87	−0.15	1.20
0.85	−0.15	0.08	3	**620**	106	0.92	−0.15	0.85
0.55	−0.10	0.04	1	**640**	125	0.96	−0.10	0.55

calls and 460 puts will expire worthless. The maximum possible value of the strangle is unlimited to the upside and limited only by zero to the downside.

Note that the cost of the Sep 460/580 strangle is significantly less than the cost of the Sep 520 straddle. The strangle costs 17 against 57 for the straddle. In the case of the long straddle, this maximum loss is only realised if BP is at exactly 520 (i.e. £5.20) on Sep expiry. In the case of the cheaper long strangle, the maximum loss of 17 is realised if BP is *between* 460 (i.e. £4.60) and 580 (i.e. £5.80) on Sep expiry. Although the maximum loss on the strangle is much smaller than that on the straddle, the range of underlying within which that loss will be realised is much wider in the case of the strangle.

So, the risk/reward for buying the 460/580 strangle at 17 is a potential loss of 17 ticks (equivalent to £170) per strangle against unlimited potential profit, favourable "odds" of infinity to 1. Why would we buy this strangle? In short, for almost exactly the same reasons that we would buy a straddle.

Remember the two key factors when deciding upon option strategy are our view on the underlying and our view on volatility (are the options cheap or expensive?). If we are buying a strangle, then we are buying both a call and a put. So do we have a view on the underlying? Are we bullish or bearish? No! If we were bullish, we would be buying only calls and not puts. If we were bearish, we would be buying puts but not calls. If we don't have a view on the underlying, it follows that we *must* have a view on volatility. We must have a view on whether the options are cheap or expensive.

Thus, the motivation for choosing a long strangle is a view on volatility. Specifically, a view that market volatility is currently too low, that the options are currently underpriced. We know that we want to be long options, that is our starting point. Because we are neither bullish nor bearish, we need to buy both calls and puts. Our view is not that the market will rise or that it will fall but that it is likely to do either. We believe that the market will be volatile, that the market will move; we just don't know which way. Hence, just as when we buy a straddle, we "cover all the bases", we buy both out-of-the-money calls *and* out-of-the-money puts, we buy a strangle.

Let's reconsider our example of a long strangle in more detail. Buying the Sep 460/580 strangle involves two legs, buying the 460 put at 10 and buying the 580 call at 7. The cost of the strangle is therefore 17 ticks (equivalent to £170) per strangle, the sum of the two premiums. This is our maximum loss, a loss that we will realise if the underlying BP share price is between 460 (i.e. £4.60) and 580 (i.e. £5.80) on Sep expiry because both the 460 put and the 580 call will expire worthless in such circumstances.

Remember that the rationale for buying the strangle is a belief that the options are too cheap because market volatility is currently too low. We expect the underlying to become more volatile, we expect BP to move away from its current price of 522 (£5.22), but we aren't sure in which direction.

If the price of BP starts to rise, then the 580 call that we own should start to gain value. The 460 put will simultaneously start to lose value but can only fall in value to zero. If the price of BP rises towards infinity, the value of the 580 call will also rise towards infinity, giving us an infinite profit! Theoretically correct but not very real world. To use a less extreme example, if the share price of BP rises to 950 (£9.50) by Sep expiry, then the value of the 580 call that we own will rise to at least 370, the intrinsic value of the option. This will give us a profit of at least 353 ticks (equivalent to £3530) per strangle, the difference between the value of the strangle and the price originally paid for it.

If the price of BP starts to fall, then the 460 put that we own should start to gain value. The 580 call will simultaneously start to lose value but can only fall in value to zero. If the price of BP falls to zero, then the value of the 460 put will be 460, giving us a profit of 443 (equivalent to £4430) per strangle. Again mathematically correct but not very real world. To use a less extreme example, if the share price of BP falls to 400 (£4.00) by Sep expiry, then the value of the 460 put that we own will rise to at least 60, the intrinsic value of the option. This will give us a profit of at least 43 ticks (equivalent to £430) per strangle, the difference between the value of the strangle and the price originally paid for it.

The expiry breakeven points for the strangle are 17 above 580 (597 or £5.97) and 17 below 460 (443 or £4.43). If the BP share price is at exactly £5.97 on Sep expiry, then the Sep 580 call will be worth exactly 17 and the 460 put will expire worthless. The 460/580 strangle will be worth 17 which is the price that we originally paid for it.

If the BP share price is at exactly £4.43 on Sep expiry, then the Sep 460 put will be worth exactly 17 and the 580 call will expire worthless. The 460/580 strangle will again be worth 17 which is the price that we originally paid for it.

This information is depicted in the expiry payoff chart shown in Figure 20.1.

Note that profit and loss is shown on the vertical axis with the BP share price shown on the horizontal. As before, the line depicts the payoff of the strategy on expiry.

Thus far we have considered the payoff of the long strangle upon expiry. But what about the value of the strangle between the trade date and expiry? Consider the following exercise.

Exercise 20.1: Long Strangles

Consider the BP Sep 460/580 strangle. The prices and the Greeks of the strangle are highlighted in Table 20.2 (repeated from Table 16.1).

Other things being equal, what will the Sep 460/580 Strangle be worth:

1. In 6 days' time?
2. If the underlying BP share price falls by 30p?
3. If market volatility increases by 4%?
4. In 10 days' time if the underlying BP share price has fallen by 50p and volatility has risen by 5%?

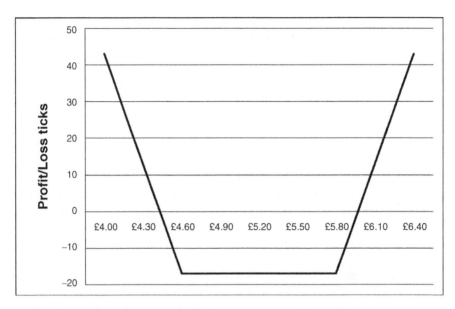

Figure 20.1   Long Sep 460/580 strangle at 17; expiry payoff

Exercise 20.1: Answers

1. The net theta of the Sep 460/580 strangle is −0.35, the sum of the theta of the 460 put (−0.15) and the theta of the 580 call (−0.20). Other things being equal, this means that the 460/580 strangle should erode by about 2 ticks over the next 6 days (6 days' decay at 0.35 per day), giving it a value at that time of about 15.

Table 20.2   LIFFE Sep BP option prices and Greeks at close on 21 July 2008 (BP share price (LSE) = 522 (i.e. £5.22))

Calls					Puts			
Vega	Theta	Delta	Price	Strike Price	Price	Delta	Theta	Vega
1.30	−0.10	0.88	86	**440**	6	0.12	−0.10	1.30
1.70	−0.15	0.79	69	**460**	**10**	**0.21**	**−0.15**	**1.70**
2.25	−0.25	0.73	53	**480**	14	0.27	−0.25	2.25
2.80	−0.40	0.64	39	**500**	20	0.36	−0.40	2.80
3.30	−0.55	0.52	28	**520**	29	0.48	−0.55	3.30
2.75	−0.50	0.40	19	**540**	40	0.60	−0.50	2.75
2.20	−0.30	0.29	12	**560**	54	0.71	−0.30	2.20
1.65	**−0.20**	**0.20**	7	**580**	70	0.80	−0.20	1.65
1.20	−0.15	0.13	4	**600**	87	0.87	−0.15	1.20
0.85	−0.15	0.08	3	**620**	106	0.92	−0.15	0.85
0.55	−0.10	0.04	1	**640**	125	0.96	−0.10	0.55

2. The net delta of the Sep 460/580 strangle is −1% (or −0.01), the sum of the −21% delta of the 460 put and the +20% delta of the 580 call. If the underlying BP share price falls by 30p, the 460/580 strangle should gain about 0.3 ticks of value, other things being equal, giving it a virtually unchanged value.
3. The net vega of the Sep 460/580 strangle is 3.35, the sum of the vega of the 460 put (1.70) and the vega of the 580 call (1.65). Other things being equal, if market volatility increases by 4%, then the 460/580 strangle should gain a little over 13 ticks of value (4 times vega of 3.35), giving it an expected value of about 30 ticks.
4. Ten days' time decay should reduce the value of the 460/580 strangle by about 3.5 ticks (10 times the net daily theta of −0.35). The underlying BP share price falling by 50p should increase the value of the strangle by about half of a tick (50p fall in the underlying times the net delta of −0.01). Market volatility rising by 5% should increase the value of the 460/580 strangle by about just under 17 ticks (5 times the net vega of 3.35). The net effect of the above changes upon the price of the 460/580 strangle should be to increase its value by about 14 ticks (vega increase of 17 plus delta increase of 0.5 less erosion of 3.5). The expected value of the strangle in these circumstances is therefore about 31 ticks.

Note that for illustrative purposes, the Greeks used in the above excercise are both exaggerated and rounded; Greeks in real life are likely to be less user friendly!

Let's summarise the Greeks for a long strangle which are, unsurprisingly, similar (though generally lesser in magnitude) than the Greeks of a long straddle. Other things being equal:

- In practice, long strangles tend to be close to delta neutral, so a change in the underlying will have little impact upon the value of a long strangle. Note that this doesn't have to be the case, since any combination of put and call may be chosen to make up a strangle (delta neutral).
- A rise in volatility will increase the value of a long strangle (long vega).
- The passage of time will erode the value of a long strangle (negative theta).

How should we choose the tenor and exact strikes of a long strangle? The answer to this question depends partly upon the main reasoning behind the trade. Are we looking to profit from market volatility spiking and our options increasing in value, or are we looking to trade our gamma, to profit from the market moving around? In practice, these two considerations are likely to be related but it is still often the case that either vega or gamma is the prime consideration.

If the trade is largely vega driven, then it makes sense to choose options that will increase significantly in value as volatility spikes, options with significant vega. Other things being equal, longer-dated options have greater vega than shorter-dated options. Of course, longer-dated options are also more expensive than comparable shorter-dated options. This means that they offer less potential for leverage, less gearing than shorter-dated options but, as ever in trading, there are pros and cons to be weighed.

If the trade is largely gamma driven, then it makes sense to choose options whose delta will change significantly as the underlying moves; options with significant gamma. Other things being equal, shorter-dated options have greater gamma than comparable longer-dated options. Since shorter-dated options are also cheaper than comparable longer-dated options, they also offer greater potential for gearing but they erode faster than comparable longer-dated options. As a rough rule-of-thumb, longer-dated options may be appropriate if we are looking to profit from an increase in market volatility and shorter-dated options may be more appropriate if we are looking to trade our long gamma. However, the appropriate choice of options in any specific situation will depend upon the exact prices and circumstances at the time.

Long straddles and long strangles are similar types of strategy. Both focus upon volatility rather than direction, both involve buying both calls and puts. In practice, straddles are unlikely to be bought because they are likely to be prohibitively expensive and to decay at an alarming rate. In reality, strangles are more likely to be bought than straddles because they are cheaper and suffer less from time decay. Broadly speaking, buying strangles is a less "punchy" trade than buying straddles.

Having looked at both straddles and strangles from a long perspective, let's now consider them from a short perspective; short straddles and short strangles.

21
Short Straddles

In an earlier chapter on the uses of options, the point was made that, due to their multifaceted nature, options give us more ways in which to trade than futures or physical. For example, suppose we believe that the underlying is going to stay exactly where it is for the next month or so. Can we use futures or physical to exploit this view? No, but we can use options to benefit enormously from such a scenario. Specifically, we can use short straddles or strangles.

What is a short straddle? A short straddle consists of two legs, a short call and a short put with the same strike and from the same series. Selling a straddle involves selling both options simultaneously. In practice, it tends to be at-the-money or close-to-the-money straddles that are sold, though this need not necessarily be the case. We will focus initially upon selling at-the-money straddles, as in the following example, before briefly considering how and why we might sell straddles away from the money.

From the matrix of Sep BP option prices (Table 21.1, repeated from Table 16.1), selling the 520 straddle consists of two legs, selling the 520 call at 28 and simultaneously selling the 520 put at 29. The price received for the straddle is 57 ticks (equivalent to £570) per straddle sold, the sum of the 28 received for the 520 call and the 29 received for the 520 put. These 57 ticks represent the maximum profit on selling the straddle. If BP is at exactly 520 (i.e. £5.20) on Sep expiry, then both the 520 calls and 520 puts will expire worthless. The maximum possible value of the straddle is unlimited to the upside and limited only by zero to the downside.

So, the risk/reward for selling the 520 straddle at 57 is potential profit of 57 ticks (equivalent to £570) per straddle against unlimited potential loss, unfavourable "odds" of infinity to 1. Why would we sell this straddle?

We know that the two key factors when deciding upon option strategy are our view on the underlying and our view on volatility (are the options cheap or expensive?). If we are selling a straddle, we are selling both a call and a put. Do we have a view on the underlying then? Are we bullish or bearish? No! If we wanted to sell options and were bullish on the underlying, we would be selling puts and not calls. And if we wanted to sell options and were bearish on the underlying, we would be selling calls

Table 21.1 LIFFE Sep BP option prices and Greeks at close on 21 July 2008 (BP share price (LSE) = 522 (i.e. £5.22))

Calls					Puts			
Vega	Theta	Delta	Price	Strike Price	Price	Delta	Theta	Vega
1.30	−0.10	0.88	86	**440**	6	0.12	−0.10	1.30
1.70	−0.15	0.79	69	**460**	10	0.21	−0.15	1.70
2.25	−0.25	0.73	53	**480**	14	0.27	−0.25	2.25
2.80	−0.40	0.64	39	**500**	20	0.36	−0.40	2.80
3.30	**−0.55**	**0.52**	**28**	**520**	**29**	**0.48**	**−0.55**	**3.30**
2.75	−0.50	0.40	19	**540**	40	0.60	−0.50	2.75
2.20	−0.30	0.29	12	**560**	54	0.71	−0.30	2.20
1.65	−0.20	0.20	7	**580**	70	0.80	−0.20	1.65
1.20	−0.15	0.13	4	**600**	87	0.87	−0.15	1.20
0.85	−0.15	0.08	3	**620**	106	0.92	−0.15	0.85
0.55	−0.10	0.04	1	**640**	125	0.96	−0.10	0.55

and not puts. Since we don't have a view on the underlying, it therefore follows that we *must* have a view on volatility. We must have a view on whether the options are cheap or expensive.

Thus, the driver behind a short straddle is a view on volatility. Specifically, a view that market volatility is currently too high, that the options are currently overpriced compared to our view on the market (that it is going to stagnate!). We know that we want to be short options, that is our starting point. Because we are neither bullish nor bearish, we need to sell both calls and puts. Our view is not that the market will rise or that it will fall but that it is unlikely to do either. We believe that the market will be calm, that the market will stay where it is. Hence we sell both at-the-money calls and puts, we sell an at-the-money straddle.

Let's reconsider our example of a short straddle in more detail. Selling the Sep 520 straddle involves two legs, selling the 520 call at 28 and selling the 520 put at 29. The price received is therefore 57 ticks (equivalent to £570) per straddle, the sum of the two premiums. This is our maximum profit, the profit that we will realise if the underlying BP share price is at exactly 520 (£5.20) on Sep expiry because both the 520 call and the 520 put will expire worthless.

Remember that the rationale for selling the straddle is a belief that the options are too expensive because market volatility is currently too high. We expect the underlying to become or remain calm, we expect BP to stay around its current price of 522 (i.e. £5.22). But what if we are wrong? What if BP *does* move?

If the price of BP starts to rise, then the 520 call that we have sold will start to gain value. The 520 put will simultaneously start to lose value but can only fall in value to zero. If the price of BP rises towards infinity, the value of the 520 call will also rise towards infinity, giving us an infinite loss! Theoretically correct but not very real world. To use a less extreme example, if the share price of BP rises to 850 (£8.50) by Sep expiry, then the value of the 520 call that we have sold will rise to at least

330, the intrinsic value of the option. This will give us a loss of at least 273 ticks (equivalent to £2730) per straddle, the difference between the value of the straddle and the price for which we originally sold it.

If the price of BP starts to fall, then the 520 put that we have sold will start to gain value. The 520 call will simultaneously start to lose value but can only fall in value to zero. If the price of BP falls to zero, then the value of the 520 put will be 520, giving us a loss of 463 (equivalent to £4630) per straddle sold. Again, mathematically correct but not very real world. To use a less extreme example, if the share price of BP falls to 450 (£4.50) by Sep expiry, then the value of the 520 put that we own will rise to at least 70, the intrinsic value of the option. This will give us a loss of at least 13 ticks (equivalent to £130) per straddle sold, the difference between the value of the straddle and the price for which we originally sold it.

The expiry breakeven points for the straddle are 57 above 520 (577 or £5.77) and 57 below 520 (463 or £4.63). If the BP share price is at exactly £5.77 on Sep expiry, then the Sep 520 call will be worth exactly 57 and the 520 put will expire worthless. The 520 straddle will be worth 57 which is the price for which we originally sold it.

If the BP share price is at exactly £4.63 on Sep expiry, then the Sep 520 put will be worth exactly 57 and the 520 call will expire worthless. The 520 straddle will again be worth 57 which is the price for which we originally sold it.

The above information is depicted in the expiry payoff chart shown in Figure 21.1.

Note that profit and loss is shown on the vertical axis with the BP share price shown on the horizontal. As before, the line depicts the payoff of the strategy on expiry.

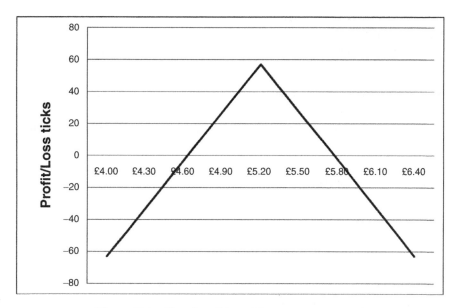

Figure 21.1 Short Sep 520 straddle at 57; expiry payoff

Table 21.2 LIFFE Sep BP option prices and Greeks at close on 21 July 2008 (BP share price (LSE) = 522 (i.e. £5.22))

Calls					Puts			
Vega	Theta	Delta	Price	Strike Price	Price	Delta	Theta	Vega
1.30	−0.10	0.88	86	**440**	6	0.12	−0.10	1.30
1.70	−0.15	0.79	69	**460**	10	0.21	−0.15	1.70
2.25	−0.25	0.73	53	**480**	14	0.27	−0.25	2.25
2.80	−0.40	0.64	39	**500**	20	0.36	−0.40	2.80
3.30	**−0.55**	**0.52**	**28**	**520**	**29**	**0.48**	**−0.55**	**3.30**
2.75	−0.50	0.40	19	**540**	40	0.60	−0.50	2.75
2.20	−0.30	0.29	12	**560**	54	0.71	−0.30	2.20
1.65	−0.20	0.20	7	**580**	70	0.80	−0.20	1.65
1.20	−0.15	0.13	4	**600**	87	0.87	−0.15	1.20
0.85	−0.15	0.08	3	**620**	106	0.92	−0.15	0.85
0.55	−0.10	0.04	1	**640**	125	0.96	−0.10	0.55

Thus far we have considered the payoff of the short straddle upon expiry. But what about the value of the straddle between the trade date and expiry? To understand how a short straddle will be affected by the underlying, time and volatility, we need to consider the Greeks. Consider the following exercise.

Exercise 21.1: Short Straddles

Consider the BP Sep 520 straddle. The prices and the Greeks of the straddle are highlighted in Table 21.2 (repeated from Table 16.1).

Other things being equal, what will the Sep 520 straddle be worth:

1. In 10 days' time?
2. If the underlying BP share price rises by 12p?
3. If market volatility falls by 3%?
4. In 10 days' time if the underlying BP share price has risen by 12p and volatility has fallen by 3%?

Exercise 21.1: Answers

1. The net theta of the Sep 520 straddle is −1.10, the sum of the theta of the 520 put (−0.55) and the theta of the 520 call (−0.55). Other things being equal, this means that the 520 straddle should erode by about 11 ticks over the next 10 days (10 days' decay at 1.10 per day), giving it a value in such circumstances of about 46.
2. The driver behind selling a straddle is a view on volatility, a view that future volatility does not justify the current option premiums, rather than a directional view on the underlying. Given this, it is not surprising that the delta of a short straddle such as the Sep 520 straddle is not particularly significant. The net delta

of the Sep 520 straddle is +4% (or +0.04), the sum of the −48% delta of the 520 put and the +52% delta of the 520 call. If the underlying BP share price rises by 12p, the 520 straddle should gain about 0.5 of a tick of value, other things being equal, giving it a virtually unchanged value.

3. The net vega of the Sep 520 straddle is 6.60, the sum of the vega of the 520 put (3.30) and the vega of the 520 call (3.30). If market volatility falls by 3%, the 520 straddle should lose about 20 ticks of value (3 times net vega of 6.60), other things being equal, giving it an expected value of about 37 ticks.

4. Ten days' time decay should reduce the value of the 520 straddle by about 11 ticks (10 times the net daily theta of −1.10). The underlying BP share price rising by 12p should increase the value of the straddle by about half of a tick (12p rise in the underlying times the net delta of +0.04). Market volatility falling by 3% should reduce the value of the 520 straddle by about 20 ticks (3 times the net vega of 6.60). The net effect of the above changes upon the price of the 520 straddle should be to reduce its value by about 30 ticks (vega decrease of 20 plus delta increase of 0.5 less erosion of 11). The expected value of the straddle in these circumstances would therefore be about 27 ticks.

Note that for illustrative purposes, the Greeks used in the above excercise are both exaggerated and rounded; Greeks in real life are likely to be less user friendly!

Let's summarise the Greeks for a short straddle. Other things being equal:

- In practice, most short straddles are either at-the-money or close-to-the-money. Such short straddles are close to delta neutral; a relatively small change in the underlying will have little impact upon the value of a short straddle although a large move in the underlying will become increasingly significant as gamma "kicks in" (delta neutral, short gamma).
- A fall in volatility will reduce the value of a short straddle and is therefore beneficial (short vega).
- The passage of time will erode the value of a short straddle and is therefore beneficial (positive theta).

Selling straddles allows us to exploit a view that the underlying will not move significantly, that the underlying will remain roughly where it is at present. We can sell both calls and puts and collect the premiums as the value of the options erodes. So far so good. The problem is when it goes wrong. Specifically, the problem with selling naked straddles is the problem with selling any options naked; significant and possibly unlimited risk. When we sell a naked straddle (i.e. with nothing against it) we have unlimited risk to the upside and significant risk to the downside (limited only by zero). Subjectively, this is not acceptable. Even if we sell a straddle for what we perceive to be a good price, taking on unlimited risk is surely a bad idea. Does this mean that we cannot sell straddles? No! If the options are unjustifiably expensive, then it is surely logical to sell them but there are "good" ways and "bad" ways of doing this, as the following chapter explains.

22
The Iron Butterfly

No one should be intimidated by the colourful names of option strategies such as the "iron 'fly". Traders have, over the years, given names to various popular strategies, the names often relating to the shape of the expiry payoff graphs of the strategies. Hence, names such as "butterfly" and "condor". These strategies also have "bodies" and "wings", another reason for the choice of names.

When selling options in practice, it is likely that the primary driver behind the trade will be the option prices themselves and/or a view that the market will become calmer. Specifically, our starting point is likely to be a view that options are too expensive because we believe that market volatility is currently unjustifiably high. As a result, we know that we want to be short of options. Our exact choice of *which* options to short will depend upon our view on the underlying market. Let's consider an example of how the decision-making process might work.

We are speculators in BP options. We believe that all BP options are currently overpriced. As ever, this view may be intuitive, a result of familiarity with BP option prices or the result of a more technical approach involving the study of implied "vols". Either way, our starting point is a view that BP options are currently too expensive. We therefore want to sell them. We want to sell BP options but which ones? This is the point at which our underlying view comes into play.

Simply, if we are bearish (or at the very least not bullish), we could sell calls. If we are right in our bearish views on both the underlying and volatility, then we will profit from both a fall in the underlying and a fall in volatility. Both dimensions of our view will work for us. If we are bullish (or at the very least not bearish), we could sell puts. If we are right in our bullish view on the underlying and bearish view on volatility, then we will profit from both a rise in the underlying and a fall in volatility. Both dimensions of our view will again work for us. And if we are neither bullish nor bearish, we could sell both calls and puts. If we are right in our view that the underlying will remain unchanged and in our bearish view on volatility, then both dimensions of our view will again work for us.

In simple terms, we match our choice of trade to our views on underlying direction and volatility. If we think that the underlying will remain at its current level, if we think that the options are currently overpriced, then we could sell a straddle. The problem is that selling naked straddles equates to unlimited risk (literally unlimited to the upside in the case of the short call leg, limited only by zero to the downside in the case of the short put leg). Selling straddles naked is unacceptable not just because of the unlimited risk that it conveys but also because *there are better choices available*. Broadly speaking, there are "good" ways and "bad" ways of selling straddles. Specifically, if we believe that options are too expensive and we expect the underlying not to change, then we should sell iron butterflies rather than outright straddles. What is an iron butterfly?

An iron butterfly is a short straddle protected by a long strangle. For this reason, iron 'flies are sometimes known as "straddle/strangles". The short straddle element of the strategy is designed to exploit a view that options are overpriced while the cheaper long strangle element of the strategy protects against unlimited risk. Consider the following example using the BP option prices shown in Table 22.1 (repeated from Table 16.1).

As before, we are speculators in BP options. We currently have no positions in BP. Our view is that Sep BP options are currently too expensive because Sep market volatility is currently too high. We therefore want to be short of Sep BP options. Our view on the underlying is that the share price of BP is likely to stay where it is between now and Sep expiry. As a result of these views, we consider selling the Sep 520 straddle naked but are not prepared to accept the unlimited risk that such a strategy involves. As a result, we sell the 520 straddle and protect it by buying the 500/540 strangle against it. We have sold an iron butterfly.

Selling the Sep 520 straddle brings in a credit of 57 ticks (equivalent to £570) per straddle sold. Buying the Sep 500/540 strangle costs 39 ticks (equivalent to

Table 22.1 LIFFE Sep BP option prices and Greeks at close on 21 July 2008 (BP share price (LSE) = 522 (i.e. £5.22))

Calls					Puts			
Vega	Theta	Delta	Price	Strike Price	Price	Delta	Theta	Vega
1.30	−0.10	0.88	86	**440**	6	0.12	−0.10	1.30
1.70	−0.15	0.79	69	**460**	10	0.21	−0.15	1.70
2.25	−0.25	0.73	53	**480**	14	0.27	−0.25	2.25
2.80	−0.40	0.64	39	**500**	20	**0.36**	**−0.40**	**2.80**
3.30	**−0.55**	**0.52**	**28**	520	29	0.48	−0.55	**3.30**
2.75	**−0.50**	**0.40**	**19**	540	40	0.60	−0.50	2.75
2.20	−0.30	0.29	12	**560**	54	0.71	−0.30	2.20
1.65	−0.20	0.20	7	**580**	70	0.80	−0.20	1.65
1.20	−0.15	0.13	4	**600**	87	0.87	−0.15	1.20
0.85	−0.15	0.08	3	**620**	106	0.92	−0.15	0.85
0.55	−0.10	0.04	1	**640**	125	0.96	−0.10	0.55

£390) per strangle purchased. The net credit for the Sep 500/520/540 iron 'fly is therefore 18 ticks (equivalent to £180) per iron 'fly (net credit of 57 received for the short straddle less 39 paid for the long strangle). Remember our rationale for selling the 500/520/540 iron 'fly is an expectation that the underlying BP share price will remain at or around 520 (i.e. £5.20) until Sep expiry. If we are right and BP is at exactly 520 on Sep expiry, then the short 520 straddle and the long 500/540 straddle will both expire worthless. None of the options making up the strategy will have any value. We will simply collect the 18 tick credit (equivalent to £180) for every iron 'fly sold. This is our maximum profit. What about if we are wrong in our view?

The maximum possible value of the Sep 500/520/540 iron 'fly is 20.

If BP is at exactly 540 (i.e. £5.40) on Sep expiry, then the 520 calls that we have sold will be worth exactly 20 and all of the other options in the strategy (long 540 call, short 520 put, long 500 put) will be worthless. If BP is above 540 (i.e. £5.40) on Sep expiry, then the 520 calls that we have sold will be worth exactly 20 more than the 540 calls that we have bought and the other options in the strategy (short 520 put, long 500 put) will be worthless. To the upside, then, the maximum possible value of the iron 'fly is 20.

If BP is at exactly 500 (i.e. £5.00) on Sep expiry, then the 520 puts that we have sold will be worth exactly 20 and all of the other options in the strategy (long 500 put, short 520 call, long 540 call) will be worthless. If BP is below 500 (i.e. £5.00) on Sep expiry, then the 520 puts that we have sold will be worth exactly 20 more than the 500 puts that we have bought and the other options in the strategy (short 520 call, long 540 call) will be worthless. To the downside then, the maximum possible value of the iron 'fly is also 20.

The maximum possible value of the Sep 500/520/540 iron 'fly in any scenario is 20. Since we sold it for 18, our maximum possible loss is 2, the difference between the maximum possible value of 20 and the price of 18 for which it was sold.

To summarise, if we sell the Sep 500/520/540 iron 'fly at 18, we can make 18 and lose 2, favourable "odds" of 9 to 1 on BP being at exactly 520 (i.e. £5.20) on Sep expiry. Our expiry breakeven points are 502 (£5.02) to the downside and 538 (£5.38) to the upside. If BP is at exactly 502 (i.e. £5.02) on Sep expiry, then the iron 'fly will be worth 18 which is the price for which we sold it. If BP is at exactly 538 on Sep expiry, then the iron 'fly will again be worth 18 which is the price for which we sold it. Consider the expiry payoff chart for selling the Sep 500/520/540 iron 'fly at 18 shown in Figure 22.1.

Note that profit and loss is shown on the vertical axis with the BP share price shown on the horizontal. As before, the line depicts the payoff of the strategy on expiry.

As previously alluded to, someone way back in the mists of trading time thought that the payoff chart in Figure 22.1 looked like a butterfly. Thus a strategy was christened. We shall address the "iron" part of the name a little later when we compare an "iron" 'fly to a regular butterfly.

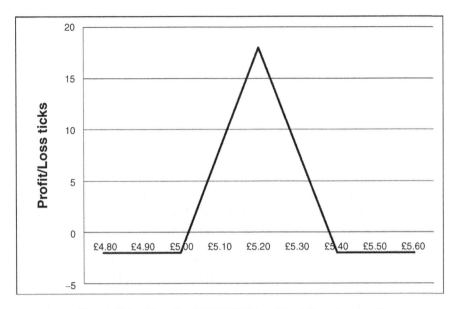

Figure 22.1   Short Sep 500/520/540 iron 'fly at 2; expiry payoff

As with all option strategies, a short iron butterfly does not have to be held to expiry. If, as we hope and expect, the underlying BP share price remains unchanged for the next few weeks, we would expect the value of the iron 'fly that we have sold to reduce, making us a profit. We may decide to take that profit or to run the strategy further towards expiry in the hope that BP stays around the same level. If we want to quantify how much we can expect to make if BP stays around the same level over the coming days and weeks, we simply need to apply the Greeks. We can use the net theta of the trade (-0.20 of a tick per day) to estimate the impact of time and we can use the net vega of the trade (-1.05 per 1%) to estimate the impact of volatility.

SHORT STRADDLES VERSUS SHORT IRON BUTTERFLIES

As speculators in BP options, we believe that the BP share price will stay at or around its current price up to Sep expiry. We consider current Sep BP options to be unjustifiably expensive. Given these views, we have two basic choices of strategy. We can sell the Sep 520 straddle outright or we can sell the Sep 500/520/540 iron 'fly. Given the option prices in Table 22.2 (repeated from Table 16.1), which is the "better" choice?

If we sell the Sep 520 straddle at 57, we can make 57 and lose an unlimited amount, "odds" of infinity to 1 against. If we sell the Sep 500/520/540 iron 'fly at 18, we can make 18 and lose only 2, "odds" of 9 to 1 in our favour.

Table 22.2 LIFFE Sep BP option prices and Greeks at close on 21 July 2008 (BP share price (LSE) = 522 (i.e. £5.22))

Calls					Puts			
Vega	Theta	Delta	Price	Strike Price	Price	Delta	Theta	Vega
1.30	−0.10	0.88	86	**440**	6	0.12	−0.10	1.30
1.70	−0.15	0.79	69	**460**	10	0.21	−0.15	1.70
2.25	−0.25	0.73	53	**480**	14	0.27	−0.25	2.25
2.80	−0.40	0.64	39	**500**	**20**	**0.36**	**−0.40**	**2.80**
3.30	**−0.55**	**0.52**	**28**	520	29	**0.48**	**−0.55**	**3.30**
2.75	**−0.50**	**0.40**	**19**	540	40	0.60	−0.50	2.75
2.20	−0.30	0.29	12	**560**	54	0.71	−0.30	2.20
1.65	−0.20	0.20	7	**580**	70	0.80	−0.20	1.65
1.20	−0.15	0.13	4	**600**	87	0.87	−0.15	1.20
0.85	−0.15	0.08	3	**620**	106	0.92	−0.15	0.85
0.55	−0.10	0.04	1	**640**	125	0.96	−0.10	0.55

In relative terms, there is no comparison between the risk/reward profiles of the two trades. The iron 'fly is surely a better "bet" than the naked straddle. In the event that we are wrong, in the event that the price of BP moves significantly away from its current level, we have unlimited potential losses on the naked short straddle and minimal potential losses (2 ticks or £20 per iron 'fly) on the short iron 'fly.

In absolute terms, the short straddle can make us 57 ticks (equivalent to £570) per straddle sold while the short iron 'fly can only make 18 ticks (equivalent to £180) per iron 'fly sold. Of course, this may be addressed by simply trading the iron 'fly in greater size. If we want a similar potential payoff, then we need to trade about three times as many iron 'flies as naked straddles. Selling one Sep 520 straddle at 57 ticks gives us a maximum potential profit of 57 ticks (equivalent to £570) and unlimited potential losses. Selling three Sep 500/520/540 iron 'flies at 18 gives us a maximum potential profit of 54 ticks (equivalent to £540) and a potential loss of 6 ticks (equivalent to £60).

Now which is "better"; +57 against minus infinity or +54 against minus 6? I rest my case. Of course, there may be greater trading costs associated with the iron 'fly. It has four legs and we may need to trade it in three times the size of the straddle to achieve a similar absolute return. But transaction costs are surely a small price to pay for limiting risk and being able to sleep at night.

This is why, *in my opinion*, selling naked straddles is unacceptable. Not only do naked short straddles convey significant (and possibly unlimited) risk but there are "better" alternatives available.

23
Short Strangles

A short strangle is similar to a short straddle. What is a short strangle? A short strangle consists of two legs, a short out-of-the-money call and a short out-of-the-money put from the same series. Selling a strangle involves selling both options simultaneously.

From the matrix of Sep BP option prices (Table 23.1, repeated from Table 16.1), selling the 460/580 strangle consists of two legs, selling the 460 put at 10 and simultaneously selling the 580 call at 7. The price received for the strangle is 17 ticks (equivalent to £170) per strangle sold, the sum of the 10 received for the 460 put and the 7 received for the 580 call. These 17 ticks represent the maximum profit on selling the strangle. If BP is between 460 and 580 (i.e. £4.60 and £5.80) on Sep expiry, then both the 460 puts and 580 calls will expire worthless. The maximum possible value of the strangle is unlimited to the upside and limited only by zero to the downside. The "odds" on selling the Sep 460/580 strangle at 17 are therefore infinity to 1 against.

Table 23.1 LIFFE Sep BP option prices and Greeks at close on 21 July 2008 (BP share price (LSE) = 522 (i.e. £5.22))

Calls					Puts			
Vega	Theta	Delta	Price	Strike Price	Price	Delta	Theta	Vega
1.30	−0.10	0.88	86	**440**	6	0.12	−0.10	1.30
1.70	−0.15	0.79	69	**460**	**10**	**0.21**	**−0.15**	**1.70**
2.25	−0.25	0.73	53	**480**	14	0.27	−0.25	2.25
2.80	−0.40	0.64	39	**500**	20	0.36	−0.40	2.80
3.30	−0.55	0.52	28	**520**	29	0.48	−0.55	3.30
2.75	−0.50	0.40	19	**540**	40	0.60	−0.50	2.75
2.20	−0.30	0.29	12	**560**	54	0.71	−0.30	2.20
1.65	**−0.20**	**0.20**	**7**	**580**	70	0.80	−0.20	1.65
1.20	−0.15	0.13	4	**600**	87	0.87	−0.15	1.20
0.85	−0.15	0.08	3	**620**	106	0.92	−0.15	0.85
0.55	−0.10	0.04	1	**640**	125	0.96	−0.10	0.55

Selling strangles is popular in practice. There are plenty of market participants who say things such as "BP *can't* go beneath £4.60" and "there's *no way* BP gets above £5.80 in the next couple of months". It is these sorts of dogmatic views that lead people to sell strangles. They hold strong views about what the market "can" or "cannot" do. They are wrong. The market can do anything. While, in the real world, it may be unlikely that the price of BP exceeds £5.80 or falls below £4.60 in the short term, it is not impossible. The low chances of BP exceeding £5.80 or falling below £4.60 in the near term are reflected in the commensurately low prices of the £5.80 calls and £4.60 puts. Remember, probability plays a key role in the option pricing process. Selling naked strangles (i.e. with nothing against them) is dangerous; it conveys unlimited risk. All of which takes us neatly onto the beautifully named "iron condor".

24
The Iron Condor

A variation on the iron butterfly is the "iron condor". We have already seen that an iron 'fly comprises a straddle traded against a strangle. An iron condor comprises a narrow strangle traded against a wider strangle. The rationale behind an iron condor is identical to that behind the iron 'fly. We want to sell options because we think that they are overpriced and we think that the underlying will stay around its current level. As a result, we decide to sell strangles. The problem is that selling naked strangles equates to unlimited risk. We are unwilling to accept this so we buy a wider strangle around our short strangle to protect it. The result is that potential losses are limited, albeit at the cost of lower potential profit. Consider an example of a short iron condor using the Sep BP option prices shown in Table 24.1 (repeated from Table 16.1).

Our view is that market volatility is currently too high and, as a result, the Sep options are overpriced. Our view on the underlying is that BP will stay between about

Table 24.1 LIFFE Sep BP option prices and Greeks at close on 21 July 2008 (BP share price (LSE) = 522 (i.e. £5.22))

Calls					Puts			
Vega	Theta	Delta	Price	Strike Price	Price	Delta	Theta	Vega
1.30	−0.10	0.88	86	**440**	6	0.12	−0.10	1.30
1.70	−0.15	0.79	69	**460**	10	0.21	−0.15	1.70
2.25	−0.25	0.73	53	**480**	14	**0.27**	−**0.25**	**2.25**
2.80	−0.40	0.64	39	**500**	20	**0.36**	−**0.40**	**2.80**
3.30	−0.55	0.52	28	520	29	0.48	−0.55	3.30
2.75	−**0.50**	**0.40**	**19**	**540**	40	0.60	−0.50	2.75
2.20	−**0.30**	**0.29**	**12**	**560**	54	0.71	−0.30	2.20
1.65	−0.20	0.20	7	**580**	70	0.80	−0.20	1.65
1.20	−0.15	0.13	4	**600**	87	0.87	−0.15	1.20
0.85	−0.15	0.08	3	**620**	106	0.92	−0.15	0.85
0.55	−0.10	0.04	1	**640**	125	0.96	−0.10	0.55

500 (i.e. £5.00) and 540 (i.e. £5.40) between now and Sep expiry. As a result of these
views, we sell the Sep 500/540 strangle at 39 (i.e. we sell the 500 put at 20 and the
540 call at 19) and buy the wider Sep 480/560 strangle at 26 (i.e. we buy the 480 put
at 14 and the 560 call at 12) against it. Our net credit on the whole trade is 13 (we
receive 39 for selling the 500/540 strangle and pay out 26 for the 480/560 strangle)
per iron condor sold. Consider the trade in tabular form:

Call Position (Price)	Strike Price	Put Position (Price)
	480	+1 (14)
	500	−1 (20)
−1 (19)	**540**	
+1 (12)	**560**	

The short iron condor may be looked at in two ways. Thus far, we have considered
it as a narrow short strangle against a wider long strangle. But if we look at the above
table, we can see that another way of breaking it down would be as a short put spread
(specifically, short the 500/480 put spread at 6) in conjunction with a short call spread
(specifically, short the 540/560 call spread at 7). We take in a credit of 6 ticks for the
put spread and a credit of 7 ticks for the call spread, giving a total credit of 13 ticks
(equivalent to £130) per iron condor sold. This 13 tick credit is our maximum profit
which we will realise if, as we expect, BP is between 500 and 540 (i.e. £5.00 and
£5.40) on Sep expiry. What will happen if we are wrong in our view and BP moves
outside this range?

Consider first what will happen if BP breaks out of the anticipated range to the
downside. The most that the short Sep 500/480 put spread can ever be worth is 20
and then only if BP is at or below 480 (i.e. £4.80) on Sep expiry. And if BP is at or
below 480 (i.e. £4.80) on Sep expiry, then the Sep 540/560 call spread that we have
sold is worthless.

Now consider what will happen if BP breaks out of the anticipated range to the
upside. The most that the short 540/560 call spread can ever be worth is 20 and
then only if BP is at or above 560 (i.e. £5.60) on expiry. And if BP is at or above
560 (i.e. £5.60) on Sep expiry, then the Sep 480/500 put spread that we have sold is
worthless.

The most that the whole strategy can ever be worth is 20 and we have sold it for
13. We can therefore make 13 and lose 7, "odds" of roughly 2 to 1 in our favour that
BP is between £5.00 and £5.40 on Sep expiry. The above information, along with
the upside and downside expiry breakeven points, are depicted in the graph shown in
Figure 24.1.

Note that profit and loss is shown on the vertical axis with the BP share price shown
on the horizontal. As before, the line depicts the payoff of the strategy on expiry.

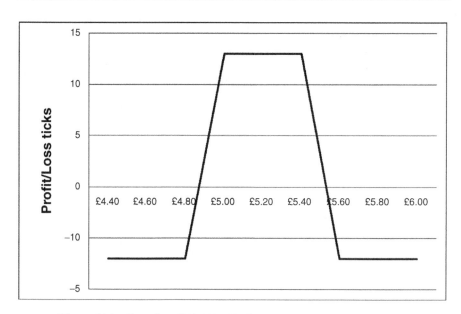

Figure 24.1 Short Sep 480/500/540/560 iron condor at 13; expiry payoff

As previously suggested, someone once thought that the payoff chart in Figure 24.1 resembled a condor. Thus another strategy was named. Condors are sometimes called "stretched butterflies", reflecting the fact that the maximum profit is achieved over a wider or "stretched" range than is the case with a butterfly.

As with short iron butterflies, a short iron condor does not have to be held to expiry. If, as we hope and expect, the underlying BP share price remains within a narrow trading range for the next few weeks, we would expect the value of the iron condor that we have sold to reduce, making us a profit. We could then decide to take that profit or run the strategy further towards expiry in the hope that BP remains range bound. If we want to quantify how much we can expect to make if BP remains range bound over the coming days and weeks, we simply need to apply the Greeks. We can use the net theta of the trade (-0.35 of a tick per day) to estimate the impact of time and we can use the net vega of the trade (-1.10 per 1%) to estimate the impact of volatility.

The following exercise seeks to reinforce the idea that selling spreads is preferable to selling outright naked options.

Exercise 24.1: Short Strangles versus Short Iron Condors

As speculators in BP options, we believe that the BP share price will stay in a range of about 460 to 520 (i.e. £4.60 to £5.20) up to Sep expiry. We consider current Sep BP

Table 24.2   LIFFE Sep BP option prices and Greeks at close on 21 July 2008 (BP share price (LSE) = 522 (i.e. £5.22))

Calls					Puts			
Vega	Theta	Delta	Price	Strike Price	Price	Delta	Theta	Vega
1.30	−0.10	0.88	86	**440**	**6**	**0.12**	**−0.10**	**1.30**
1.70	−0.15	0.79	69	**460**	**10**	**0.21**	**−0.15**	**1.70**
2.25	−0.25	0.73	53	**480**	14	0.27	−0.25	2.25
2.80	−0.40	0.64	39	**500**	20	0.36	−0.40	2.80
3.30	**−0.55**	**0.52**	**28**	**520**	29	0.48	−0.55	3.30
2.75	**−0.50**	**0.40**	**19**	**540**	40	0.60	−0.50	2.75
2.20	−0.30	0.29	12	**560**	54	0.71	−0.30	2.20
1.65	−0.20	0.20	7	**580**	70	0.80	−0.20	1.65
1.20	−0.15	0.13	4	**600**	87	0.87	−0.15	1.20
0.85	−0.15	0.08	3	**620**	106	0.92	−0.15	0.85
0.55	−0.10	0.04	1	**640**	125	0.96	−0.10	0.55

options to be unjustifiably expensive. Given these views, we have two basic choices of strategy. We can:

(a) Sell the Sep 460/520 strangle outright
(b) Sell the Sep 440/460/520/540 iron condor

The option prices are shown in Table 24.2, repeated from Table 16.1.

1. Compare the expiry payoffs for the two trades.
2. If, in 10 days' time, BP is still trading at 522 and market volatility has fallen by 2%, how much do we expect to make or lose on each of the two strategies?
3. If, in 3 days' time, BP has risen in price to £5.38 and market volatility has spiked by 5%, how much do we expect to make or lose on each of the two strategies?

Exercise 24.1: Answers

1. Selling the Sep 460/520 strangle outright at 38 gives us a maximum profit of 38 ticks (equivalent to £380) per strangle sold and unlimited potential losses, "odds" against us of infinity to 1. Selling the Sep 440/460/520/540 iron condor at 13 gives us a maximum profit of 13 ticks (equivalent to £130) and a maximum loss of 7 ticks (equivalent to £70) per iron condor sold, "odds" of roughly 2 to 1 in our favour. We therefore need to trade the iron condor in about three times the size as the strangle to have roughly the same *absolute* potential profit on expiry.
2. We would expect the Sep 460/520 strangle to lose about 17 ticks of value, giving us a profit of £170 per strangle sold. This 17 tick loss of value breaks down into 7 ticks of time decay (0.70 of a tick positive theta per day for 10 days) and 10 ticks of vega (2 times vega of −5.00). We would expect the Sep 440/460/520/540 iron condor to lose about 3 ticks of value, giving us a profit of £30 per iron condor

sold. This 3 tick loss of value breaks down into 1 tick of time decay (0.10 of a tick positive theta per day for 10 days) and about 2 ticks of vega (2 times vega of −0.95).

3. We would expect the Sep 460/520 strangle to gain about 28 ticks of value, giving us a loss of £280 per strangle sold. This 28 tick loss breaks down into about 5 ticks of loss due to negative delta (underlying rise of 16 times net delta of −31%), 2 ticks of time decay in our favour (0.70 of a tick positive theta per day for 3 days) and 25 ticks of vega against us (5 times vega of −5.00). We would expect the Sep 440/460/520/540 iron condor to gain just under 5 ticks of value, giving us a loss of about £50 per iron condor sold. This 5 tick gain in value breaks down into about 0.5 of a tick of rise in value due to negative delta (underlying rise of 16 times net delta of −3%), 0.3 of a tick of time decay in our favour (0.10 of a tick positive theta per day for 3 days) and 4.75 ticks of vega against us (5 times vega of −0.95).

Note that for illustrative purposes, the Greeks used in the above excercise are both exaggerated and rounded; Greeks in real life are likely to be less user friendly!

To summarise the above comparison, we can see that selling the iron condor is "safer" than selling the strangle outright in that the iron condor limits potential downside. Specifically, selling the strangle outright offers a potential reward of 38 versus unlimited risk. Selling the iron condor offers a potential reward of 13 versus a potential risk of 7. Even allowing for the fact that trading is a largely subjective endeavour, selling the iron condor is surely the "better" choice. We can see that if we want to make the same absolute amount from selling iron condors as from selling outright strangles, then we need trade in bigger sizes; we should sell more iron condors than we would outright strangles. How much bigger depends upon the premiums being taken in. In the above example, it makes intuitive sense to sell roughly three times as many iron condors as outright strangles to get a similar absolute potential return.

In practice, the size in which we are allowed to trade is limited by the amount of money in our trading account and the amount of margin that we are subsequently able to provide. The amount of margin required to cover a particular position will relate to the risk associated with that position. Since the short iron condor is infinitely less risky than the outright short strangle (in the above example, risk of 7 against unlimited risk), it will require less margin than the short strangle. Given a finite amount in our trading account, we are therefore able to sell more iron condors than we can sell outright strangles.

SUMMARY OF CHAPTERS 15–18 AND 22–24

We know that the two key considerations when deciding upon option strategy are:

- Our view upon volatility; are the options relatively cheap or expensive?
- Our view on the underlying; up, down or sideways?

If we believe that options are currently overpriced because volatility is relatively high, then we know that we want to sell options. We want to sell calls if our view on the underlying is bearish, we want to sell puts if our view on the underlying is bullish and we want to sell both calls and puts if our view on the underlying is that it is going to stay where it is. The problem is the risk that such strategies convey. To address this problem, we buy further out-of-the-money, cheaper options to protect us against unlimited risk. We trade spreads. Specifically, if we want to reduce the risk of shorting options, we should consider adopting the following broad principles:

- Don't sell naked calls, sell call *spreads*
- Don't sell naked puts, sell put *spreads*
- Don't sell naked straddles, sell *iron butterflies*
- Don't sell naked strangles, sell *iron condors*

As a general rule, the wider the strategy, the wider apart the individual strikes, the more aggressive the strategy. The narrower the strategy, the closer together the individual strikes, the more conservative the strategy.

HEALTH WARNINGS!

Remember, all trading is largely subjective. The principles stated above are broad in nature. As ever, the choice of trade in a specific set of circumstances will depend upon the trader's exact views, desire for reward and appetite for risk.

Don't "lift a leg" of a spread. In other words, a spread is only a spread as long as both legs are in place. If we trade out of one of the strategy's legs, then it is no longer a spread but rather an outright trade with a completely different risk/reward profile to the original spread.

25
Calendar Spreads

The following four chapters will consider calendar spreads. These involve trading options with different expiry dates against one another, hence their alternative name of "time spreads". Just as call and put spreads are sometimes known as "vertical" spreads, calendars are sometimes referred to as "horizontal" spreads.

What is a calendar spread? A calendar spread involves two options with the *same strike* but *different expiry dates* traded against one another. We can trade both call calendars (a longer-dated call against a shorter-dated call) and put calendars (a longer-dated put against a shorter-dated put). Buying a calendar spread involves buying a more expensive, longer-dated option and selling a cheaper, shorter-dated option against it. Selling a calendar involves selling a longer-dated option and buying a shorter-dated option against it. This is the market convention.

Whatever we are doing with the longer-dated leg (i.e. buying or selling) is what we are doing with the calendar. If we are buying the longer-dated leg, we are buying the calendar, and vice versa. Note that this is the exact opposite of the market convention for quoting futures spreads. In the futures markets, whatever we are doing with the nearer-dated future is what we are doing with the spread. For example, if we are buying a Sep/Dec FTSE futures spread, we are buying Sep and selling Dec. For the sake of avoiding errors, it is worth spelling out to your broker exactly what you want to do with each leg of a calendar.

Calendar spreads offer us the following four choices:

- Long call calendar spread (long a longer-dated call vs short a shorter-dated call)
- Short call calendar spread (short a longer-dated call vs long a shorter-dated call)
- Long put calendar spread (long a longer-dated put vs short a shorter-dated put)
- Short put calendar spread (short a longer-dated put vs long a shorter-dated put)

We will consider a long call calendar in some detail before briefly considering short call calendars, long put calendars and short put calendars.

Table 25.1   LIFFE Sep and Dec FTSE 100 option prices as at close on 26 August 2008 (Sep FTSE 100 future = 5494, Dec FTSE 100 future = 5528)

Sep Calls	Strike	Sep Puts
221	5325	53
150	5425	82
93	5525	124
51	5625	181
Dec Calls	Strike	Dec Puts
384	5325	185
320	5425	220
262	5525	259
207	5625	303

We will use the matrix of LIFFE FTSE 100 derivatives prices shown in Table 25.1 for our examples. Note that the Sep and Dec futures closed at different prices on the day in question. There is a "spread" of 34 ticks between the two months. This inter-month futures spread, the Sep/Dec spread, can move around. It may widen or it may narrow and even move into "backwardation", whereby the longer-dated Dec futures price falls below the nearer-dated Sep futures price. However, due to cost-of-carry, we would normally expect the Dec future to trade at a higher price than Sep. In the real world, as one month rises, the other month tends to rise as well. One may rise more than the other or they may rise by exactly the same amount. There are no hard and fast rules and in theory the spread can widen to infinity in either direction. In practice, however, the different futures months do tend to move broadly together, except in unusual circumstances.

26
Long Call Calendars

A long call calendar involves buying a longer-dated call against selling a shorter-dated call. For example, from the matrix of Sep and Dec FTSE 100 option prices shown in Table 26.1 (repeated from Table 25.1), buying the Sep/Dec 5625 call spread consists of two legs, buying the Dec 5625 call at 207 ticks (equivalent to £2070) per contract and simultaneously selling the Sep 5625 call at 51 ticks (equivalent to £510) per contract. The cost of the calendar is therefore 156 ticks (equivalent to £1560) per calendar spread purchased, the difference between the 207 paid for the Dec call and the 51 received for the sale of the Sep call. Why would we do such a trade?

Remember the two main reasons that option spreads have evolved; to reduce the cost of owning options and/or to reduce the risk of shorting options. In the case of a long calendar, we are looking primarily to *reduce the cost* of owning options. We want to buy some out-of-the-money Dec calls but want to reduce the cost of the

Table 26.1 LIFFE Sep and Dec FTSE 100 option prices as at close on 26 August 2008 (Sep FTSE 100 future = 5494, Dec FTSE 100 future = 5528)

Sep Calls	Strike	Sep Puts
221	**5325**	53
150	**5425**	82
93	**5525**	124
51	**5625**	181

Dec Calls	Strike	Dec Puts
384	**5325**	185
320	**5425**	220
262	**5525**	259
207	**5625**	303

trade by selling some similarly out-of-the-money Sep calls at the same time. Not surprisingly, by reducing cost, we are simultaneously limiting profit potential.

What views on the underlying and volatility would lead us to choose such a trade? Intuitively, since we are spending money on out-of-the-money calls, we have a bullish view on the underlying. We are not aggressively bullish otherwise we would simply buy outright FTSE calls, thus giving ourselves unlimited upside potential. Since we are selling the Sep 5625 calls, it makes sense that this is our upside target between now and Sep expiry. Our view on the underlying is mildly bullish.

In actual fact, FTSE expiring at exactly 5625 in September is our ideal scenario. If, on Sep expiry, the FTSE 100 Index is at exactly 5625, the Sep 5625 calls that we have sold will expire worthless. The Dec 5625 calls that we have bought will still have 3 months to run and are will be *at*-the-money. They are likely to be worth around 200 to 250 ticks per contract (the current value of 3 month at-the-money calls), depending upon what has happened to market volatility. Since we originally paid 156 ticks for the calendar, we will have a healthy profit in such circumstances of around 70 ticks per calendar. So much for the ideal scenario. What about if we are wrong?

Remember the views behind our choice of buying the Sep/Dec 5625 call calendar? We believe that the underlying FTSE 100 Index will rise to around 5625 by Sep expiry. There are two ways in which this view may be significantly wrong.

First, the FTSE may fall between now and Sep expiry. If this happens, both our long Dec 5625 calls and our short Sep 5625 calls will lose value. Since they have a higher delta, the Dec 5625 calls will fall by more than the Sep 5625 calls. Our long call calendar will lose value. In the event of an extreme move to the downside, both the Sep and Dec 5625 calls will fall towards zero. In such circumstances, our worst case scenario is the loss of our initial investment, the 156 ticks that we have paid for the calendar.

The second way in which our view may be significantly wrong is if the FTSE rallies too sharply between now and Sep expiry. In the event of an extreme move to the upside, both the Sep and Dec 5625 calls will become deep in-the-money calls and their prices will move towards intrinsic value. Both options will move towards having zero time value. As with a large downward move, our worst case scenario is that we lose our initial investment, the 156 ticks that we originally paid for the calendar. One further complication in this scenario is that the underlying FTSE futures spread may change, either for or against us. As previously stated, the Sep/Dec futures spread can move infinitely in either direction. In practice, however, there are limits to how much the futures spread is likely to change. Nonetheless, it is important to be aware of the possibilities.

In summary, if we buy the Sep/Dec 5625 call calendar for 156, then our best case scenario is that the FTSE is at exactly 5625 on Sep expiry. In such circumstances, the Sep 5625 call that we are short will expire worthless and we will be long a "cheap" at-the-money (5625) Dec call. Our worst case scenario is an extreme move in either direction. At these extremes, (unless the Sep/Dec spread widens massively), we can only lose the price that we have paid for the calendar, our maximum loss is known.

Having looked at the limits of profit and loss, we now need to consider what will happen to our calendar spread under less extreme circumstances. As ever, to do this accurately, we need to consider the Greeks.

Before addressing the effects of the underlying, time and volatility upon the value of long calendar spreads, we need to consider the nature of calendar spreads in practice. In reality, the majority of calendar spreads traded tend to be *out*-of-the-money. That is to say, both the short-dated and long-dated legs are usually out-of-the-money. Of course, this is not a rule; calendar spreads don't have to be out-of-the-money, just as short outright calls don't have to be out-of-the-money, they just usually are.

First, let's consider the impact of changes in the underlying upon a long call calendar spread. Intuitively, since the trade is entered to exploit a bullish view, the calendar spread should increase in value as the underlying rises and vice versa. Other things being equal, it will perform well to the upside (excluding the extreme upside) and poorly to the downside. Broadly speaking, if we buy an out-of-the-money call calendar spread, we expect to profit if the underlying rises and lose if the underlying falls.

If we want to quantify the extent of these potential profits and losses, then we need to consider the net delta of the spread. Let's return to our example of a long call calendar spread, buying the Sep/Dec 5625 call spread at 156. Our long Sep/Dec 5625 call calendar consists of a long Dec 5625 call and a short Sep 5625 call, both of which are out-of-the-money. The Dec 5625 call will have a larger delta than the Sep 5625 call giving the Sep/Dec calendar a net long delta. If the Dec 5625 call has a delta of $+0.35$ and the Sep 5625 call has a delta of $+0.25$, then the net delta of the Sep/Dec 5625 call calendar is $+0.10$ (long a $+0.35$ delta call and short a $+0.25$ delta call).

If we buy the calendar spread for 156 and the FTSE instantly rallies by 20, then the value of the calendar spread should rise by around 2 ticks (making a profit of about £20) per spread, equivalent to about 10% (the net delta of the spread) of the 20 tick rise in the underlying FTSE 100 Index.

If the underlying FTSE falls by 10, then we expect the value of the calendar spread we have bought to fall by about 1 tick (making a loss of about £10) per spread, again equivalent to about 10% (the net delta of the spread) of the fall of 10 in the underlying FTSE 100 Index. By using the net delta of the spread in this way, we can estimate the likely effect of an instantaneous move in the underlying upon the value of the calendar spread. If the instant underlying move is particularly large, then we need to bear the effects of gamma in mind. This is particularly important in relation to calendar spreads. Remember that our long Sep/Dec 5625 call calendar consists of long a Dec 5625 call and short a Sep 5625 call. Gamma tends to be greater for shorter-dated options than for longer-dated options. The gamma of our long Dec 5625 call is likely to be smaller than the gamma of our short Sep 5625 call. Our long calendar spread is therefore likely to be net short gamma. A slow move upwards in the underlying is good but, as we have already seen, extreme upward moves in the underlying are bad.

How will time affect a long call calendar? Consider our example, long the Sep/Dec 5625 call calendar. Both legs, the long Dec 5625 call and the short Sep 5625 call are currently out-of-the-money. The passage of time will erode both legs of the spread in the same way but to different degrees.

Remember, shorter-dated options tend to erode at a faster rate than longer-dated options. Specifically, time will erode our short Sep 5625 call more quickly than it erodes our long Dec 5625 call. Right now, the net effect of the passage of time upon our long call calendar spread is to increase its value.

If we want to quantify this effect, we need to consider the net theta of the call spread. If, for example, the theta of the Sep 5625 call is −1.60 and the theta of the Dec 5625 call is −0.60, then the net theta of the Sep/Dec 5625 call calendar is −1.00, the difference between the two individual thetas. In lay terms this means that, other things being equal, our long Sep/Dec 5625 call calendar should gain about 1 tick (equivalent to £10 per spread) per day. Over a 5 day period, other things being equal, the spread should gain about 5 ticks (equivalent to £50 per spread).

At some point in the future, as the value of the Sep 5625 call falls towards zero, the net theta of the calendar spread is likely to turn against us. This is a function of the fact that, other things being equal, the value of the near-dated call that we are short will fall towards zero quicker than the longer-dated call that we are long. And when the value of the near-dated call falls to zero, it can fall no more. Erosion ceases to affect the near-dated call but it is still impacting the longer-dated call that we own. This point is reinforced in the summary below.

Notwithstanding the above, and depending upon the exact strikes in question, long call calendars tend to gain value due to the passing of time. If the underlying remains unchanged to Sep expiry, then we can expect to make a small profit on our long call calendar. Our long call calendar is short gamma but making from the passage of time.

How will changes in volatility impact the value of calendar spreads? Buying a call calendar spread involves buying a call that is longer dated and selling a call that is shorter dated. The longer-dated call that we are long has more time value than the shorter-dated call that we are short because it has more time to expiry. The longer-dated call will therefore gain more value due to volatility rising than the shorter-dated call. The longer-dated call has a higher vega than the shorter-dated call.

As ever, if we want to quantify the effects of volatility upon the value of call calendar spreads, we need to consider the net vega of the spread.

Consider our previous example of a long call calendar spread, buying the Sep/Dec 5625 calendar call spread at 156. In terms of the effect of volatility upon our spread, if the Sep 5625 call has a vega of 4.3 and the Dec 5625 call has a vega of 7.8, then the net vega of the spread is +3.5 (short a 4.3 vega call and long a 7.8 vega call). Other things being equal, this means that the Sep/Dec 5625 call calendar spread should increase in value by 3.5 ticks (equivalent to £35) per spread for a 1% rise in volatility.

Let's summarise the Greeks in relation to long call calendar spreads. Other things being equal:

- A rise in the underlying (as long as the move is neither too fast nor too great) is likely to be beneficial since it will tend to increase the value of a long out-of-the-money call calendar spread and vice versa (long delta).
- A rise in volatility will tend to increase the value of a long out-of-the-money call calendar spread (positive vega) and is therefore likely to be beneficial.
- A rise in volatility will tend to decrease the value of long in-the-money call calendar spreads (negative vega) and is therefore likely to be detrimental.
- The passage of time will tend* to increase the value of long out-of-the-money call calendar spreads (positive theta) and is therefore beneficial.

Broadly speaking, buying call calendar spreads is a cheaper alternative to buying naked out-of-the-money calls. We might buy out-of-the-money call calendars to exploit a mildly bullish view on the underlying or to exploit a bullish view on volatility.

How should we choose the tenor and constituent strikes of a calendar call spread? As ever, the exact nature of our views on volatility and the underlying is key.

Note that calendar spreads cease to exist when the short-dated leg expires. At that point, we are simply left with a position in the longer-dated option, a position that we can then cut, run or hedge. This point is important in the context of choosing the appropriate strikes of a long calendar. The key decision is the choice of the short leg, the option that we are selling to finance the longer-dated options.

If we are buying a call calendar because of a bullish view on the underlying, then common sense dictates that we should choose to sell calls with a strike price and expiry date that line up with our views on the timing and extent of the anticipated upward move. For example, if we are anticipating that the FTSE will rise to 5625 over the next month, then it makes sense to sell the 1 month 5625 call. If our view is that the FTSE will rise to 5850 between now and year-end, then it seems sensible to sell Dec 5850 calls. As is often the case with option spreads, we should sell our target because this is the optimal choice given our views.

In summary, long call calendars may be used in a variety of ways. They may be employed as a way of buying "cheap" longer-dated calls, the sale of the shorter-dated call reducing the cost of owning the longer-dated option. Alternatively, more sophisticated traders may use long call calendars as a way of "safely" selling shorter-dated calls, the longer-dated option providing the ultimate protection.

Having considered long call calendars in some detail, let's now briefly consider short call calendars.

---

* Note that this positive theta may turn negative when the value of the short call becomes insignificant. At this point, the decay of this short leg may become less than the erosion of the long leg, with the result that the net theta of the spread turns negative. The long call calendar starts to erode. At this point, if possible, the short leg of the calendar should be bought back. Why bother being short an option for such a small amount of potential reward?

27
Short Call Calendar Spreads

A short call calendar involves selling a longer-dated call against buying a shorter-dated call. For example, from the matrix of Sep and Dec FTSE 100 option prices shown in Table 27.1 (repeated from Table 25.1), selling the Sep/Dec 5625 call spread consists of two legs, selling the Dec 5625 call at 207 ticks (equivalent to £2070) per contract and simultaneously buying the Sep 5625 call at 51 ticks (equivalent to £510) per contract. The price of the calendar is therefore 156 ticks (equivalent to £1560) per contract, the difference between the 207 received for the Dec call and the 51 paid for the Sep call. What is the thinking behind such a trade?

Remember that option spreads have evolved for two main reasons; to reduce the cost of owning options and/or to reduce the risk of shorting options. In the case of a short calendar, we are looking primarily to reduce the risk of selling options. We want to sell some out-of-the-money Dec calls but are not willing to accept the unlimited risk that such a trade conveys. We reduce the risk of the trade by buying

Table 27.1 LIFFE Sep and Dec FTSE 100 option prices as at close on 26 August 2008 (Sep FTSE 100 future = 5494, Dec FTSE 100 future = 5528)

Sep Calls	Strike	Sep Puts
221	**5325**	53
150	**5425**	82
93	**5525**	124
51	**5625**	181

Dec Calls	Strike	Dec Puts
384	**5325**	185
320	**5425**	220
262	**5525**	259
207	**5625**	303

some similarly out-of-the-money Sep calls at the same time. We protect the sale of the Dec calls by buying some Sep calls. Unsurprisingly, by capping risk, we are simultaneously limiting our profit potential.

So short call calendars are a "safer" way of selling calls, a protected way of being short longer-dated calls. Why would we want to be short calls in the first place? The answer, of course, is that we believe that the underlying will fall and/or that the options are overpriced. In either case, we want to be short of calls but know that short outright calls equate to unlimited risk. Hence, we decide to buy some cheaper, shorter-dated calls to limit our exposure; we sell a call calendar.

If we are right and the underlying falls in price, then the value of the Dec calls that we have sold is likely to fall by more than the Sep calls that we have bought. The calendar is likely to fall in value and we will make a profit. If we are right and market volatility falls, then again the value of the Dec calls that we have sold is likely to fall by more than the Sep calls that we have bought and we are again likely to make a profit. Aside from unusual circumstances such as the Sep/Dec spread going into extreme backwardation (i.e. the Dec future trading far below the Sep future), our maximum profit is the price for which we have sold the calendar, 156 ticks (equivalent to £1560) per calendar, in the above example. We will make this maximum profit if the underlying FTSE falls far enough that both the Sep and Dec 5625 calls are worthless, or if it rises far enough that both options are deep enough in-the-money to be worth only their intrinsic value. To illustrate this, consider the following exercise.

Exercise 27.1: Short Call Calendars

We sell one FTSE Sep/Dec 5625 call calendar at 156 ticks (equivalent to £1560) per spread.

1. What are the two "legs" of this trade?
2. What is the short calendar likely to be worth if the underlying FTSE Index falls to 3000 over the next few weeks? (Note the use of the word "likely"; an exact answer is not expected.)
3. What is the short calendar likely to be worth if the underlying FTSE Index rises to 8000 over the next few weeks? Assume that the Sep/Dec futures spread remains unchanged at 34. (Again, note the use of the word "likely"; an exact answer is not expected.)

Exercise 26.1: Answers

1. A short FTSE Sep/Dec 5625 call calendar has two legs; buying a (shorter-dated) Sep 5625 call and selling a (longer-dated) Dec 5625 call. The two legs are high-lighted in Table 27.2 (repeated from Table 25.1).
2. In the event that the underlying FTSE Index falls to 3000 over the next few weeks, both the Sep and Dec 5625 calls are likely to be worthless, since both options

Table 27.2 LIFFE Sep and Dec FTSE 100 option prices as at close on 26 August 2008 (Sep FTSE 100 future = 5494, Dec FTSE 100 future = 5528)

Sep Calls	Strike	Sep Puts
221	**5325**	53
150	**5425**	82
93	**5525**	124
51	**5625**	181

Dec Calls	Strike	Dec Puts
384	**5325**	185
320	**5425**	220
262	**5525**	259
207	**5625**	303

would be far out-of-the-money in such circumstances. In turn, this means that the Sep/Dec 5625 call calendar is also likely to be worthless. Of course, such a huge fall in the underlying would almost certainly increase volatility significantly which might mean that the Dec 5625 calls retain a little value. It is for this reason that the word "likely" is included in the question and answer.

3. In the event that the underlying FTSE Index rallies to 8000 over the next few weeks, both the Sep and Dec 5625 calls are likely to be worth only their intrinsic values, since both options would be very deep in-of-the-money in such circumstances. Assuming that the Dec FTSE future is still trading 34 ticks above the Sep future, then the Dec 5625 call will be worth 34 ticks more than the Sep 5625 call. In turn, this means that the Sep/Dec 5625 call calendar is likely to be worth 34, the difference in intrinsic value between the two options. As with scenario (2), such a huge move in the underlying would almost certainly increase volatility significantly which might mean that the Dec 5625 calls retain a little more time value than the Sep 5625 calls. Again, it is for this reason that the word "likely" is included in the question and answer.

As with long call calendars (and indeed all other option strategies), we don't have to hold short call calendars to expiry, we may trade in and out of them at will. To quantify the impact of a move in the underlying, the passing of time and/or changes in volatility upon a short call calendar, we need to consider the Greeks. Again, as with long calendar spreads, short calendars in practice tend to be *out*-of-the-money. For that reason, we will consider the Greeks in relation to short out-of-the-money call calendars, which are as follows.

Other things being equal:

• A fall in the underlying is likely to be beneficial since it will tend to decrease the value of an out-of-the-money call calendar spread and vice versa (short delta).
• A fall in volatility will tend to decrease the value of an out-of-the-money call calendar spread (negative vega) and is therefore likely to be beneficial.

- The passage of time will tend* to increase the value of out-of-the-money call calendar spreads (negative theta) and is therefore detrimental.

SUMMARY OF CHAPTERS 25–27

In summary, call calendars may be bought or sold. We may view long call calendars as a "cheaper" way of being long calls than buying calls outright. Cost is reduced at the expense of profit potential. Short call calendars may be viewed as a "safer" way of being short calls than selling calls outright. Risk is reduced at the expense of profit potential.

Calendars may also be used to trade the Greeks. Buying call calendars tends to equate to being long delta, long vega and long theta (profiting from the passage of time). Selling call calendars tends to equate to being short delta, short vega and short theta (losing due to time passing). Having considered call calendars from both a long and short perspective, let's now turn our attention to put calendars.

---

* Refer to the notes on theta relating to long call calendars.

28
Long Put Calendar Spreads

A long put calendar involves buying a longer-dated put against selling a shorter-dated put. For example, from Table 28.1 (repeated from Table 25.1) of Sep and Dec FTSE 100 option prices, buying the Sep/Dec 5325 put calendar consists of two legs (highlighted), buying the Dec 5325 put at 185 ticks (equivalent to £1850) per put and simultaneously selling the Sep 5325 put at 53 ticks (equivalent to £530) per put. The price of the calendar is therefore 132 ticks (equivalent to £1320) per spread, the difference between the 185 paid for the Dec put and the 53 received for the Sep put. What is the thinking behind such a trade?

Remember that option spreads have evolved for two main reasons; to reduce the cost of owning options and/or to reduce the risk of shorting options. In the case of a long put calendar, we are looking primarily to reduce the cost of owning options.

Table 28.1 LIFFE Sep and Dec FTSE 100 option prices as at close on 26 August 2008 (Sep FTSE 100 future = 5494, Dec FTSE 100 future = 5528)

Sep Calls	Strike	Sep Puts
221	**5325**	**53**
150	**5425**	82
93	**5525**	124
51	**5625**	181

Dec Calls	Strike	Dec Puts
384	**5325**	**185**
320	**5425**	220
262	**5525**	259
207	**5625**	303

We want to buy some out-of-the-money Dec puts but are not willing to buy them outright, either because we do not perceive them to be cheap enough and/or because we do not expect the underlying FTSE Index to fall sufficiently. We reduce the cost of the trade by selling some similarly out-of-the-money Sep puts at the same time. We part-finance the purchase of the Dec puts by selling some Sep puts. Unsurprisingly, by reducing cost, we are simultaneously limiting our profit potential.

Buying put calendars is a cheaper alternative to buying puts outright, a "cheap" way of being long puts. Why would we want to be long puts in the first place? The answer, of course, is that we believe that the underlying will fall. We would like to buy some outright puts to exploit this view but consider the options too expensive to do so. Hence, we decide to sell some cheaper, shorter-dated puts to limit the cost; we buy a put calendar.

What views on the underlying and volatility would lead us to choose such a trade? Intuitively, since we are spending money on out-of-the-money puts, we have a bearish view on the underlying. We are not aggressively bearish otherwise we would simply buy outright FTSE puts, thus giving ourselves significant profit potential to the downside (with potential profit limited only by zero). Since we are selling the Sep 5325 puts, it makes sense that this is our downside target between now and Sep expiry. Our view on the underlying is best summed up as mildly bearish.

Our ideal scenario is the FTSE expiring at exactly 5325 in September. If, on Sep expiry, the FTSE 100 Index is at exactly 5325, then the Sep 5325 puts that we have sold will expire worthless. The Dec 5325 puts that we have bought still have 3 months to run and will be *at*-the-money. They are likely to be worth around 200 ticks per contract (the current value of a 3 month at-the-money put), depending upon what has happened to market volatility. Since we originally paid 132 ticks for the calendar, we have a healthy profit of around 70 ticks per spread under such circumstances. So much for the ideal scenario. What about if we are wrong?

Remember the views behind our choice of buying the Sep/Dec 5325 put calendar? We believe that the underlying FTSE 100 Index will fall to around 5325 by Sep expiry. We are mildly bearish. There are two ways in which this view may be significantly wrong.

First, we may get direction wrong. The FTSE may rise between now and Sep expiry. If this happens, both our long Dec 5325 puts and our short Sep 5325 puts will lose value. Since they have a higher delta, the Dec 5325 puts will fall in value by more than their Sep counterparts. Our long put calendar will lose value. In the event of an extreme move to the upside, the price of both the Sep and Dec 5325 puts will fall towards zero. In such circumstances, our worst case scenario is to lose our initial investment, the 132 ticks that we originally paid for the calendar. The second way in which our view may be significantly wrong is if we are wrong about volatility and the FTSE falls too sharply between now and Sep expiry. Remember that the driver behind this trade is a mildly bearish view on the underlying. In the event of an extreme move to the downside, both the Sep and Dec 5325 puts will become deep in-the-money puts and their prices will move towards intrinsic value. As a result, both options will move towards having zero time value. Assuming that the Sep/Dec futures spread doesn't change, our worst case scenario is that we lose our initial investment, the 132 ticks that we originally paid for the calendar plus the futures spread of 34.

For example, if the Sep FTSE future falls to 2000 and the Dec FTSE future falls to 2034, keeping the Sep/Dec spread unchanged at 34, then the Sep 5325 put is likely to be worth its intrinsic value of 3325 (put strike price of 5325 minus Sep futures price of 2000) and the Dec 5325 put is likely to be worth its intrinsic value of 3291 (put strike price of 5325 minus Dec futures price of 2034). The value of the Sep/Dec 5325 put calendar under such circumstances is minus 34 since the Sep 5325 put is worth more than the Dec 5325 put. While this is clearly an extreme example chosen for the purpose of illustration, it is important to understand that the maximum possible loss when buying a put calendar is *not* limited to the price originally paid.

In summary, if we buy the Sep/Dec 5325 put calendar for 132, then our best case scenario is that the FTSE is at exactly 5325 on Sep expiry. In such circumstances, the Sep 5325 put that we are short will expire worthless and we will be long a "cheap" at-the-money (5325) Dec put. Our worst case scenario is an extreme move in either direction.

Having looked at the limits of profit and loss, let's now consider what will happen to our calendar spread under less extreme circumstances. To do this accurately, we need to consider the Greeks.

As with call calendar spreads, put calendars in practice tend to be *out*-of-the-money. For that reason, we will consider the Greeks in relation to long out-of-the-money put calendars, which are as follows.

Other things being equal:

- A fall in the underlying is likely to be beneficial since it will tend to increase the value of an out-of-the-money put calendar spread and vice versa (short delta)
- A rise in volatility will tend to increase the value of an out-of-the-money put calendar spread (positive vega) and is therefore likely to be beneficial
- The passage of time will tend* to increase the value of out-of-the-money put calendar spreads (positive theta) and is therefore likely to be beneficial

In terms of choosing the tenor and strikes of a long put calendar, common sense again prevails. When do we expect the market to move, and by how much? Common sense dictates that, if we expect the FTSE to fall to around 5325 by Sep expiry, then we

---

* Note that, as with long call calendars, this positive theta may turn negative when the value of the short put becomes insignificant. At this point, the decay of this short leg may become less than the erosion of the long leg, with the result that the net theta of the spread turns negative. The long put calendar starts to erode. At this point, if possible, we should consider buying back the short leg of the calendar. Why bother being short an option for such a small amount of potential reward?

should sell the Sep 5325 put and buy a longer-dated 5325 put against it. If, on the other hand, we expect the FTSE to fall to around 5175 by year end, we should sell the Dec 5175 put and buy a longer-dated 5175 put against it.

We have now considered call calendars from both a long and short perspective, as well as long put calendars. The final part of this section on calendars focuses upon a short put calendar, the one type of calendar not yet considered.

29
Short Put Calendar Spreads

Consider the following exercise.

Exercise 29.1: Short Put Calendars

1. Selling the Sep/Dec 5425 put calendar comprises two "legs". What are they?
2. What is the price of the spread?
3. What views upon the underlying and volatility lie behind such a trade?
4. If we sell this put calendar, where do we want the FTSE to be on Sep expiry?
5. What do we *not* want to happen?

Table 29.1 LIFFE Sep and Dec FTSE 100 option prices as at close on 26 August 2008 (Sep FTSE 100 future = 5494, Dec FTSE 100 future = 5528) – repeated from Table 25.1

Sep Calls	Strike	Sep Puts
221	**5325**	53
150	**5425**	82
93	**5525**	124
51	**5625**	181

Dec Calls	Strike	Dec Puts
384	**5325**	185
320	**5425**	220
262	**5525**	259
207	**5625**	303

Exercise 29.1: Answers

1. Selling the Sep/Dec 5425 put calendar comprises the following two legs; buying the (shorter-dated) Sep 5425 put and selling the (longer-dated) Dec 5425 put.
2. The price of the spread is 138 ticks (equivalent to £1380), the difference between the 220 ticks received for the Dec 5425 put and the 82 ticks paid for the Sep 5425 put.
3. The views behind this trade are a bullish/non-bearish view on the underlying and/or a belief that market volatility will fall.
4. If we sell the Sep/Dec 5425 put calendar, we want the FTSE either to rally as far as possible or to fall as far as possible. In either event, the time value of both the Sep and Dec options will fall towards zero and we will collect the net premium received.
5. Our worst-case scenario is the underlying FTSE being at exactly 5425 on Sep expiry. In this event, the Sep 5425 put that we own will expire worthless and the Dec 5425 put that we have sold will have significant value. We will effectively be short a 3 month at-the-money put for 138. Broadly speaking, a September FTSE expiry anywhere between the current FTSE level and 5425 is likely to be bad for us.

SUMMARY OF CHAPTERS 25–29

Calendar spreads are also known as horizontal or time spreads. As the various names imply, such spreads involve the simultaneous purchase and sale of two options of the same type (call or put) and same strike price but with different expiry dates.

Long calendar spreads involve buying the more expensive, longer-dated option and selling the cheaper, shorter-dated option against it. The difference between the premium paid out for the more expensive option and the premium received for the cheaper option is the cost of the spread. Except in unusual circumstances (such as the underlying futures spread widening excessively), this is the maximum loss. This maximum loss will be realised in the event of an extreme up- or downward move in the underlying.

The maximum profit is made in the event that the underlying is at the strike price of the options upon the expiry of the shorter-dated leg. In this event, the shorter-dated option will expire worthless while the (now at-the-money) longer-dated leg still has some time to run. Except in unusual circumstances, both potential risk and potential reward are approximately known. The cost of owning longer-dated options is reduced by selling some nearer-dated options, but in doing so, potential profit is also limited.

Long calendar spreads may be viewed as a conservative way of trading a directional view. Specifically, long call calendars may be used to exploit a mildly bullish view on the underlying and long put calendars may be used to exploit a mildly bearish view on the underlying.

Short calendar spreads involve selling the more expensive, longer-dated option and buying the cheaper, shorter-dated option against it. The difference between the premium received for the more expensive option and the premium paid out for the cheaper option is the price received for the spread. Except in unusual circumstances (such as the underlying futures spread widening excessively), this is the maximum profit. This maximum profit will be realised in the event of an extreme up- or downward move in the underlying.

The maximum loss is incurred in the event that the underlying is at the strike price of the options upon the expiry of the shorter-dated leg. In this event, the shorter-dated option will expire worthless while the (now at-the-money) longer-dated leg still has some time to run. As with long calendars, except in unusual circumstances, both potential risk and potential reward are approximately known. The risk associated with shorting longer-dated options is reduced by buying some nearer-dated options for protection. However, in capping risk, potential profit is also limited.

Short calendar spreads may be viewed as a "safer" way of selling options either as a result of a directional view or a belief that options are overpriced because market volatility is too high.

Calendar spreads may be as wide or as narrow as desired. In terms of tenor, the expiry dates may be adjacent or far apart. Broadly speaking, the narrower the spread, the more conservative the trade and vice versa.

Calendar spreads should be entered as a spread (i.e. both legs executed simultaneously) and, if exited before the first expiry, closed as a spread. Don't be tempted to "leg out" of calendar spreads (i.e. trade out of one leg and leave the other leg open) unless you are closing the short leg first and are aware that you then have a long outright position.

While all serious option market participants will be familiar with calendars, they tend to be traded less frequently than vertical or volatility spreads. Option brokers should understand such spreads but it is well worth spelling out exactly what you want to do to avoid any confusion.

Calendar spreads are not, in my humble opinion, quite as simple and user-friendly as vertical spreads. As such, calendars are probably most appropriate for those with some existing knowledge and experience of spread trading. Having considered calendar spreads in some detail, let's now briefly consider a variation of the calendar spread; the "diagonal".

30
Diagonal Spreads

"Diagonals" are a refinement of calendar spreads. As such, we will briefly consider the nature of such spreads and the reasons for their use without going into greater detail.

What does diagonal mean? A diagonal line goes up or down as well as across; it is a combination of horizontal and vertical. Intuitively, then, what is a diagonal spread? A spread that is a combination of a horizontal spread (same series, same strike, different expiries) and a vertical spread (same series, same expiry, different strikes).

A call diagonal is a spread where a shorter-dated call is traded against a longer-dated call with a different strike.

A put diagonal is a spread where a shorter-dated put is traded against a longer-dated put with a different strike.

Consider the following examples taken from the FTSE option prices shown in Table 30.1 (repeated from Table 25.1).

An example of a call diagonal is the Sep 5525/Dec 5625 call diagonal. This diagonal consists of two legs (highlighted in the table), either buying the Sep 5525 call against selling the Dec 5625 call or vice versa. The value of this spread is 114 ticks (equivalent to £1140) per one lot of the spread, the difference between the prices of the two calls.

If we buy the Sep 5525/Dec 5625 call diagonal at 114, we are buying the (longer-dated) Dec 5625 call at 207 and simultaneously selling the (shorter-dated) Sep 5525 call at 93 against it. We are part-financing our purchase of the Dec 5625 calls by selling the Sep 5525 calls against them. Why would we do this? Simply, we are buying the Dec 5625 calls because we are bullish. If we were aggressively bullish, then this is all that we would do; we would buy the calls outright. In this case, because we are selling the Sep 5525 calls to part-finance the trade, we are not aggressively bullish but mildly bullish. Specifically, we believe that the FTSE will rally, but not beyond 5525 by Sep expiry. This is the ideal scenario for our diagonal. If the FTSE

Table 30.1   LIFFE Sep and Dec FTSE 100 option prices as at close on
26 August 2008 (Sep FTSE 100 Future = 5494, Dec FTSE 100 Future = 5528)

Sep Calls	Strike	Sep Puts
221	**5325**	53
150	**5425**	82
93	**5525**	124
51	**5625**	181

Dec Calls	Strike	Dec Puts
384	**5325**	185
320	**5425**	220
262	**5525**	259
207	**5625**	303

is at exactly 5525 on Sep expiry, then the Sep 5525 calls that we have sold will expire worthless and we will simply be long the Dec 5625 calls. At this point, the Dec 5625 calls will almost certainly be worth significantly more than the 114 ticks that we originally paid for the diagonal spread. Upon Sep expiry, upon expiry of the shorter-dated options, the diagonal ceases to exist and we must decide whether to run the Dec 5625 calls, sell them or delta hedge them with FTSE futures. So much for the ideal scenario. What about if we are wrong; what is our worst case scenario?

There are two ways in which this trade can hurt us badly. Given that the diagonal was bought in response to a mildly bullish view on the underlying, it is no surprise that either a fall in the underlying (contra to the bullish nature of our underlying view) or a sharp upward move in the underlying (contra to the mildly bullish nature of our underlying view) will cost us money. Specifically, if the underlying FTSE falls between now and expiry, then both the Sep 5525 calls that we have sold and the Dec 5625 calls that we have bought are likely to lose value. If the FTSE falls enough, then both the Sep and Dec calls may become worthless. In this event, our maximum loss is the initial investment of 114 ticks (equivalent to £1140) per spread.

If the underlying FTSE rallies significantly between now and expiry, then both the Sep 5525 calls that we have sold and the Dec 5625 calls that we have bought are likely to increase in value. If the FTSE rallies enough, then both the Sep and Dec calls will move deep into-the-money and their value will become purely intrinsic. If this happens and the Sep/Dec futures spread remains at 34, then the Dec 5625 calls that we own will be worth exactly 66 ticks less than the Sep 5525 calls that we have sold (the 100 tick difference between the strikes of 5525 and 5625 less the Sep/Dec spread of 34). Given that we originally paid 114 ticks for the diagonal, our maximum loss in this scenario is 180 ticks (114 plus 66) equivalent to £1800 per one lot of the spread.

An example of a put diagonal is the Sep 5525/Dec 5325 put diagonal. This diagonal consists of two legs, either buying the Sep 5525 put against selling the Dec 5325 put or vice versa. The value of this spread is 61 ticks (equivalent to £610) per one lot, the difference between the prices of the two puts.

If we buy the Sep 5525/Dec 5325 put diagonal at 61, we are buying the (longer-dated) Dec 5325 put at 185 and selling the (shorter-dated) Sep 5525 put at 124 against it. We are part-financing our purchase of the Dec 5325 puts by selling the Sep 5525 puts against them. We are reducing the cost of owning options, one of the two main reasons for using option spreads. The other main reason for using option spreads is to reduce the risk associated with selling options, and it is for this reason that short diagonal spreads tend to be employed. A short put diagonal involves selling a longer-dated option and buying a shorter-dated option with a different strike. Broadly speaking (and depending upon the exact strikes under consideration), short diagonals are a less risky way of shorting options than outright short options.

In summary, the reasons for trading diagonals are, unsurprisingly, similar to those for trading ordinary calendar spreads. By trading one option against another, we are either reducing the cost of owning options and/or reducing the risk of selling options.

Diagonals may be attractive to option buyers because they can be set up to be zero (or close to zero) cost. While cost is clearly an important consideration when deciding upon option strategy, it is not desirable to focus upon cost to the exclusion of other considerations such as our view on the underlying and future volatility.

As with regular calendar spreads, diagonals are probably most appropriate for those with some existing knowledge and experience of spread trading. Since diagonals in practice are often zero (or close to zero) cost, it is doubly important to be absolutely clear when quoting and trading such spreads. It is well worth stating exactly what we want to do with each leg of the trade.

SUMMARY OF CHAPTERS 11–30

Remember our list of the most popular and widely used option spreads from Chapter 11:

Collars/fences
Call spreads and put spreads
Straddles and strangles
Butterflies and condors
Calendars and diagonals

We have now considered the above spreads in some detail. As also stated in Chapter 11, the list is by no means exhaustive. There are far more option spreads than those listed, increasingly complex combinations of the simpler spreads, often with increasingly colourful names such as jelly-rolls, seagulls, Christmas trees, "toofers" and so on. Those are for another day and another book. The spreads that we have considered are the building blocks of option spreads, the most commonly used strategies and a good starting point for the newcomer to option trading.

Of the list of spreads that we have covered, the majority are used primarily to speculate, the exception being the collar or fence. Of the strategies listed above, only the collar/fence is a truly defensive strategy; that is, a strategy used primarily to hedge an existing position in the underlying. The collar is likely to be the starting point for anyone looking primarily to protect an existing portfolio, whether fund managers or private investors. For those interested primarily in speculation, strategies such as call and put spreads are as good a place to start as any.

Remember, the majority of these option strategies have evolved for one of two reasons:

* To reduce the *cost* of owning options
* To reduce the *risk* of selling options

Broadly speaking, we know that owning options gives us significant profit potential against limited risk. The problem is that options cost money and lose value over time. Spreads such as long verticals and long calendars address this problem; they reduce cost.

Broadly speaking, we know that being "naked" short of options gives us significant, possibly unlimited risk, an unacceptable state of affairs to many, myself included. Spreads such as short verticals, short calendars, butterflies and condors address this problem; they limit risk. Let's conclude our study of option spreads by rounding up some of the "ground rules" of option spread trading. "Health warnings" have been given at various points in the preceding text and they bear repetition.

When getting a spread quote, ask for a two-way (i.e. both bid and offer) quote in the spread. Don't tell the broker which way round you are (i.e. whether you are a buyer or a seller); brokers in turn should not have to tell market-makers whether they are looking to buy or sell. Ask for an *underlying reference price* for the quote. In other words, find out the underlying stock or index price upon which the market-maker based the spread quote. This should not only stop any wriggling when you come back to trade, but also reveal to both broker and market-maker that you know what you are doing, even if you don't!

Further information that is worth requesting, both for its own sake and to increase your credibility (thus improving your chances of being treated well), include the *delta* and *implied volatility* of the option price. Any option broker worth their salt should have such information to hand.

Option spreads should be quotes as spreads, not as individual legs. For instance, let's assume we are looking to buy the 400/420 call spread. The 400 call is trading at 12 and the 420 call is trading at 7. We should ask for a two-way quote in the 400/420 call spread, *not* for a quote in the 400 calls and a separate quote in the 420 calls. Not only will the combined bid/offer spread almost certainly be wider if we try to trade the individual legs, we may also get filled on one side of the trade but not the other; we may have a "leg up".

Spreads should be entered as spreads and exited as spreads. Don't be tempted to "leg out" of option spreads (i.e. trade out of one leg and leave the other leg open) unless you are closing the short leg first and are aware that you then have a long outright position.

Pricing some option spreads (e.g. verticals, butterflies, etc.) is relatively easy and straightforward. We know that a vertical or a 'fly will always cost us money. If we receive a quote on such a spread of "13 bid at 16" from our broker, we know that the market-maker is prepared to buy the spread for 13 and sell it at 16. No problem. But some option spreads such as collars and diagonals may not be so straightforward. We may trade a collar or a diagonal for a credit or a debit. If the price of the spread is close to zero because the two individual options comprising the spread are roughly the same price, then there is plenty of room for confusion. Be assured, it is not just option novices who suffer in such circumstances, professionals may make a mistake on pricing just as easily. For this reason, it is worth being absolutely clear, absolutely explicit in such circumstances. Ask for a two-way quote on the spread, then inform your broker exactly what you want to do. For example, suppose we want to trade the 400/440 collar. Our broker gives us a quote of "minus 1 bid at plus 2, put over". The market-maker is prepared to buy the 400 put against selling the 440 call for "minus 1", for a credit of 1. And the market-maker is prepared to buy the 440 call against selling the 400 cut for "plus 2", for a credit of 2. If and when you decide to trade, it is well worth stating exactly what you want to do with each leg of the collar. For example, you may ask your broker to "pay 1 over to buy the put and sell the call". No worthwhile broker will begrudge you the extra time and care in such circumstances.

Having considered trading options outright (Chapter 10) and option spreads (Chapters 11–30), over the following two chapters we will consider the ways in which options may be traded against the underlying. We have, in fact, already considered one key way in which options may be traded against their underlying when we looked at using options to hedge. We saw that options may be bought to protect an underlying position; they may be used as price "insurance policies". A further refinement of this use, the collar, was studied in some detail in Chapter 11. Aside from this fundamental use of options as hedging tools, options may be combined with their underlying in various other ways. We will consider two such combinations. First, we will consider *yield enhancement*, a popular way of trading stock options against the underlying share. Then we will consider the way in which the underlying may be traded around a long option position; *gamma trading*.

31
Yield Enhancement

The strategy of yield enhancement, also known as "covered calls", involves selling out-of-the-money calls against an existing underlying stock holding. Unsurprisingly, given the name "yield enhancement", the purpose of this call sale is to enhance the return, to enhance the yield on the underlying stock holding.

Investors tend to hold equities for two basic reasons; capital appreciation (the hope that the share price will rise) and/or income (dividends received). The strategy of yield enhancement is best used by investors holding equities primarily for income, investors who are attracted to a stock by the dividends payable upon it. That is not to say that yield enhancement cannot be used by those looking primarily for capital appreciation, just that it is perhaps best used by those investing in shares primarily for income.

Consider the following example. This is a simple, theoretical example for the purposes of illustration. We are stock market investors interested primarily in holding shares for income, for the dividends payable. We have decided to buy shares in company ABC because of the dividend that the share pays and because we believe ABC to be a good company in which to invest.

We buy 1000 ABC shares at 500 (i.e. £5.00). A dividend of 20 (i.e. £0.20) is payable on ABC, the shares going "ex-div" in 4 months' time. Three month ABC stock option prices are shown in Table 31.1. One ABC stock option equates to 1000 ABC shares.

The dividend yield on ABC is 4% (i.e. dividend of £0.20 divided by a share price of £5.00). To enhance this yield, we sell one 3 month 540 call at 13 (i.e. £0.13). Our upside exposure on selling one upside call is limited because we own the equivalent number of underlying shares. Our upside risk is covered by our ABC holding, hence the name of "covered calls". What is the effect on our overall position of selling the call? Consider the various possible outcomes.

Table 31.1   Three month ABC stock option prices
(ABC = 500 (i.e. £5.00))

Calls	Strike Prices	Puts
69	440	10
55	460	15
42	480	22
30	500	30
21	520	41
13	540	53
7	560	66

If ABC stays at its current price between now and expiry, then we receive the dividend of 20p and the premium of 13 received from the sale of the 540 call. Our return on the overall position is enhanced by a little over 2.5% (13p divided by £5.00).

If ABC falls in price between now and expiry, then we again receive the dividend of 20p and the premium of 13 received from the sale of the 540 call. As before, our return on the overall position is enhanced by a little over 2.5% (13p divided by £5.00).

If ABC rallies to, say, £5.25 between now and expiry, then we still receive the dividend of 20p, we still make the premium of 13 from the call sale and the value of our ABC shares is increased by 25p. As before, the return on the overall position is enhanced by a little over 2.5% (13p divided by £5.00).

If the ABC share price is above £5.40 on expiry, then the £5.40 calls that we are short will be exercised; we will be assigned and be obliged to sell our 1000 ABC shares at the strike price of £5.40. We no longer own the shares and therefore no longer receive the dividend. We miss out on our income from the dividend but we make £0.40 on the share price itself and we still collect the premium of 13 from the call sale, a return of 10.6% (£0.53 divided by £5.00).

Selling the calls improves our return in every scenario. There is an opportunity cost in the case of a significant rally; in the event that ABC rallies to, say, £6.00, we will be assigned on our short calls and obliged to sell our shares at the strike price of £5.40. Our upside potential is limited to £5.40.

Further, selling the calls gives us only limited protection in the case of a fall in ABC's share price. However, this strategy of covered calls is based upon a view that it is worth holding ABC shares, a view that ABC will not fall significantly in price.

The widespread popularity of this strategy is unsurprising, given that it improves returns in every scenario except a significant rally. Even then, it is opportunity cost that is incurred; the overall position is still making a healthy profit thanks to the appreciation in the share price.

Let's consider the question of when this strategy of yield enhancement should be employed. Remember the key considerations when deciding upon option strategy. What is our view on the underlying and what is our view on volatility; are the options relatively cheap or expensive?

As we have already seen, the strategy of yield enhancement comprises two "legs"; long the underlying stock and short out-of-the-money calls. To undertake such a strategy, we must be bullish on the underlying stock that we are holding (or at the very least not bearish), but not aggressively bullish since we are prepared to sell out-of-the-money calls. If we were aggressively bullish, we would surely not be willing to give away our "blue-sky" upside profit potential.

Further, if we are selling out-of-the-money calls, we must believe that the calls are worth selling; we must believe that the premium received for the calls justifies the profit potential that is sacrificed by selling them. To take an extreme example, if we are looking to enhance yield, is it worth selling an out-of-the-money call for 0.5 of a penny? Probably not, since the resulting enhancement of yield is tiny yet we have limited our upside potential. The calls must be worth selling.

In practice, many investors use the yield enhancement strategy automatically. Rather than consider each trade as a separate trading decision, they trade on auto-pilot, selling calls against their stock regardless of the option prices. This is clearly a mistake. Yield enhancement is appropriate when we are mildly bullish on the underlying stock and when the options are not cheap. Why give away "blue sky" if we are aggressively bullish? Why sell calls if we perceive them to be "cheap"?

Having considered in general terms when it might be appropriate to trade covered calls, let's consider the very best time to employ this strategy, the type of scenario in which this strategy really comes into its own.

In equity markets, when are options at their most expensive? In other words, in what market conditions does volatility tend to be at its highest? The answer is during sharp downward movements, during stock market crashes. Nobody would ever suggest that buying stocks in sharply falling markets is easy. Buying shares in such testing circumstances is known as "bottom fishing" or "catching knives", colourful descriptions for a hazardous practice. Investors brave enough to buy selected stocks while others panic may be rewarded not only with attractive dividend yields but also healthy option premiums (due to high market volatility) that make yield enhancement an interesting and potentially lucrative choice.

SUMMARY OF CHAPTER 31

Yield enhancement (aka covered calls) is a strategy involving buying a share, usually for dividend income, then selling out-of-the-money calls against it to enhance the overall yield on the shareholding.

Yield enhancement is most appropriate when we are moderately bullish on the stock and when market volatility is high enough to ensure that the calls are worth selling.

As the name suggests, yield enhancement is all about improving the return on a position; yield enhancement does *not* provide downside protection. To limit our downside exposure, we could use the proceeds of the out-of-the-money call sale to buy some protective out-of-the-money puts. If we did this, our covered call position would be converted into a long collar, a strategy designed to protect an existing underlying position (see Chapter 12).

Yield enhancement is one of the most widely used equity option strategies, a highly effective way of trading options in conjunction with the underlying stock. Another way of combining options with the underlying is "trading gamma", the subject of the next chapter.

32
Gamma Trading

In Chapter 9, we considered the primary Greeks; delta, theta, vega and rho. Remember that the primary Greeks tell us how much an option price should change in response to changes in the underlying share price, time, volatility and interest rates.

The most important of the secondary Greeks is gamma which tells us how much an option delta should change in response to a move in the underlying. For example, other things being equal, if the delta of the Sep FTSE 5825 call is 0.500 (or 50.0%) at the current underlying price of 5825 and would be 0.501 (or 50.1%) if the underlying FTSE rose by 1 tick to 5826, then the gamma of the Sep 5825 call is 0.001 (or 0.1%), the difference between the delta of the call at the different underlying prices.

Because gamma tends to be of a relatively small magnitude for a 1 tick move in the underlying, traders in the real world tend to look at gamma over larger movements. So much for the theory, what of practice? How do option traders use "gamma"? How do we "trade gamma"? Consider the following FTSE example. For the purposes of clear illustration, the numbers used in our example are both exaggerated and rounded.

We are speculators in FTSE options. We are not looking to hedge an existing position. We are simply looking to trade FTSE options profitably. We believe that the FTSE will be volatile over the coming period and that FTSE options are currently underpriced. We do not have a directional view. We believe that the market will move but we are not sure in which direction. As a result of these views, we decide to buy some at-the-money options.

The 1 month FTSE future is trading at 5825 so we buy 10 lots of the 1 month 5825 calls. Since we have no directional view, we delta hedge these 10 calls by selling 5 FTSE futures at 5825. The combined position is delta neutral. We are long of volatility, "long vol" to use trader-speak. We want the market to move and we don't care which way.

As in all good examples, we are correct in our belief that the market will move and the underlying FTSE future falls from 5825 to 5725. Remember, we are long of 10 lots of the 5825 calls. These calls are no longer at-the-money because the underlying

FTSE future has fallen. The calls no longer have a delta of 50%. Since the 5825 calls have moved 100 out-of-the-money, they now have a delta less than 50%; they have a delta of, say, 30%.

The correct delta hedge for the 10 5825 calls that we own is short 3 futures. We originally sold 5 futures, so we now need to buy 2 lots back at the prevailing price of 5725 in order to maintain delta neutrality.

Now the FTSE future surges back up to 5825, the original level at which we bought the calls. Our 5825 calls are at-the-money once more. The delta of the calls has risen back to 50%. The correct delta hedge for the 10 5825 calls that we own is short 5 futures. We are only short 3 futures, so we now need to sell 2 more futures at the prevailing price of 5825 to maintain delta neutrality.

All through the above example, we were long 10 lots of the 5825 calls. As the underlying FTSE future moved around, from 5825 down to 5725 then back up to 5825, we adjusted our futures hedge to maintain a delta neutral position.

We originally sold 5 futures to hedge our long 10 calls. As the future fell to 5725 we bought 2 futures back because of gamma, because the delta of the calls had fallen. And as the future rose back to 5825 we sold those 2 futures out because of gamma, because the delta of the calls had risen back to 50%.

All through the process we were long 10 lots of the 5825 calls. All through the process we remained delta neutral. We bought 2 futures at 5725 and sold 2 futures at 5825. We made a profit of 100 ticks on 2 futures, a profit of 200 FTSE ticks (equivalent to £2000). We traded our gamma. Consider the above example as a timeline.

Trade 1: Buy 10 5825 calls (delta 50%)
        Sell 5 futures @ 5825 (delta hedge)
        Combined position (futures and options) is delta neutral
FTSE future falls from 5825 to 5725
Position: Long 10 5825 calls (now delta 30%)
        Short 5 futures @ 5825
Trade 2: *Buy 2 futures @ 5725* (adjustment of delta hedge)
Updated position: Long 10 5825 calls (delta 30%)
        Short 3 futures (correct delta hedge)
        Combined position (futures and options) is delta neutral
FTSE rallies back up to 5825
Position: Long 10 5825 calls (now delta 50%)
        Short 3 futures
Trade 3: *Sell 2 futures @ 5825* (readjustment of delta hedge)
Updated position: Long 10 5825 calls (delta 50%)
        Short 5 futures (correct delta hedge)
        Combined position (futures and options) is delta neutral

The "gamma trading" is italicised. Our gamma profit is the 200 ticks made by buying 2 futures at 5725 and selling them out at 5825. So far so good. However, a few key pieces of information are missing. What price did we pay for the 5825 calls? Did we buy calls with a relatively low volatility or did we pay too much for them? And what about the timeframe?

If the above trading took place over an hour, then we have almost certainly made a healthy profit. But if the above process took a month, then the options that we bought will have eroded, lost value due to the passage of time, and we may not have made an overall profit.

This relationship between time and opportunity, between theta and gamma, is known as "gamma rent". Gamma rent addresses the question: "How much movement in the underlying is needed to pay for the time decay on a long option position?"

If we are long options then we can trade our gamma, trade the underlying *against* our long option position. Long options equate to long gamma. It therefore follows that short options equate to short gamma. Just as gamma works for us when we are long options, gamma works against us when we are short options. Let's consider an example of this.

As before, we are speculators in FTSE options. We believe that the FTSE will be relatively calm ("unvolatile") over the coming period and that FTSE options are currently overpriced. We believe that the FTSE will not rise over the coming period; that it will stay where it is or fall a little.

As a result of these views, we decide to sell some call options. The 1 month FTSE future is trading at 5825 and we sell 10 lots of the 1 month 5925 calls at 10 ticks (equivalent to £100) per call sold. If we are correct in our view that both volatility and the underlying will fall, then we will make a profit on the trade. The calls will erode due to the passage of time, will lose value as the underlying falls, and lose further value as volatility declines.

We can then either buy the calls back at a lower price or run the trade to expiry and collect the whole premium. But what if we are wrong? What if the underlying FTSE rallies?

Remember, we have sold 10 lots of the 1 month 5925 calls at 10 ticks per contract. As the FTSE starts to rally from its current level of 5825 towards the call strike of 5925, the value of the 5925 calls is likely to rise, because the probability of breaching the call strike is increasing. We have various choices at this stage.

We can do nothing and hope that the market stops rallying. Alternatively, we can buy the calls back and take a loss. Or we can delta hedge the short calls by buying futures to reduce (but not eliminate) our upside exposure. Which is the right choice?

If we do nothing, if we maintain the short call position in the hope that it will "come right", then we are clearly taking a risk. If the underlying FTSE keeps rallying, then the calls that we have sold may move into the money; they may gain intrinsic value. And there is no limit (in theory) to the amount of intrinsic value that the calls may gain.

If the FTSE rallies to 6025, then the 5925 calls that we sold for 10 will be worth at least 100 each, a loss of at least 90 ticks (equivalent to £900) per contract.

If the FTSE rallies to 6525, then the 5925 calls that we sold for 10 will be worth at least 600 each, a loss of at least 590 ticks (equivalent to £5900) per contract.

And if the FTSE rallies towards infinity (admittedly rather unlikely in practice!) then the value of the calls that we sold for 10 will move towards infinity, delivering us the unpalatable prospect of infinite losses.

So doing nothing is a distinctly questionable course of action. What else could we do as the market moves against us? We could cut our position by buying the calls back. We could recognise that we got it wrong and take our loss. Realising losses is never pleasant (though market wisdom has it that "the first cut is the cheapest"). If we buy the calls back and the market falls back to its original level, then the options may eventually expire worthless and we will be annoyed at not having had the courage to hold the position. What else could we do?

There is a third alternative to doing nothing (too risky) or taking our losses (unpalatable). We could delta hedge the short calls.

Remember that we have sold 10 lots of the 1 month 5925 calls at a price of 10 ticks (equivalent to £100) per contract, with the underlying FTSE trading at 5825. If the FTSE rallies to 5925, then we have to take some action to protect ourselves against increasing losses in the event that the FTSE continues to rally.

We don't want to buy the calls back and realise a loss. Instead, we decide to delta hedge the short calls by buying some FTSE futures. Given that we have sold 10 5925 calls and that the underlying is now at exactly 5925, the delta of the calls is 50% because they are exactly at-the-money. To delta neutralise the trade, we need to buy 5 FTSE futures at 5925 (i.e. 10 lots of short calls times a 50% delta). The combined trade is now delta neutral. By hedging the short calls with long futures, we have reduced our exposure to further upside movement but not eliminated that risk completely. In the event that the underlying FTSE keeps on rallying, we need to buy more futures if we want to stay delta neutral.

For example, if the FTSE rallies up to 6025, the delta of our short calls will rise to, say, 70%. If we want to remain delta neutral, we need to be long a total of 7 futures against the short 10 calls. We need to buy another 2 futures at 6025 to add to the 5 futures that we bought at 5925. We are further reducing our exposure to continuing upside movement but not eliminating that risk completely. Furthermore, if the FTSE now falls back to 5925, we will need to sell out the 2 futures that we bought at 6025 in order to remain delta neutral. We will take a gamma loss of 100 ticks on 2 futures, a loss of £2000. This "reverse jobbing" (buying high and selling low) due to gamma working against us is known as "being whip-sawed" or, more colourfully, "being whipped". This phrase describes all too closely the way that short option players feel in volatile markets.

As with the previous long gamma example, let's consider the above short gamma example as a timeline.

Trade 1: Sell 10 5925 calls "naked" (i.e. with nothing against them)
FTSE future rises from 5825 to 5925
Position: Short 10 5925 calls (delta 50%)
Trade 2: *Buy 5 futures @ 5925* (delta hedge)
Updated position: Short 10 5925 calls (delta 50%)
      Long 5 futures (correct delta hedge)
      Combined position (futures and options) is delta neutral
FTSE continues to rise up to 6025
Position: Short 10 5925 calls (delta 70%)
      Long 5 futures
Trade 3: *Buy 2 more futures @ 6025* (adjustment of delta hedge)
Updated position: Short 10 5925 calls (delta 50%)
      Long 7 futures (correct delta hedge)
      Combined position (futures and options) is delta neutral
FTSE now falls back to 5925
Position: Short 10 5925 calls (delta 50%)
      Long 7 futures
Trade 4: *Sell 2 futures @ 5925* (readjustment of delta hedge)
Updated position: Short 10 5925 calls (delta 50%)
      Long 5 futures (correct delta hedge)
      Combined position (futures and options) is delta neutral

The "gamma trading" is italicised. Our gamma loss is the 200 ticks made by buying 2 futures at 6025 (trade 3) and selling them out at 5925 (trade 4). We have been "whipped". At what price did we originally sell the 5925 calls? We sold them for 10 ticks (equivalent to £100) each. We took in a total of 100 ticks for the 10 calls, giving us a maximum profit on the trade of £1000 (10 lots times £100). Our delta hedging cost us 200 ticks, a monetary cost of £2000. We have clearly lost money. And it doesn't end there.

We are still short of the 10 calls. We are still exposed to further movements. In fact, by delta hedging the calls, while reducing the immediate impact of a move in the underlying FTSE, we have now exposed ourselves to unlimited losses *in both directions*. We may get whipped again and again by further volatility, by further movements in the underlying between now and expiry. And if we finally decide to buy the calls back, to take our losses, then we may well find that they have increased in value in response to the increased volatility in the market.

We can see that, given the subsequently volatile nature of the underlying FTSE, we sold the calls too cheaply. The 5925 calls were underpriced at 10 ticks. Time worked in our favour; the calls will have lost a little time value due to the passage of time, but this theta profit is dwarfed by the losses due to gamma (certainly) and vega (very possibly).

Whenever I explain long gamma to traders previously unfamiliar with options, they are immediately seduced by the idea. Buying options and trading the underlying profitably around the options seems like a very attractive proposition. Of course, in the real world, things are not quite so simple. It is rare that we are able to buy "cheap" options and that the underlying immediately becomes volatile. More often than not, options are "cheap" for a reason; nothing much is happening. On countless occasions through my trading career, I have bought options that I perceived as cheap, only to see them "bleed" time value over the days and weeks, a kind of slow death by theta. Nonetheless, I know that, over time, if I buy options at the right prices, I am likely to occasionally be long options as the market suddenly enters a period of volatility. Those occasional periods, the crashes, the company failures, the political upheavals, they pay for the other occasions when nothing happened. Remember, options are all about chances, about probability. If we buy options at the right prices, then, over the long run, we are likely to profit. And if we sell options too cheaply, then, over the long run, it becomes increasingly likely that we will suffer, that we will run into a stock market crash or other seismic event.

Exercise 32.1: Trading Gamma

We are speculators in FTSE options. We believe that the FTSE will be volatile over the coming period and that FTSE options are currently underpriced; they are "cheap". We do *not* have a directional view. We believe that the market will move but we are not sure in which direction. As a result of these views, we decide to buy some at-the-money options. Specifically, with the 1 month FTSE future trading at 5825, we decide to buy 10 lots of the 1 month 5825 puts.

1. Since we have no directional view, we decide to delta hedge the 10 lots of 5825 puts that we have bought. Given that the puts are at-the-money, what futures trade should we execute in order that our combined options and futures position is delta neutral?
2. Given this delta neutral position, what do we now want the FTSE to do?
3. If the FTSE rises to 5925 and, as a result, the delta of the 5825 puts falls to 30%, what futures trade should we now execute in order that our combined options and futures position remains delta neutral?
4. Given this delta neutral position, what do we now want the FTSE to do?
5. If the FTSE now rises further to 6025 and, as a result, the delta of the 5825 puts falls to 20%, what futures trade should we now execute in order that our combined options and futures position remains delta neutral?
6. Given this delta neutral position, what do we now want the FTSE to do?
7. If the FTSE now falls back to 5825, what futures trade should we execute in order that our combined options and futures position remains delta neutral?

8. We have successfully traded our gamma, traded our view upon the market. How much gamma profit have we made?

Exercise 32.1: Answers

1. Since the 5825 puts are at-the-money, they have a delta of 50%. To delta hedge the 10 lots of 5825 puts that we own, we therefore need to buy 5 futures (10 lots times 50% delta) in order that our combined options and futures position is delta neutral.
2. We now want the underlying FTSE Index to be volatile, to move as much as possible.
3. If the FTSE rises to 5925 and, as a result, the delta of the 5825 puts falls to 30%, we need to sell 2 futures at 5925 in order that our combined options and futures position remains delta neutral.
4. We still want the underlying FTSE Index to be volatile, to move around as much as possible.
5. If the FTSE now rises further to 6025 and, as a result, the delta of the 5825 puts falls to 20%, we need to sell 1 more future at 6025 in order that our combined options and futures position remains delta neutral.
6. We are still long options, still long volatility and we still want the underlying FTSE Index to be as volatile as possible.
7. If the FTSE now falls back to 5825, then the delta of the 5825 puts will be 50%. We need to buy back 3 futures at 5825 in order that our combined options and futures position remains delta neutral.
8. We have successfully traded our gamma, traded our view upon the market. We sold 2 futures at 5925 (3), sold 1 more future at 6025 (5), then bought these 3 futures back at 5825 (7). We have made a total of 400 ticks (100 ticks on 2 futures plus 200 ticks on 1 future), equivalent to £4000. This is our gamma profit, the profit made from trading our view that the market would be volatile.

What we have *not* considered is erosion, the effect of time passing upon our options. Depending upon the timeframe of the above example, the passage of time will have reduced the value of our options. This theta loss must be set against the gamma profit.

Further, we have *not* considered vega, the effect of volatility changing upon our options. Given the significant moves in the underlying in the above example, it is likely (though not certain) that market volatility will have risen. Since we are long options, this is clearly in our favour.

Having considered the mechanics of gamma trading, we now need to turn our attention to a couple of further considerations, a couple of FAQs:

1. Where should we delta hedge? At what levels? After how much movement in the underlying should we rebalance our delta hedge?
2. How often should we hedge? Every hour, every day; at what intervals?

In answering these questions, it is first necessary to make an important point. Large, discrete movements in the underlying will tend to make us more gamma profit than steady moves of a similar magnitude. If we hedge and rehedge our long options at regular intervals during a directional move, we will make less gamma profit than if the underlying moves in one sharp movement and we only adjust our hedge once, at the extreme of the move. Consider the following example.

We are long some delta-hedged options (it doesn't matter whether they are hedged calls or hedged puts). If the underlying falls by 4% throughout the trading day, then we could buy futures at various intervals in order to remain delta neutral.

We could, for example, buy some futures when the underlying is down 1%, buy some more futures when the underlying is down 2%, buy more when we are down 3% and buy more when the underlying is down 4%. We have remained delta neutral by buying futures against our long options at an average underlying price of down about 2.5% (i.e. the sum of 1%, 2%, 3% and 4% divided by 4).

Alternatively, instead of hedging at various intervals throughout the day, we could wait until the end of the day to adjust our delta hedge. We could buy all of our futures against our long options when the underlying is down 4%. Clearly, this is better than buying our futures at an average of down 2.5%. However, we are relying on the underlying moving steadily in one direction.

If the underlying fell by 2% then bounced back to unchanged, we would be better off buying our futures at regular intervals than waiting for a bigger move. It all depends upon our underlying view.

In the real world, many traders pick arbitrary levels at which to trade their gamma. Traders may buy or sell the underlying when they have "created" an underlying position of a certain size, when they become long or short 5 futures for instance, or long or short 1000 shares. This approach, while being (option) technically correct, doesn't seem to provide the best chance of maximising profit.

Although the rationale for buying options and trading long gamma is a belief that the underlying will move rather than a directional view, it is nonetheless true that we can identify key levels in the underlying at which it might be sensible to buy or sell. Technical analysis can provide insight in this context. Support levels might be smart places at which to consider buying deltas back. Resistance levels might be smart places at which to consider selling deltas out. The same might be applied to retracement levels, with pullbacks in the underlying.

How can we execute such a strategy most effectively in practice? By using "trailing stops". If, for example, we are long some delta hedged options and the underlying starts to rally, we will have some deltas to sell due to our positive gamma. What we could do is place a "stop-loss order" to sell our deltas out if the underlying stops rallying and falls back a little. If this happens, we will have foregone a little gamma profit. However, if the underlying keeps rising in a steady upward trend, then we are creating more and more long deltas as the underlying moves higher and higher. We are running our profits. To make sure that we don't miss out on too much opportunity, we could bring our "stop" up behind the rising underlying, increasing the size of the underlying "stop" by the appropriate amount. The "stop" trails behind the rising underlying, hence its name "trailing stop". Consider the following example.

We are speculators in FTSE options. We believe that the FTSE will be volatile over the coming period and that FTSE options are currently underpriced; the options are "cheap". We do *not* have a directional view. We believe that the market will move but we are not sure in which direction.

As a result of these views, we decide to buy some at-the-money options. Specifically, with the 1 month FTSE future trading at 5825, we decide to buy 10 lots of the 1 month 5825 calls.

Since we have no directional view, we delta hedge these long 10 calls by selling 5 FTSE futures at 5825. The combined position is delta neutral. We are "long vol", long of volatility. We want the market to move.

As in all good examples, we are correct in our belief that the market will move and the underlying FTSE future rallies to 5900. The 5825 calls that we own are now 75 FTSE points *in*-the-money and now have a delta of, say, 60%. The correct delta hedge for the 10 5825 calls that we own is now short 6 futures. We originally sold 5 futures, so we could sell one more future at 5900 to maintain delta neutrality.

However, we want to run our profits and so, instead of selling a future at 5900, we place an order to sell the future at, say, 5890 "on stop". If the future falls back to 5890, then we will be "stopped out" at or around 5890. We will have missed out on 10 ticks of profit. However, we are hoping and/or expecting that the underlying FTSE will continue to rally; we are running our gamma profits.

Now the FTSE continues to rise, rallying all the way up to 6050. The 5825 calls that we own are now 225 points in-the-money and now have a delta of, say, 80%. The correct delta hedge for the 10 5825 calls that we own is now short 8 futures. We originally sold 5 futures, so we could sell 3 more futures at 6050 to maintain delta neutrality. However, as before, we want to run our profits and so, instead of selling 3 futures at 6050, we place an order to sell 3 futures at, say, 6025 "on stop". (This replaces our earlier "stop" which was not triggered.) If the future falls back to 6025, then we will be "stopped out" at or around 6025. We will have missed out on the last 25 ticks of profit on 3 futures. However, we are still hoping and/or expecting that the underlying FTSE will continue to rally; we are continuing to run our gamma profits.

Now the FTSE continues to rise, rallying all the way up to 6200. The 5825 calls that we own are now 375 points in-the-money and now have a delta of nearly 100%. The correct delta hedge for the 10 5825 calls that we own is now short 10 futures. We originally sold 5 futures, so we could sell 5 more futures at 6200 to maintain delta neutrality. However, as before, we want to run our profits and so, instead of selling 5 futures at 6200, we place an order to sell 5 futures at, say, 6165 "on stop". (Again, this replaces our earlier "stops" which were not triggered.) If the future falls back to 6165, then we will be "stopped out" at or around 6165. We will have missed out on the last 35 ticks of profit on 5 futures. However, we are still hoping and/or expecting that the underlying FTSE will continue to rally; we are continuing to run our profits.

As long as we believe that there is a chance that the FTSE will continue to rally, we can continue this process of running our profits with a trailing stop ad infinitum. At any point, our worst-case scenario is that the FTSE falls back a little, triggering our stop. And if we have run our profits all the way up to 6200, then our worst-case scenario still results in a significant gamma profit. Selling the 5 extra futures that our long gamma position has "created" at 6165 is a significantly more profitable choice than selling one future at various levels throughout the rally. One note of caution; stops are not necessarily guaranteed. That is to say, in normal market conditions we can be reasonably confident that our stops will be filled close to our limit price. But in extreme circumstances after large, discrete moves, our stops may be filled a long way away from the desired level.

Employing a strategy of "trailing stops" in a trending market has allowed us to observe the first commandment of trading; "run profits and cut losses". It is also an example of the way in which different disciplines may be used together; in this case the successful combination of gamma trading with technical analysis.

SUMMARY OF CHAPTER 32

Gamma is the amount by which delta changes in response to a change in the underlying. Gamma works in our favour when we are long options and against us when we are short options.

Hedging and rehedging a long option position with the underlying in order to maintain delta neutrality is known as "trading gamma".

Hedging and rehedging a short option position with the underlying in order to maintain delta neutrality is known as "being whipped".

Either way, the key relationship is that between gamma and theta.

When long options, gamma will work in our favour but theta (time decay) is against us. When short options, gamma will work against us but theta (time decay) is in our favour.

33
Resources

Markets are infested with jargon, technical language used by market professionals as a weapon, as a barrier to entry. The glossaries provided both before certain chapters and at the end of this book should help the reader to understand some of the more commonly used language in the options world. Beyond that, there are a number of websites that provide explanations of financial terms. My personal preference is www.investopedia.com but there are plentiful alternatives.

On the subject of websites, all of the major derivatives exchanges provide a wide range of information, both market related and educational, the vast majority of which is free. LIFFE publish the settlement prices, deltas, implied volatilities, etc. of every option traded on the exchange on a daily basis. Further, LIFFE provide lots of useful educational material on all of the various derivatives traded upon the exchange. Web addresses of some of the major exchanges are listed below.

LIFFE (derivatives arm of NYSE Euronext group): www.liffe.com
EDX (derivatives arm of LSE): www.londonstockexchange.com/en-gb/edx
EUREX (German/Swiss exchange): www.eurexchange.com
Chicago Mercantile Exchange (CME): www.cmegroup.com
Intercontinental Exchange (ICE): www.theice.com
NASDAQ: www.nasdaq.com
New York Mercantile Exchange (NYMEX): www.nymex.com

One key resource that is often overlooked is brokers. A good option broker will be able to provide all kinds of valuable information both verbally and via their website. Some of the better brokers provide educational seminars, often at minimal (or zero) cost. One such broker, Sucden, offers free access to an option pricing model on its website (www.sucden.co.uk/html/content_5.htm).

In terms of further written material, the reader is spoilt for choice. Large numbers of books have been written on the subject of options, the majority of which are highly mathematical in nature, the main reason why I chose to approach this subject from a more intuitive angle. For those of you that wish to continue studying options, my personal recommendations are Sheldon Natenberg's *Option Volatility and Pricing*, a copy of which could be found in most dealing rooms and, for the more mathematically orientated reader, John Hull's *Options, Futures, and Other Derivatives*.

34
Summary

Options are called "options" because they convey choice, which is why they command a price. Options give us the right to do something without an equivalent obligation. Options may be bought or sold; they are freely tradable.

The risk/reward profiles of options are similar to those of insurance policies. When we buy options (take out insurance), we can only ever lose the premium paid and have significant profit potential (like an insurance claim). When we sell options (write insurance), we can only ever make the premium received and have significant risk (the counterparty making a claim). Options, just like insurance, are neither inherently good nor inherently bad. It all depends on how they are used. Options, just like insurance, were originally designed to manage price risk, to be used as hedging tools. But options are equally well suited to speculation, because of the potential for gearing that they offer.

If we are using options to speculate, then we need to address two key questions. First, do we perceive the options to be "cheap" (because market volatility is relatively low) or "expensive" (because market volatility is relatively high)? Second, what is our view on the underlying? Are we bullish, bearish or neutral? The answers to these two questions allow us to determine the appropriate option strategy.

If we perceive the options to be relatively cheap, then our life is relatively simple. We may choose to buy calls if we are bullish, puts if we are bearish and both (straddle or strangle) if we are unsure.

It is when we perceive that the options are *not* "cheap" that our world becomes more complicated. In a wider context, what do we do with anything that we perceive to be overpriced? We sell it! The problem is that selling options on their own (outright or "naked") exposes us to significant and possibly unlimited risk. Subjectively, unlimited risk is unacceptable and this is where option spreads enter the equation. Selling option spreads rather than outright options allows us to limit risk, to "draw a line in the sand". Hence my (subjective!) "rules" at the end of Chapter 24:

- Don't sell naked calls, sell call *spreads*
- Don't sell naked puts, sell put *spreads*
- Don't sell naked straddles, sell *iron butterflies*
- Don't sell naked strangles, sell *iron condors*

If the reader takes just one message from all of the information contained within this book, it should be; "DO NOT SELL OPTIONS NAKED". This is *my* view, *my* trading credo. Others may disagree – I can only agree to disagree with them. In my defence I can invoke Nick Leeson and Barings, Warren Buffett ("Financial WOMD!") and, more recently, any one of a vast number of banks and funds who are finding out about derivatives risk the hard way. Enough preaching – I shall stop banging the drum.

For those starting out in options, for those who have no experience, the good news is that it is easy to start trading options in a "safe", "cheap" way either by buying moderately priced options or by trading simple spreads such as call or put spreads. By starting in such a conservative fashion, newcomers can limit their downside, quantify their maximum exposure from the moment that they trade.

For those reluctant to put hard cash, no matter how little, upon the table, "paper trading" (theoretical trading) is a good idea. The only rider that I would add is that theoretical positions are vastly easier to manage than real ones. Just because a particular strategy works wonderfully on paper, don't assume it will translate smoothly into the real world.

And remember that option pricing leans heavily upon probability. The laws of probability are least applicable to one-off trades; hence, the law of large numbers. In lay terms, we can be lucky or unlucky on a small number of occasions. But over the long run, doing the "right" thing will almost certainly result in profit; bad practice will almost certainly result in loss.

I sincerely hope that this book has achieved the purpose that its title suggests, to explain equity and index options. Thank you for your time and attention . . . good hunting!

Glossary

American style
An option that may be exercised *at any time* up until expiry

Arbitrage
The exploitation of anomalies in pricing between different markets and instruments

Asian option
An average price option

Assignment
The exact equal and opposite of an option exercise

At-the-money
Term used to describe an option with a strike price close to the prevailing underlying price

Backwardation
Term used to describe a futures market where the nearer months are trading at a premium to further months (opposite of "contango")

Bearish
View that something will *fall* in value (opposite of "bullish")

Bear spread
Any spread designed to benefit from a *fall* in the underlying

Broker
An intermediary paid to execute orders on clients' behalf

Bullish
View that something will *rise* in value (opposite of "bearish")

Bull spread
Any spread designed to benefit from a *rise* in the underlying

Calendar spread (aka time spread)
Strategy involving the simultaneous purchase and sale of two options of the same type (call or put) and same strike price but with *different expiry dates*

Call
An option to *buy* the underlying

Call spread
Strategy involving the simultaneous purchase and sale of two calls with the same expiry date but *different strike prices*

Cash-settled
A method of settlement of profit/loss involving cash transfer based upon the closing expiry price (EDSP) of a contract

Class
Group of options of the same type (call or put) with the same expiry date and based upon the same underlying asset

Clearing house
Central counterparty for trades on an exchange

Clearing member
Firm that is a member of an exchange and can therefore process clients' trades upon that exchange

Collar (aka fence)
Protective option strategy involving buying calls and selling puts or vice versa

Compound option
Option where the underlying is another option

Contango
Term used to describe a futures market where the further months are trading at a premium to nearer months (opposite of "backwardation")

Contract specification
Official specification of an exchange-traded derivative

Cost of carry
The interest rate cost of holding a long stock position

Cylinder
Alternative name for a "collar" or "fence"

Deep in-the-money
Term used to describe an option with a relatively large amount of intrinsic value

Delta
Sensitivity of an option price to moves in the underlying

Delta neutral
A position that has no net delta

Diagonal spread
Strategy involving the simultaneous purchase and sale of two options of the same type (call or put) with different strikes and different expiry dates

DTE
Days to expiry; self-explanatory

EDSP
Exchange delivery settlement price; the official settlement price of a contract on expiry, used for the purpose of calculating final profit and loss

Erosion
The loss of an option's value due to the passing of time

ETO
Exchange traded option; self-explanatory

European style
An option that may only be exercised *upon expiry*

Ex-dividend date
Day on which a share starts to trade without the right to receive the dividend

Exercise
The act of exercising the right to buy (call) or sell (put) the underlying at the strike price

Expiry (aka expiration)
Date on which an option expires

Extrinsic value
US term for time value

Fair value
Theoretical value of an option

Far out-of-the-money
Term used to describe an option with a relatively small price, reflecting the relatively low probability that it may expire in-the-money

Fence (aka collar)
Protective option strategy involving buying calls and selling puts or vice versa

"Fill or kill"
Order that is automatically cancelled if it is not filled immediately, more formally known as an "IOC" (immediate or cancel)

Flex option
Option traded on an exchange where certain features of the option (e.g. expiry, strike, etc.) are negotiable

Forward contract
OTC agreement to deliver or receive an asset on a date in the future

Futures contract
Exchange-traded agreement to deliver or receive an asset on a date in the future

Gamma
Sensitivity of an option *delta* to moves in the underlying

GTC
Order that remains active until execution, cancellation or expiration; the *only* type of order that remains active after the day's close

Guts
Strangle where both legs are *in*-the money; an *in*-the money strangle

Hedge ratio
Alternative term for delta

Hedging
The removal or reduction of existing price risk

Historical volatility
Statistical measure of the previous movement of the price of a particular asset

Horizontal spread
A calendar (time) spread

Implied (market) volatility
Volatility trading in the market at the moment, the volatility implied by current market option prices

Index option
Option where the underlying is a share index

Initial margin
Money deposited with the clearing house when a trade is first established; effectively, a security deposit to protect against default

In-the-money
Term used to describe an option which currently has intrinsic value

Intrinsic value
The value of an option if it were exercised now

IOC (immediate or cancel)
Order that is automatically cancelled if it is not filled immediately, informally known as "fill or kill"

Jelly roll
Option strategy involving a synthetic long futures position in one month against a synthetic short futures position in another month, effectively a synthetic futures spread using options with the same strike but different expiry dates

Kappa
US term for vega

Leg
Constituent part of an option spread or strategy

LIFFE
The London International Financial Futures Exchange, the derivatives arm of the NYSE Euronext group

Limit order
Order specifying the maximum buying price or the minimum selling price

Local
An independent, professional trader

Long
A net positive position in a particular asset or instrument

Margin
Money deposited with the clearing house to ensure the performance of counterparties to a trade

Margined options
Options that do *not* have to be paid for in full at the time of trading, margin being paid instead (as opposed to premium-paid options)

Marking-to-market
Valuation of open positions against prevailing market prices, usually calculated on a daily basis against the official settlement prices

MIT (market if touched)
Order activated when a specified price is reached

MOC (market on close)
Order executed close to the end of the trading session

(option) Market-maker
Market professional specialising in the provision of two-way prices in options

Market order
Order to trade at the best price currently available in the market

Naked
Option market slang used to describe a short option position with no other position against it

OCO (one cancels other)
Two orders placed together, either of which may be executed, the result being the cancellation of the other order

OTC (over-the-counter)
Any derivative not traded on an exchange

Out-of-the-money
Term used to describe an option which currently has *no* intrinsic value

Pin risk
Risk to an option seller arising from uncertainty as to whether at-the-money options will be exercised upon expiry

Premium
The price of an option

Premium-paid
Options that have to be paid for in full at the time of trading (as opposed to margined options)

Pricing model
Software that calculates theoretical values ("fair values") of options

Put
An option to *sell* the underlying

Put spread
Strategy involving the simultaneous purchase and sale of two puts with the same expiry date but *different strike prices*

Ratio spread
Call or put spread where the number of long options is different to the number of short options (e.g. 2 for 1 call spread, 3 to 2 put spread, etc.)

Rho
Sensitivity of an option price to a change in interest rates

Series
Options with the same strike price, same expiry date and based upon the same underlying asset

Settlement price
Price at which an instrument closes at the end of the trading session

Short
A net negative position in a particular asset or instrument

Skew
Difference in implied volatilities of options with different strikes ("strike skew") or different expiries ("time skew")

Speculation
Risk taking in the hope or expectation of making profit

Stock option
An option where the underlying is a share

Stop-loss order
Order activated if the market trades at a pre-specified level, designed to limit market risk

Straddle
Strategy involving the simultaneous purchase or sale of calls and puts with the same strike price and same expiry date

Strangle
Strategy involving the simultaneous purchase or sale of out-of-the-money calls and puts with the same strike price and same expiry date

Strike price
Price at which the underlying may be bought (call) or sold (put)

Swap
Agreement to exchange ("swap") different cash flows, most commonly an interest rate swap involving the exchange of a variable rate for a fixed rate or vice versa

Synthetic (long) call
Long puts combined with long underlying to create the risk profile of long calls

Synthetic (long) put
Long calls combined with short underlying to create the risk profile of long puts

Synthetic (long) underlying
Long calls combined with short puts to create the risk profile of long underlying (shares, futures, etc.)

Teenie
Option market slang for a far out-of-the-money option with a commensurately small price

Theoretical value
Option value calculated using a pricing model

Theta
Sensitivity of an option price to the passage of time

Time spread (aka calendar spread)
Strategy involving the simultaneous purchase and sale of two options of the same type (call or put) and same strike price but with *different expiry dates*

Time value
All of an option's value that is *not* intrinsic

(option) Type
Specification of an option as either a call or put

Underlying
Asset or instrument upon which an option (or other type of derivative) is based

Variation margin
Money paid into (in the event of a profit) or taken from (in the event of a loss) a trading account at the end of each day; effectively the running profit or loss on open positions

Vega
Sensitivity of an option price to changes in market/implied volatility

Vertical spread
Call or put spread; an option strategy involving the simultaneous purchase and sale of two options with the same expiry date but *different strike prices*

Volatility
Measure of the extent to which an asset price is moving around

Warrant
Essentially, a stock option that is issued by a company (rather than listed by an exchange)

Writer
Option seller

Yield enhancement
Strategy involving selling out-of-the-money calls against a long underlying stock position

Index

actuaries 52
agricultural origin of options 19–20
American-style options
  see also options
  concepts 10–11, 16–17, 47–8
  definition 10
  intrinsic value 48
anonymity factors, trading 1, 13
answers *see* exercises and answers
arbitrage
  concepts 31, 36, 38, 46–7
  definition 31
  put/call parity 36, 38
Aristotle 19
assignments
  concepts 13–17
  exercises and answers 14–17
'at market' prices 28
at-the-money options
  concepts 38, 39–41, 49–50, 55–9, 61–70,
    78–80, 82–5, 91–2, 96–104, 128–37,
    164–5, 173–7, 206–8, 228–32
  skew 59, 61–70
automatic exercise 16

Barings 236
bear call spreads *see* short call spreads
bear markets 22, 25, 57–8, 65, 100–4,
    127–37, 139–46, 157–60, 161–5,
    168–72, 173–7, 180–3, 205–8, 235–6
bear put spreads *see* long put spreads
Bear Sterns 153
'being whipped' 92, 226–32

bid/offer spreads, concepts 33–8, 112–13
Black, Fischer 20, 43, 44–5, 59
Black, Scholes and Merton option pricing
    models 20, 43, 44–5, 59
Bloomberg 56, 67–8, 82
bonds 9, 54
'bottom fishing' 221
BP 1, 2, 10, 11, 13–17, 46–7, 51–4, 80,
    97–8, 117, 119–26, 127–37, 139–46,
    148–9, 151–5, 161–4, 167–71, 173–7,
    180–3, 187–91
Brent Crude 54
brokers 16–17, 81–2, 216–17, 233–4
  delta 81–2, 216–17
  information resources 233–4
  quotes 216–17
  two-way quotes 216–17
Buffett, Warren 236
bull call spreads *see* long call spreads
bull markets 22, 25–30, 57–8, 65, 95–104,
    110–18, 119–26, 147–9, 151–5,
    157–60, 161–5, 168–72, 173–7, 180–3,
    195–9, 213–15, 221–2, 235–6
bull put spreads *see* short put spreads
butterflies, concepts 105, 117, 160, 180–3,
    187–92, 215–17, 236

calendar spreads
  see also long call . . . ; long put . . . ; short
    call . . . ; short put . . .
  concepts 105, 117, 193–211, 215–17
  critique 210–11
  definition 193

calendar spreads (*Continued*)
  diagonal spreads 213–17
  summary 210–11
  types 193–4
  uses 193–4, 195–9, 201–4
  vertical spreads 211
call calendars *see* long call calendar spreads;
    short call calendar spreads
call diagonal spreads
  concepts 213–15
  definition 213
call options 2–5, 9–11, 13–17, 22, 24–5,
    26–30, 31–8, 45–59, 61–70, 71–93,
    95–104, 108–18, 119–26, 151–5,
    157–60, 161–5, 167–72, 173–7,
    193–211
  see also long . . . ; option . . . ; short . . .
  concepts 2–5, 9–11, 13–17, 22, 24–5,
    26–30, 31–8, 45–59, 61–70, 71–93,
    95–104, 108–17, 119–26
  definition 2, 5
  examples 2–5, 13–17, 22, 24–5, 26–30,
    31–8, 51, 61–70, 119–26
  formal definition 5
  house examples 2–5
  intrinsic value 31–2, 33–8, 45–50,
    225–32
  moneyness concepts 39–41, 45–6,
    49–50
  option price determinants 3, 4–5, 24–5,
    26–7, 33–8, 43–59, 71–2, 121–2,
    143–6
  option strategies 95–104
  perspectives of buyers/sellers 3–4
  put/call parity 35–8, 78–80
  speculation 26–30
  time value 33–8, 49–50, 82–3
  yield enhancement 217, 219–22
call spreads
  see also long . . . ; short . . . ; vertical . . .
  concepts 105–6, 117–18, 119–26, 134–7,
    139–46, 151–5, 157–60, 192, 215–17,
    236
  definition 119, 139
  directional trades 120, 124–6, 139–46,
    151–5, 157–60

examples 119–26, 192
exercises and answers 134–7
long/short-vertical alternatives 157–60
uses 119–20, 126, 134–7, 139–46, 151,
    157–60, 192, 236
Capita 134–7
capital efficiency 25–30
cash transactions, concepts 2
CBOE *see* Chicago Board Options Exchange
CBOT *see* Chicago Board of Trade
CFDs 95, 100–1
chartists *see* technical analysis
cheapness/expensiveness of options
  delta 77–82, 228–32
  option strategies 100–4, 110–18, 120–6,
    129–37, 161–5, 167–72, 220–2,
    228–32, 235–6
  volatility 54–8, 77, 100–4, 110–18, 120–6,
    129–37, 161–5, 220–2, 228–32, 235–6
Chicago Board Options Exchange (CBOE)
    20
Chicago Board of Trade (CBOT) 10, 20
Chicago Mercantile Exchange (CME) 9, 233
Christmas trees 215–16
clearing houses, concepts 1–2, 16–17
Clearnet 1
CME *see* Chicago Mercantile Exchange
cocoa 33, 34–6, 114–17
coffee 9, 32–3, 54, 65
collars
  concepts 22, 25, 105–6, 107–18, 215–17,
    222
  cost-reduction efforts 108–13
  decision-making processes 110–14
  definition 107
  examples 108–14
  exercises and answers 114–17
  profits and losses 109–18
  terminology 107
  time factors 112–18
  trading motivations 109–10
  uses 108–14, 222
  zero costs 113–14
combos *see* collars
commodities 10, 37, 47–8, 65–70, 107
  see also margined options

collars 107
  skew 65–70
condors, concepts 105, 117, 160, 187–92,
  215–17, 236
contracts
  see also futures; options; specifications
  concepts 1–8, 9–11, 13–17
copper 5, 7
cost-of-carry
  concepts 38, 43, 44–7, 50–2, 79, 98, 106
  definition 43
cost-reduction efforts, options 106, 108–18,
  195, 216–17
covered calls see yield enhancement
CQG 56, 67–8, 82
crashes 63, 221–2
currency options 9

decision tree, hedging 22
deep in-the-money options 39–41, 47–8,
  91–2
deeper in-the-money options 39–41
deepest in-the-money options 39–41
defensive strategies
  see also collars; hedging
  concepts 105–6, 107–18
delta
  see also gamma; underlying assets
  alternative interpretations 76–9
  brokers 81–2, 216–17
  cheapness/expensiveness of options
    77–82, 228–32
  concepts 46, 72–82, 85–93, 122, 130–7,
    143–6, 147–9, 154–5, 157–60, 162–5,
    168–72, 174–7, 180–91, 197–9, 203–4,
    206–8, 216–17, 223–32
  definition 72–3, 76, 91, 93
  examples 72–5, 76–7, 86–93, 122, 130–7,
    143–6, 147–9, 154–5, 157–60, 162–5,
    168–72, 174–7, 180–91, 197–9, 203–4,
    206–8, 223–32
  exercises and answers 74–5, 78–9, 80–1,
    87–93, 147–9
  in-the-money options 76–82, 231–2
  information sources 81–2
  mathematical properties 75–82

neutrality 223–32
positive/negative values 75–7
put/call parity 78–80
straddles 78
uses 72–82, 86–93, 122, 130–7, 143–6,
  147–9, 154–5, 157–60, 216–17,
  223–32
'what-ifs' 87–93
delta hedging, concepts 81, 223–32
deregulated markets 19–20
derivatives
  see also futures; options; swaps
  concepts 1–8, 9–11, 19–30, 68–9, 105–6,
    107–18, 235–6
  definition 1
  hedging uses 19–25, 105–6, 107–18
  speculation uses 25–30, 68–9, 105–6,
    235–6
  tax advantages 25–6
  types 1–2, 9–11
  uses 19–30, 68–9, 105–6, 107–18, 235–6
diagonal spreads
  see also calendar spreads
  concepts 105, 117, 213–17
  definition 213
  uses 213, 215
directional trades 120, 124–6, 127–37,
  139–46, 151–5, 157–60
  see also underlying assets
  call spreads 120, 124–6, 139–46, 151–5,
    157–60
  put spreads 127–37, 151–5, 157–60
dividends 35–6, 44–5, 46–7, 54–5, 59, 71,
  219–20
downside exposure, concepts 22–3, 63,
  108–18, 155, 221–2
downside moves, skew 63–4, 67, 70
Dutch tulip-traders 19

EDX 233
emotions 63–7, 70
  see also fear
Enron 153
equities
  ex-div stocks 47, 219–20
  yield enhancement 217, 219–22

equity options 9, 10, 22–5, 37–8, 44–5,
    54–5, 65–70, 107–18, 219–22,
    235–6
    see also dividends; options; premium-paid
        options
    hedging 22–5, 68–9, 235
    skew 65–70
    volatilities 54–5, 220–2
erosion *see* time decay
ETOs *see* exchange-traded options
Eurex 10, 20, 233
Euribor options 9–10, 54
Eurodollars 54
Europe
    major exchanges 20, 233
    underlying assets 10
European-style options
    see also options
    concepts 10–11, 47–8
    definition 10
evolution of options 19–20
ex-div stocks 47, 219–20
exact tailoring benefits of options 29–30
exchange-traded options (ETOs), concepts
    1–2, 9–11, 17, 20, 82
exercise rights
    see also American-style options;
        European-style options
    concepts 10–11, 13–17, 47–8
    definition 10
    exercises and answers 14–17
exercises and answers
    assignments 14–17
    call spreads 134–7
    collars 114–17
    delta 74–5, 78–9, 80–1, 87–93, 147–9
    exercise rights 14–17
    gamma trading 228–9
    hedging 22–5, 114–17
    in-the-money options 40–1
    intrinsic value 32, 34–6
    iron condors 189–91
    long call spreads 134–7, 158–60
    long put spreads 134–7, 158–60
    long strangles 169–72
    option basics 4–5

option price determinants 4–5, 6–7, 23–4,
    48–9, 56–8
option strategies 100–1
out-of-the-money options 40–1
pricing 48–9
put spreads 134–7, 147–9, 152–5
put/call parity 36–7, 78–80
short call calendar spreads 202–3
short put calendar spreads 209–10
short put spreads 147–9, 158–60
short straddles 176–7
short strangles 189–91
skew 68–9
specifications 11
time value 34–6
volatility 56–8
expensiveness/cheapness of options
    delta 77–82, 228–32
    option strategies 100–4, 110–18, 120–6,
        129–37, 161–5, 167–72, 220–2,
        228–32, 235–6
    volatility uses 54–8, 77, 100–4, 110–18,
        120–6, 129–37, 161–5, 167–72, 220–2,
        228–32, 235–6
expire worthless circumstances 14, 21, 28,
    30
expiry dates
    see also calendar spreads
    concepts 1–2, 3, 5, 7–8, 10–11, 16–17, 35,
        85, 112–18, 119–26, 127–37, 151–60,
        193–211
    definition 5, 8, 10
    vega 85
    vertical spreads 119–26, 127–37, 151–60
expiry payoffs, option strategies 98–104,
    120–6, 127–37, 158–60, 163–5,
    169–72, 175–7, 181–3, 189–91
extrinsic value *see* time value

fair value calculation, forwards 46–7, 50–2
far out-of-the-money options 39–41, 91–2
fear 63–7, 70
    see also emotions
fences *see* collars
forex markets, collars 107
forwards

see also futures
concepts 2, 20–1, 22, 24–5, 46–9, 50–2
definition 20, 46–7
examples 20–1, 46–7
fair value calculation 46–7, 50–2
hedging 22, 24–5
FTSE 5, 7, 10–11, 22–5, 38, 39–41, 50,
54–9, 62–7, 73–92, 103, 107–12, 165,
193–4, 195–9, 202–3, 205–10, 213–15,
223–32
further out-of-the-money options 39–41,
145–6
furthest out-of-the-money options 40–1, 85
futures
see also derivatives; forwards; initial
margin
concepts 1–2, 9–11, 13, 20, 22, 23, 24–6,
32–8, 39–41, 46–7, 69, 88–93, 100–4,
107–18, 194, 223–32
definition 20
examples 1, 2, 9–10, 22, 23, 24–30, 46–7,
88–93, 107–8
expiry dates 10
fair value calculation 46–7, 50–2
hedging 22, 23, 24–5, 69
options comparisons 25–30, 107–8
speculation 25–30
stop-loss orders (stops) 28–30, 69,
230–2
Futuresource 56, 82

gamma
see also delta; underlying
'being whipped' 92, 226–32
concepts 74, 81–2, 91–2, 164–5, 171–2,
197–9, 217, 222, 223–32
definition 92, 223
examples 91–2, 197–8, 223–32
exercises and answers 228–9
option strategies 74, 81–2, 91–2, 93,
164–5, 171–2, 197–9, 217, 222, 223–32
theta 225–32
uses 92–3, 223–4
gamma rent, concepts 225–32
gamma trading
concepts 92, 217, 222, 223–32

examples 223–32
exercises and answers 228–9
FAQs 229–32
uses 223–4
gearing 25–30
glossary 237–45
the 'Greeks'
see also delta; gamma; rho; theta; vega
concepts 46, 49, 71–93, 122, 130–7,
143–6, 154–5, 157–60, 165, 169–72,
177, 203–4, 223–32
definition 72
secondary 'Greeks' 74, 81–2, 91–3,
223–32
'what-ifs' 87–93

health warnings 192, 216–17, 236
hedging
concepts 19–25, 68–9, 81, 105–6, 107–18,
235–6
decision tree 22
delta hedging 81, 223–32
equity options 22–5, 68–9, 235
examples 20–5, 108–18
exercises and answers 22–5, 114–17
forwards 22, 24–5
futures 22, 23, 24–5, 69
index options 22–5
options 19–25, 68–9, 105–6, 107–18,
235–6
put options 21–5
historical volatility
see also volatility
concepts 53–9
definition 53, 58
horizontal spreads
see also calendar spreads
concepts 193–211
vertical spreads 211
houses
insurance put examples 6–7, 21–2, 24–5,
43–4, 52–3, 108, 217, 235
option examples 2–5
Hull, John 234

ICE *see* Intercontinental Exchange

implied volatility
    see also skew; volatility
    concepts 53–9, 65–70, 216–17
    definition 53–4, 58
    examples 55–6, 65–70
in-the-money options
    see also deep . . .
    concepts 39–41, 45–8, 61–4, 76–82, 91–2,
        123–6, 132–7, 145–6, 154–5, 199,
        231–2
    delta 76–82, 231–2
    examples 39–40
    exercises and answers 40–1
    levels 39–41
index options 5, 7, 10–11, 22–5, 37–8,
        39–41, 50, 54–9, 62–70, 73–92, 103,
        107–18, 165, 235–6
    see also option . . . ; premium-paid options
    concepts 10, 22–5, 37–8, 54–5, 65–70
    hedging 22–5
    skew 65–70
    volatilities 54–5
information sources
    delta 81–2
    resources 233–4
initial margin 26–7
    see also futures
insurance put examples 6–7, 21–2, 24–5,
        43–4, 52–3, 108, 217, 235
Intercontinental Exchange (ICE) 233
interest rate markets, collars 107
interest rate options 9, 47–8
interest rates 9, 37, 43, 44–8, 50–2, 58–9, 72,
        85–6, 91–3, 107
    see also rho
    concepts 50–2, 58–9, 72, 85–6, 91–3
    cost-of-carry 38, 43, 44–7, 50–2, 79, 98
    option price determinants 50–2, 58–9, 72,
        85–6, 91–3, 143–6
intra-day trading, concepts 1–2, 13
intrinsic value
    see also moneyness . . . ; strike prices
    American-style options 48
    call options 31–2, 33–8, 45–50, 225–32
    concepts 31–8, 39–41, 45–50, 133–4,
        225–32

definition 31–2
    examples 31–8, 39–41
    exercises and answers 32, 34–6
    negative amounts 32
    put options 31–2, 33–8, 45–6, 49–50,
        133–4
    time value relationships 32–3, 49–50
iron butterflies
    see also long strangles; short straddles
    concepts 160, 180–3, 187–92, 215–17,
        236
    definition 180
    examples 180–3
    uses 180–1, 192, 236
iron condors
    see also strangles
    concepts 160, 186, 187–92, 215–17, 236
    definition 187
    examples 187–9
    exercises and answers 189–91
    uses 187–9, 192, 236
IT developments 19–20

Japanese rice traders 19–20

kappa *see* vega

law of large numbers 236
LCH Clearnet 1, 13
Leeson, Nick 236
leg, definition 119
Lehman 153
leverage 25–30
LIFFE 1, 9–10, 13–17, 20, 21, 24, 26, 32–7,
        40–1, 47–8, 50, 51, 54–6, 62–5, 73–89,
        97, 107–17, 128–35, 140–2, 148–9,
        162, 170, 174–6, 183, 188, 190, 194,
        214, 233
Lloyds TSB 14–16
London Stock Exchange (LSE) 1, 25–6, 81,
        174, 233
long call calendar spreads
    concepts 193–4, 195–9
    definition 195
    examples 195–8
    'Greeks' summary 199

uses 195–9
long call spreads
    see also call spreads
    concepts 118, 119–26, 134–7, 151–5,
        157–60, 192
    definition 119–20, 123–4, 139
    examples 119–26
    exercises and answers 134–7, 158–60
    perspectives 124–5, 134
    uses 119–20, 126, 134–7, 151, 157–60,
        192
long calls 15–17, 80–2, 92–3, 98–104, 118,
    119–26, 134–7, 151–5, 157–60, 161–5,
    167–72, 192, 225–32
long collars 109–18
    see also collars
long positions, concepts 1–2, 6, 13, 14–17,
    25, 26–7, 43, 80–2, 92–3, 98–104,
    105–6, 107–18, 119–26, 151–5,
    157–60, 161–5, 167–72, 225–32
long put calendar spreads
    concepts 193–4, 205–8
    definition 205
    examples 205–8
    'Greeks' summary 207–8
    uses 205–6
long put spreads
    see also put spreads
    concepts 118, 126, 127–37, 147, 151–5,
        157–60, 192
    definition 127, 147
    examples 127–37
    exercises and answers 134–7, 158–60
    perspectives 132–3
    uses 128–30, 132–7, 157–60, 192
long puts 15–17, 80–2, 92–3, 101–4,
    108–18, 126, 127–37, 147, 151–5,
    157–60, 161–5, 167–72
long straddles 78, 160, 161–5, 172
    see also straddles
    concepts 160, 161–5, 172
    definition 161
    examples 161–5
    'Greeks' summary 165
    uses 161–2, 165, 172
long strangles

    see also iron butterflies; strangles
    concepts 160, 165, 167–72, 180–3
    definition 167
    examples 167–72
    exercises and answers 169–72
    'Greeks' summary 171–2
    uses 167–8, 171–2, 180–3
longer-dated options 4–5, 171–2, 193–217
    see also calendar spreads
losses
    see also profits . . .
    'run profits and cut losses' principle 232
    time decay 49–50, 58, 71, 98–104, 123–6,
        131–7, 144–6, 157–60, 177, 199,
        229–32
LSE *see* London Stock Exchange

Marconi 153
margin uses 25–30
margined options 37–8
    see also commodities
marked-to-market 37
market prices, option prices 44–5, 49
market volatility *see* implied volatility
market-makers, definition 43
marking-to-market 25–30
Merton, Robert 20, 43, 44–5, 59
metals 107
Microsoft 54
min/max *see* collars
moneyness concepts 39–41, 45–6
    see also at-the-money . . . ; in-the-money
        . . . ; out-of-the-money . . .

'naked' options 104, 141–6, 149, 151–5,
    158–60, 177, 182–3, 186, 189, 192,
    216–17, 236
NASDAQ 233
Natenberg, Sheldon 234
natural long
    see also long . . .
    concepts 105–6, 107–18
    definition 105–6
natural short
    see also short . . .
    definition 105–6

negative amounts, intrinsic value 32
negative/positive values
    delta 75–7
    skew 65–7, 69–70
net positions, concepts 1–2, 13–14
New York Mercantile Exchange (NYMEX)
    233
'noise' 28–9
    see also short-term price corrections
Northern Rock 153
NYMEX *see* New York Mercantile
    Exchange
NYSE Euronext group 233
    see also LIFFE

oil 54, 66–7
opportunity costs 4, 21
option positions
    see also long … ; short …
    underlying positions 79–82
option premiums *see* option prices
option prices (premiums)
    see also intrinsic value; time value
    Black, Scholes and Merton option pricing
        models 20, 43, 44–5, 59
    concepts 3, 4–5, 6–8, 20, 21, 23–5, 26–7,
        28–30, 31–8, 43–59, 61–70, 71–92,
        96–104, 105–6, 121–6, 143–6, 163–5
    determinants 4–5, 6–7, 26–7, 30, 41,
        43–59, 71–2, 96–104, 121–6, 130–7,
        143–6, 163–5
    exercises and answers 4–5, 6–7, 23–4,
        48–9, 56–8
    the 'Greeks' 46, 49, 71–93, 122, 130–7,
        143–6, 154–5, 157–60, 165, 169–72
    interest rates 50–2, 58–9, 72, 85–6, 91–3,
        143–6
    margined options 37–8
    market prices 44–5, 49
    premium-paid options 37–8
    put/call parity 35–8, 78–80
    skew 59, 61–70
    time factors 4–5, 6–7, 27–8, 44–5, 49–50,
        58, 71–2, 82–3, 85–93, 96–104,
        112–18, 121–6, 130–7, 143–6, 163–5,
        229–32

underlying assets 4–5, 7, 26–7, 44–9,
    52–9, 71–82, 85–93, 96–104, 121–6,
    130–7, 143–6, 163–5, 197–9
volatility 4–5, 7, 44–5, 52–9, 71–2, 83–93,
    96–104, 121–6, 130–7, 143–6, 154–60,
    163–5, 197–9, 220–2
option spreads 104, 105–6, 117–18, 119–26,
    127–37, 139–46, 147–9, 151–5,
    157–92, 193–211, 215–17,
    235–6
    see also calendar … ; call … ; put … ;
        straddles; strangles
    concepts 104, 105–6, 205, 216–17, 235–6
    two-way quotes 216–17
option strategies
    butterflies 105, 117, 160, 180–3, 187–92,
        215–17, 236
    calendar spreads 105, 117, 193–211,
        215–17
    call spreads 105–6, 117–18, 119–26,
        134–7, 139–46, 151–5, 157–60, 192,
        215–17, 236
    cheapness/expensiveness of options
        100–4, 110–18, 120–6, 129–37, 161–5,
        167–72, 220–2, 228–32, 235–6
    collars 22, 25, 105–6, 215–17, 222
    concepts 29–30, 56, 93, 95–104, 105–6,
        107–18, 120–6, 128–37, 215–17,
        235–6
    condors 105, 117, 160, 187–92, 215–17,
        236
    cost-reduction efforts 106, 108–18, 195,
        216–17
    diagonal spreads 105, 117, 213–17
    examples 97–100
    exercises and answers 100–1
    expiry payoff 98–104, 120–6, 127–37,
        158–60, 163–5, 169–72, 175–7, 181–3,
        189–91
    gamma 74, 81–2, 91–2, 93, 164–5, 171–2,
        197–9, 217, 222, 223–32
    iron butterflies 160, 180–3, 187–92,
        215–17, 236
    iron condors 160, 186, 187–92, 215–17,
        236
    long call calendar spreads 193–4, 195–9

long call spreads 118, 119–26, 134–7, 151–5, 157–60, 192
long put calendar spreads 193–4, 205–8
long put spreads 118, 126, 127–37, 147, 151–5, 157–60, 192
long straddles 78, 160, 161–5, 172
long strangles 160, 165, 167–72, 180–3
'naked' options 104, 141–6, 149, 151–5, 158–60, 177, 182–3, 186, 189, 192, 216–17, 236
put spreads 105–6, 117, 118, 124, 126, 127–37, 147–9, 151–5, 157–60, 192, 215–17, 236
short call calendar spreads 193–4, 201–4
short call spreads 118, 119–20, 137, 139–46, 157–60, 192
short put calendar spreads 193–4, 209–11
short put spreads 118, 140–1, 147–9, 151–5, 157–60, 192
short straddles 160, 173–7, 180–3
short strangles 160, 185–6
straddles 78, 105, 117, 161–5, 172, 180–3, 215–17, 236
strangles 105, 117, 160, 165, 167–72, 180–3, 185–6, 215–17, 236
time factors 96–104, 112–18, 121–6, 130–7, 229–32
two-part decision-making process 96–104, 107–18, 120–6, 128–37, 161–2, 191–2, 216–17, 235–6
types 95–104, 105–6, 107–18
underlying assets 95–104, 110–18, 121–6, 130–7, 191–2, 197–9, 217, 219–22, 223–32
vertical spreads 119–26, 127–37, 151–5, 157–60
volatility 95–104, 121–6, 130–7, 154–92, 197–9, 220–2, 235–6
yield enhancement 217, 219–22
Option Volatility and Pricing (Natenberg) 234
options
    see also call . . . ; derivatives; intrinsic value; put . . .
    agricultural origin of options 19–20

basics 1–8, 235–6
benefits over other instruments 25–30
concepts 1–8, 9–11, 13–17, 107–18, 235–6
cost-reduction efforts 95, 106, 108–81, 216–17
critique 26–30, 210–11, 215–17, 235–6
definitions 1, 2, 5, 235
evolution 19–20
examples 1–5, 6–7, 14–17, 21–2, 23–30
futures comparisons 25–30, 107–8
hedging uses 19–25, 68–9, 105–6, 107–18, 235–6
historical background 19–20, 43
house examples 2–5
perspectives of buyers/sellers 3–4, 6–7
prices 3, 4–5, 6–8, 20, 21, 23–5, 26–7, 28–30, 31–8, 41, 43–59, 71–2, 96–104, 121–6, 130–7, 143–6, 163–5
profits 10–11, 13–14, 24–5, 98–104
specifications 5, 7, 9–11
speculation uses 25–30, 68–9, 105–6, 235–6
types 2–5, 10–11
uses 19–30, 68–9, 105–6, 107–18, 235–6
yield enhancement 217, 219–22
Options, Futures, and Other Derivatives (Hull) 234
OTC *see* over-the-counter transactions
out-of-the-money options
    concepts 39–41, 45–6, 61–5, 67, 69–70, 85, 91–2, 123–6, 131–7, 143–6, 154–5, 157–60, 167–72, 185–6, 195–9, 203–8, 219–22
    examples 39–40
    exercises and answers 40–1
    yield enhancement 217, 219–22
over-the-counter transactions (OTC), concepts 9, 17, 20–1

'paper trading' 236
payoffs, option strategies 98–104, 120–6, 127–37, 158–60, 163–5, 169–72, 175–7, 181–3, 189–91
physical delivery of the underlying assets 2, 10

positions
  see also long . . . ; short . . .
  concepts 1–2
positive/negative values
  delta 75–7
  skew 65–7, 69–70
premium-paid options
  see also equity options; index options
  concepts 37–8
  definition 37
premiums see option prices
prevailing price of the underlying
  see also intrinsic value; moneyness . . .
  concepts 31–8, 39–41, 44–9, 71–82,
    85–93, 98–104, 110–18, 120–6,
    127–37, 167–72, 197–9, 223–32
prices of forwards/futures, calculation 46–7,
    50–2
prices of options see option prices
primary 'Greeks' see delta; rho; theta; vega
proactive behaviour, option buyers 3, 6
probabilities
  option price determinants 4–5, 7, 44–5,
    52–9, 61–4, 236
  volatility links 7, 44–5, 52–9
profits and losses
  collars 109–18
  gamma trading 92, 217, 222, 223–32
  options 10–11, 13–14, 24–30, 98–104,
    232
  payoffs 98–104, 120–6, 127–37,
    158–60, 163–5, 169–72, 175–7, 181–3,
    189–91
  'run profits and cut losses' principle 232
  speculation 25–30
  time decay 49–50, 58, 71, 98–104, 123–6,
    131–7, 144–6, 157–60, 177, 199,
    229–32
put calendars see long put calendar spreads;
    short put calendar spreads
put diagonal spreads
  concepts 213–15
  definition 213
put options 15–17, 80–2, 92–3, 99–104,
    108–18, 126, 127–37, 140–1, 147–9,

    151–5, 157–60, 161–5, 167–72, 173–7,
    193–211
  see also long . . . ; option . . . ; short . . .
  concepts 2, 5–8, 9–11, 13–17, 21–5, 31–8,
    45–59, 61–70, 71–93, 95–104, 108–17,
    127–37
  definition 2, 6, 7
  examples 6–7, 14–17, 21–2, 23–5, 31–8,
    43–4, 51, 61–70, 127–37
  formal definition 7
  hedging uses 21–5
  insurance examples 6–7, 21–2, 24–5,
    43–4, 52–3, 108, 217, 235
  intrinsic value 31–2, 33–8, 45–6, 49–50,
    133–4
  moneyness concepts 39–41, 45–6, 49–50
  option price determinants 6–7, 43–59,
    71–2
  option strategies 95–104
  perspectives of buyers/sellers 6–7
  time value 33–8, 49–50, 82–3
put spreads 105–6, 117, 118, 124, 126,
    127–37, 147–9, 151–5, 157–60, 192,
    215–17, 236
  see also long . . . ; short . . . ; vertical . . .
  concepts 126, 127–37, 147–9, 151–5,
    157–60, 192, 215–17, 236
  definition 127
  directional trades 127–37, 151–5, 157–60
  exercises and answers 134–7, 147–9,
    152–5
  long/short-vertical alternatives 157–60
  'naked' options 149, 151–5, 158–60, 192,
    236
  uses 128–30, 132–7, 157–60, 192, 236
put/call parity
  arbitrage opportunities 36, 38
  concepts 35–8, 78–80
  definition 35
  delta 78–80
  exercises and answers 36–7, 78–80
Pythagoras 19

'quick and dirty' assessments 121, 129
quotes, brokers 216–17

Railtrack 153
reactive behaviour, option sellers 3, 6
regional variations, underlying assets 10
resources 233–4
'reverse jobbing' 226–7
reward
   see also profits . . .
   risk 24–5, 27–8, 98–104, 120–6, 129–37,
     139–46, 154–5, 157–60, 161–5, 192,
     235–6
rho
   see also interest rates
   concepts 72, 85–6, 91–3, 223
   definition 85, 91, 93
risk 4–5, 24–5, 27–8, 98–104, 106, 117–18,
     120–6, 129–37, 139–46, 154–5,
     157–60, 161–5, 192, 216–17, 235–6
   'naked' options 104, 141–6, 149, 151–5,
     158–60, 177, 182–3, 186, 189, 192,
     216–17, 236
   option price determinants 4–5, 7
   reward 24–5, 27–8, 98–104, 120–6,
     129–37, 139–46, 154–5, 157–60,
     161–5, 192, 235–6
'run profits and cut losses' principle 232

Scholes, Myron 20, 43, 44–5, 59
secondary 'Greeks'
   see also gamma
   concepts 74, 81–2, 91–3, 223–32
settlement prices
   concepts 31, 37–8
   definition 31
shape changes, skew curves 67–8
short call calendar spreads
   concepts 193–4, 201–4
   definition 201
   examples 201–2
   exercises and answers 202–3
   'Greeks' summary 203–4
   uses 201–2, 203–4
short call spreads
   see also call spreads
   concepts 118, 119–20, 137, 139–46,
     157–60, 192

   definition 139
   examples 142–6
   perspectives 140–1
   uses 139–46, 157–60, 192
short calls 15–17, 80–2, 92–3, 109–18,
     119–20, 137, 139–46, 157–60,
     173–7, 185–6, 192, 193–4, 201–4,
     225–32
short collars 109–18
   see also collars
short positions, concepts 1–2, 6, 13, 14–17,
     25, 46, 49–50, 69, 80–2, 92–3, 99–104,
     105–6, 109–18, 119, 173–7, 185–6,
     216–17, 225–32
short put calendar spreads
   concepts 193–4, 209–11
   exercises and answers 209–10
short put spreads
   see also put spreads
   concepts 118, 140–1, 147–9, 151–5,
     157–60, 192
   definition 147
   exercises and answers 147–9, 158–60
short puts 15–17, 80–2, 92–3, 99–104, 118,
     140–1, 147–9, 151–5, 157–60, 173–7,
     185–6, 192
short straddles
   see also iron butterflies; straddles
   concepts 160, 173–7, 180–3
   definition 173
   examples 173–7, 182–3
   exercises and answers 176–7
   'Greeks' summary 177
   uses 173–6, 180–3
short strangles
   see also strangles
   concepts 160, 185–91
   definition 185
   exercises and answers 189–91
short-term interest rates (STIRs) 54
short-term price corrections 28–9
   see also 'noise'
shorter-dated options 4–5, 171–2, 193–
     217
   see also calendar spreads

skew
  see also volatility
  commodities 65–70
  concepts 59, 61–70
  definition 61, 63, 69–70
  downside moves 63–4, 67, 70
  equity options 65–70
  examples 62–4
  exercises and answers 68–9
  graphical display methods 65, 70
  index options 65–70
  negative/positive skew 65–7, 69–70
  observation methods 65, 70
  shape changes 67–8
  steepening curves 67, 69
Soros, George 19
specifications
  see also contracts
  concepts 5, 7, 9–11
  exercises and answers 11
speculation
  alternative methods 25–7
  concepts 19, 25–30, 68–9, 105–6, 140–1,
      182–3, 235–6
  definition 25
  examples 25–9
  futures 25–30
  options 25–30, 68–9, 105–6, 235–6
  stop-loss orders (stops) 28–30, 69,
      230–2
speed considerations, volatility 63
spot transactions, concepts 2
stamp duty 25–6
  see also tax . . .
standard deviation
  see also volatility
  concepts 53–9
steepening skew curves 67, 69
STIRs *see* short-term interest rates
stop-loss orders (stops), concepts 28–30, 69,
      230–2
'stopped out' problems 28, 230–2
straddles
  see also long . . . ; short . . .
  concepts 78, 105, 117, 161–5, 172, 173–7,
      180–3, 215–17, 236

definitions 161, 173
delta 78
strangles
  see also iron condors; long . . . ; short . . .
  concepts 105, 117, 160, 165, 167–72,
      180–3, 185–92, 215–17, 236
  definitions 167, 185
strike prices
  see also call spreads; intrinsic value;
      moneyness . . . ; put spreads; underlying
      assets
  concepts 5, 7–8, 10–11, 13–14, 31–8,
      39–41, 45–9, 65–70, 73–93, 112–18,
      119–26, 127–37, 151–60, 167–72,
      193–211
  definition 5, 7, 10
  vertical spreads 119–26, 127–37,
      151–60
swaps
  see also derivatives
  concepts 2
synthetics, concepts 38

tax advantages
  see also stamp duty
  derivatives 25–6
technical analysis 56
term structure, concepts 47
tertiary 'Greeks' 91, 93
  see also 'Greeks'
Thales 19, 43
theta
  see also time factors
  concepts 49, 72, 82–3, 85–93, 123–6,
      131–7, 144–6, 147–9, 154–5, 157–60,
      162–5, 168–72, 174–7, 180–91, 197–9,
      204, 207–8, 223, 225–32
  definition 82, 91, 93
  examples 82–3, 86–93, 123, 131–2,
      144–6, 147–9, 154–5, 157–60, 162–5,
      168–72, 174–7, 180–91, 197–9, 204,
      207–8, 229–32
  gamma 225–32
  uses 82–3, 86–93, 123, 131–2, 144–6,
      154–5, 157–60, 225–32
  'what-ifs' 87–93

time decay, concepts 49–50, 58, 71, 98–104,
  123–6, 131–7, 144–6, 157–60, 177,
  199, 229–32
time factors
  see also theta
  collars 112–18
  longer-dated options 4–5, 171–2, 193–
    217
  option price determinants 4–5, 6–7, 27–8,
    44–5, 49–50, 58, 71–2, 82–3, 85–93,
    96–104, 112–18, 121–6, 130–7, 143–6,
    163–5, 229–32
  option strategies 96–104, 112–18, 121–6,
    130–7, 229–32
time spreads *see* calendar spreads
time value
  call options 33–8, 49–50, 82–3
  concepts 31, 32–3, 41, 49–50, 58, 82–3
  definition 32, 41
  examples 33–4
  exercises and answers 34–6
  intrinsic value relationships 32–3, 49–
    50
  put options 33–8, 49–50, 82–3
'toofers' 215–16
trading
  see also exchange-traded . . . ;
    over-the-counter . . .
  anonymity factors 1, 13
  concepts 1–8, 9–11, 13–17, 36, 92,
    109–10, 217, 222, 223–32, 235–6
  gamma trading 92, 217, 222, 223–32
  historical background 19–20, 43
  IT developments 19–20
  methods 9–11, 13, 19–20, 235–6
trading costs 26
  see also stamp duty
trailing stops 230–2
two-way quotes 216–17

UK 1, 5, 7, 10–11, 20, 22–6, 38, 39–41, 50,
  54–9, 62–7, 73–92, 103, 107–12, 165,
  174, 193–4, 195–9, 202–3, 205–10,
  213–15, 223–32, 233
  FTSE 5, 7, 10–11, 22–5, 38, 39–41, 50,
    54–9, 62–7, 73–92, 103, 107–12, 165,

  193–4, 195–9, 202–3, 205–10, 213–15,
    223–32
  LSE 1, 25–6, 81, 174, 233
  major exchanges 20, 233
  underlying assets 10
underlying assets
  see also delta; gamma; strike prices
  collars 22, 25, 105–6, 107–18, 222
  concepts 1–8, 9–11, 19–20, 44–9, 52–9,
    71–82, 85–93, 95–104, 110–18, 120–6,
    130–7, 143–6, 157–60, 191–2, 197–9,
    217, 223–32
  directional trades 120, 124–6, 127–37,
    139–46, 151–5, 157–60
  gamma trading 92, 217, 222, 223–32
  option price determinants 4–5, 7, 26–7,
    44–9, 52–9, 71–82, 85–93, 96–104,
    121–6, 130–7, 143–6, 163–5, 197–9
  option strategies 95–104, 110–18, 121–6,
    130–7, 191–2, 197–9, 217, 219–22,
    223–32
  physical delivery 2, 10
  prevailing price of the underlying 31–8,
    39–41, 44–9, 71–82, 85–93, 98–104,
    110–18, 120–6, 127–37, 167–72,
    197–9, 223–32
  regional variations 10
  types 1, 5, 9, 11, 19–20
  yield enhancement 217, 219–22
underlying positions, option positions
  79–82
underlying reference prices, quotes 216–17
universal stock futures, concepts 26
'upfront' premiums *see* premium-paid
  options
upside exposure, concepts 22–3, 108–18,
  120–6, 128–37, 219–20
USA
  CBOE 20
  CBOT 20
  CME 9, 233
  major exchanges 20, 233
  NYMEX 233
  underlying assets 10

value factors, underlying assets 4, 44–9

vega
  see also volatility
  concepts 72, 83–93, 122–6, 131–7, 143–6,
    147–9, 154–5, 157–60, 162–5, 168–72,
    174–7, 180–91, 197–9, 203–4, 207–8,
    223, 227–32
  definition 83–4, 91, 93
  examples 84–5, 86–93, 122–3, 131–2,
    143–6, 147–9, 154–5, 157–60, 162–5,
    168–72, 174–7, 180–91, 197–9, 203–4,
    207–8, 227–8, 229–32
  expiry dates 85
  uses 84–5, 86–93, 122, 131–2, 143–6,
    147–9, 154–5, 157–60, 229–32
  'what-ifs' 87–93
vertical spreads
  see also call spreads; put spreads
  calendar spreads 211
  concepts 119–26, 127–37, 151–5, 157–60
  definition 119, 159–60
  horizontal spreads 211
  long/short-vertical alternatives 157–60
Vodafone 2
volatility
  see also historical . . . ; implied . . . ; skew;
    standard deviation; vega
  cheapness/expensiveness of options 54–8,
    77, 100–4, 110–18, 120–6, 129–37,
    161–5, 167–72, 220–2, 228–32,
    235–6
  concepts 7, 44–5, 52–9, 61–70, 71–2,
    83–93, 95–104, 122–6, 129–37,
    154–92, 197–9, 220–2, 235–6
  definition 52–3

exercises and answers 56–8
market direction 63–4, 70
option price determinants 4–5, 7, 44–5,
  52–9, 71–2, 83–93, 96–104, 121–6,
  130–7, 143–6, 154–60, 163–5, 197–9,
  220–2
option strategies 95–104, 121–6, 130–7,
  154–92, 197–9, 220–2, 235–6
probability links 7, 44–5, 52–9
speed considerations 63
types 53–6
uses 53–8, 77, 84, 100–4, 110–18, 120–6,
  129–37, 161–5, 167–72, 220–2,
  228–32, 235–6
volatility smiles 70
  see also skew
volatility smirks 70
  see also skew
volatility strategies 160–92
  see also iron butterflies; iron condors;
    straddles; strangles

weather derivatives 9
website resources 233–4
'what-ifs', the 'Greeks' 87–93
Worldcom 153

yield enhancement
  concepts 217, 219–22
  definition 217, 219
  examples 219–21
  uses 219–20

zero cost collars 113–14

Printed and bound by CPI Group (UK) Ltd, Croydon, CR0 4YY

16/04/2025

14658500-0003